Christine Teague
121 Duke St
Granite Falls NC 28630

from J. J.

Doc Jones

Doc Jones

✦

A small town physician's story

Martin E. Jones, MD

Writers Club Press
New York Lincoln Shanghai

Doc Jones
A small town physician's story

All Rights Reserved © 2002 by Martin E. Jones M.D.

No part of this book may be reproduced or transmitted in any form or by any means, graphic, electronic, or mechanical, including photocopying, recording, taping, or by any information storage retrieval system, without the written permission of the publisher.

Writers Club Press
an imprint of iUniverse, Inc.

For information address:
iUniverse, Inc.
2021 Pine Lake Road, Suite 100
Lincoln, NE 68512
www.iuniverse.com

ISBN: 0-595-26289-9 (pbk)
ISBN: 0-595-65571-8 (cloth)

Printed in the United States of America

To my wife Dorothy,
my children Phyllis, Gail, Mary, Marty and Susie
and to my patients *and*

Christine

Dr. Jones

And further, by these, my son, be admonished: of making many books there is no end; and much study is a weariness of the flesh.

Let us hear the conclusion of the whole matter: Fear God, and keep his commandments: this is the whole duty of man.

—Ecclesiastes, Chapter 12

Do what the Bible says.

Contents

Foreword

❖

My take on Doc Jones

During his many years of private practice in the town of Granite Falls, N.C., Dr. Martin E. "Doc" Jones was an astute observer of human behavior and nature. His wit and wisdom are evident in these pages, as are his keen eye and memory for detail.

The following excerpt illustrates that. It describes one of the many house calls Doc made over the years, this one to an elderly man whose son had called early one morning with concerns about his father's health.

I checked his pulse and blood pressure. This was all right. I inquired about his water. He had not been able to hold his urine and had to urinate right away with each urge or he would wet his clothes. I smelt urine in the living room and the kitchen. His pants were wet now. I told his son his father might have uremia from kidney blockage. He would need to bring him to the office Monday morning where I could do more testing. We would probably send him to the hospital.

I closed my medical bag preparing to leave. The old man turned to me.

"Are you going to leave me without doing something for me?" he asked.

"Yes, I am going now," I replied. "I will see you the first thing Monday morning in the office. Tom will stay with you today and if you have any bad trouble he will call me. I will be in town all day."

"I might die before Monday," he said.

"If you do, and go up, put in a good word for me," I responded from the kitchen door. "If you go down, tell them you don't know me."

The following pages only give a brief glimpse of Doc's life, a window into his thoughts and actions from 1978 to early 1982. It was a rather turbulent time when he was intermittently distracted from tending to the problems of his patients by complications in his personal life. Like most parents, he was concerned about the uncertain future of his children. He owned a theater building in town that hosted a string of unsuccessful and sometimes raucous events. But the biggest worries during that period came from his legal and political battle with Town Hall as he fought his firing from the Alcohol Beverage Control (ABC) board by the Granite Falls Town Council.

Although his leadership in bringing a liquor store to the community might seem contrary to his Hippocratic oath to do no harm—in fact several of his patient accounts deal with the destructive health effects of alcohol abuse—his objective was to provide additional funding to the town's schools. Doc's desire to help the community and its residents is a continuing theme throughout this book.

In editing his pages I often erred on the side of verbosity, leaving in passages that I thought his most interested readers—family members and friends—would like to see preserved. For the most part they include simple glimpses into his life at that time, notations about the weather and his relationships that may seem irrelevant or unimportant to the public at large, but not to devotees of the subject of this autobiographical tome.

Readers will also no doubt note a few syntax violations that I intentionally left alone, despite my training and the insistence of Microsoft Word's grammar check, because I believe the passages as written better communicated what Doc wanted to say in the unique and folksy form in which they were written by him.

I enjoyed reading about this slice of Doc Jones' life and I hope you will as well.

RICHARD TUTTELL
8-18-2002

Preface

✦

My last days of general practice

This writing is an account of my last days of medical practice as a general practitioner in a small Southern town with a population of about 2,500 people. It is my hometown. I decided to set up practice here because I liked the people. My wife Dorothy and I have brought up our five children here. They attended the public school and the Methodist Church. They are all married now and live someplace else.

My interest in recording my experiences was started by a visit from my elder sister, Ann. Whenever the phone rang or someone came to the door she wanted to know what was going on. One evening after dinner I was called to the office to see a patient with a toothache. When I returned she was surprised when I told her I had pulled the tooth. She said she didn't know I was a dentist too. I told her I did anything I could to help my patients; pull teeth, sew up cuts and occasionally sewed up their pets.

I stopped delivering babies about ten years ago. I found it difficult to recall all of the events for her so I made little notes each day. This gave me the idea of keeping a record so that you might know what the last years of my life were like.

To best understand my life you must think of me as captain of a ship sailing on life's broad uncharted sea. My qualifications for being captain are ten years of training in schools and hospitals, two years in the army in World War II, and about forty years of general practice and community service. The sea we are sailing on is the sea of humanity, dealing with all kinds of people. In ways they are all alike and in ways they are all different which makes plotting a course difficult. I will use all my teachings and experiences to plot a smooth course, but all people react differently so it is difficult to accept things for certain.

In recording my experiences I have attempted to follow something of the outline of a man sailing on a sea without being able to determine where he is going. My first records of sailing were rather tranquil like on a calm sea. My activities in the community extended beyond the health of my patients. I worked with the United Fund, the Social Service Board and the Health Department. I helped establish the recreation center and supported the tax vote to support it. I helped bring a new bank to town and financial support to the schools by working to bring into the community an Alcoholic Beverage Control store that has been a good source of revenue for the town and schools. This project now seems destined to be my ruin. Through it I am in a lawsuit against the town for eight million dollars and in political turmoil that seems never to end. During the five years of reporting I relate many medical and political events that are very trying.

As I approach the concluding chapters, I find a very rewarding philosophy of life. Also, I found that involvement in politics is like a quotation a friend gave when asked to give an answer to infinity. It goes like this:

Once upon a time about a thousand years ago a little band of robbers sat around their campfire. The lightning flashed, the thunder roared and the rain came down in torrents. Suddenly their leader arose and said "Robin, my boy, tell us a story." Robin arose and began, "Once upon a time a thousand years ago a little band of robbers sat around their campfire. The lightning flashed, the thunder roared and the rain came down in torrents. Suddenly their leader arose and said, "Robin, my boy, tell us a story." And so it goes.

So goes the struggle of men in politics. In your hometown unknown to you little groups of men and women gather with the aim of gaining control and influence over other people.

In addition to relating my medical experience, this is an account of groups of men striving against other groups for control over them. As my story progresses you can see the power of the newspaper to influence people.

When Dorothy and I first began practice here we were unaware of this activity, political power and the influence of newspapers. Now I realize it was all around us having its subtle effect on us and our children. After reading this narrative you may notice it in your own community too.

Martin E. Jones, MD

Acknowledgements

A special thanks to my friend Richard Tuttell for all the work he did to help in the publication of this book. Thanks also to my daughter Mary who provided the original artwork for the cover of this book, a painting representing all my patients.

1

Not foundered sick

2-20-1978 ✓

My first report begins on a melancholy winter evening about nine o'clock. Now it is beginning to snow. My wife Dorothy is playing bridge with some lady friends at the community center in Hickory. Hickory is a neighboring community six miles east of here. It is across the Catawba River and has a population of about 25,000 people. On this side of the river there is a long hill leading to the bridge. The hill will get pretty slick if the snow continues. Where they are playing bridge there is no phone. I called the Hickory police to go by and warn them about the snow.

Earlier in the evening I went out to the old movie theater on Main Street. It is on the lot joining my office in the old church building. I purchased it in 1976 for $10,000. It is 110 feet long and 40 feet wide. I purchased it because it had not been in use for four or five years. I thought it would make a good place for community activities. I'll tell you more about it later as we go along.

My first activity in it is to be a boxing match managed by one of my patients, Larry, a young married man about twenty-two years old. For the last six weeks he has been training boys to box in the theater and they have a boxing match planned for Saturday night. I have had some other people interested in the theater since the boxers started their training. They want to use it for country music shows.

On the way home I stopped to visit my brother Melvin. He is about eight years older than I and has a small office on North Main Street in a garage my father built in 1924 to sell Model T Fords in. He is retired and has a lot of friends in town who stop to talk with him. They talk about gardening, cars, traveling, fishing and politics. This is the time of year they begin their talk on gardening and fruit trees. While in his office he showed me a catalogue of fruit trees. He said I should plant some below the house now that my horse and children are gone.

I built my house on the southwest side of a hill a few blocks from the center of town. Founded a century ago, Granite Falls is about three miles square with main street running east and west on a ridge through the center of town. From this ridge there are other ridges running off at right angles north and south. I am on the southwest side of the second ridge. The land was originally a cow pasture. When I was young my friends and I played a game called "Peggie" in this cow pasture. It consisted of laying a stick about six inches long on a peg and hitting it with a broom handle when it flew up. We also played cowboys and Indians. Later we played Tarzan by swinging from one pine tree to another. Sometimes in the summer we caught tadpoles and frogs in a little stream in the north end of the pasture. Even after purchasing the property in 1955 I still found a good way to play in this little stream. I built a hydraulic ram to water my garden.

Melvin said if I planted the fruit trees I could water them from this stream in the summer. I selected six nectarine trees. They are a little like a plumb. Melvin said he would call the company and get them headed our way today. He is a bit impatient, likes to do things now.

Now to return to the beginning of my story, while I have been writing it has stopped snowing. Dorothy should have no trouble getting up the river hill.

To let you know just how close we are to nature here let me tell you about the house call I made last night. It was about eleven o'clock. Lester called for me to come to see his wife Jeraldine. They have been my patients for a long time. Jeraldine is about seventy-two years old. They live alone in the east end of town and for the last twenty years have been in good health. This was my first call to see them in a long time. Her complaint was nausea and diarrhea of about twenty-four hours duration.

After examining her I couldn't find anything wrong. Her husband and I agreed that her condition might be from something she had eaten a day or two ago. Lester said about two weeks ago he had the same condition after eating some leftover Christmas candy. It made him terribly sick. He was so sick he said his bowel movements reminded him of a foundered cow. "Droppings from a foundered cow are green and watery; regular cow droppings are round and a little firm" he said. "Jeraldine's are not that bad yet, she is not foundered sick yet," he said.

Jeraldine didn't argue. She wanted something to relieve her nausea and diarrhea. I gave her an injection of medicine to relieve the nausea and some tablets for the diarrhea. Her husband was to call me if she wasn't relieved in three hours.

Lester called me this morning and said she had a good night, but was sick again this morning. I referred her to the hospital where they think she may have some trouble with her large bowel.

2

ABC troubles begin

2-21-1978 ✓

After breakfast Dorothy wanted the paper. There was a light snow on the ground and some on the paper. I called for Jack, our dog, to bring it to me. He is a small species of German shepherd that came to our house five years ago. Susie, our youngest daughter, claimed the dog, but left the training to me when she left for college. He is about ten years old. He went willingly to the front street for it, picked it up and started proudly carrying it back to me. When he was about ten feet away from the door something attracted his attention. He dropped the paper and ran out into the field in front of the house leaving it for me to bring in. I think he smelt a cat. On the way to the office I stopped in to tell Melvin where I wanted the fruit trees planted. He wasn't in his office.

I concluded he must be sick or taking what is called a "snow day" meaning a day when one just stays at home because of the snow. Snow has an exciting effect on people. I will tell you about it soon. I was leaving Melvin's office when Lee, his assistant and handyman pulled up in his pickup truck. I told him Melvin wasn't open and would he mind driving over to his house to get a piece of plywood for me to make a sign for the theater. By sending him after the plywood I could find out when he returned whether or not Melvin was sick.

After leaving Melvin's office I stopped in town at Jim Moore's clothing store to get some long handle underwear. With the cold weather I needed more than just pants to stay warm. Jim took over the clothing store when his father died. We are about the same age and have lived in Granite Falls all our lives. He is about a foot taller than I am so when we go fishing and seine for minnows he takes the deeper side of the net. When I asked about the underwear he said the army had bought it all due to the cold weather.

Leaving Jim's store I walked down the street to Dwight's store. He runs a gift shop with all kinds of nice gifts, china, pictures, flower arrangements and furniture. All the ladies in town frequent his shop for gifts and the latest gossip.

You can't have a good funeral without having Dwight sing his favorite hymn, "How Great Thou Art." It's the one where you stand in awesome wonder at the rolling thunder. One day he was so good he had a dog howling at the front door of the church.

As I passed his door he called out to tell me that Jeraldine had been operated on for obstruction of the bowels. I thanked him and went on to the hardware store where I purchased a few screws to hold pictures in the theater. I wondered how Dwight had found out so soon about my patient I had referred to the hospital last night. I hadn't heard from the hospital yet myself. News travels fast in a little town.

At the office there were several patients waiting. One had a sore throat with some fever; another was a young man waiting for an insurance examination. Shortly after starting his examination, he said this was the first time he had ever been in a church to see the doctor. He was referring to my office being in the Sunday school part of a church. I told him a lot of people make some comment about my office.

My office is in the old Baptist Church on Commerce Avenue. It would probably be fair to say I was a bit shaken up on the day I purchased the church. It was in 1964. I was on my way to make a house call going down a small street along Falls Mill on the South side of Main Street. Across the street there was a group of people gathered in the churchyard and since it was a Saturday morning I wondered what the gathering was about. My attention was brought back to my car by a sudden jar and a tearing of metal. I had driven through the intersection and caught the bumper of another car. After a little discussion and some mutual understanding I gave the man fifty dollars for the damages to his car. I then went across the street to investigate the meeting in the churchyard.

They were holding an auction to sell the church property. I had never been to an auction. The church is a large brick building with two bell towers and a Sunday school built onto the East side. In all the church is seventy-five feet wide and 100 feet long with beautiful stained glass windows. The auctioneer started the bidding off and before I knew it I had purchased the church.

After buying the church there were lots of jokes made about it. Some people said if I couldn't get my patients well with pills I could do it with praying and laying on of hands. I didn't mind this. I really considered it something of a compliment. I have a lot of faith in prayer. Another pun was now that I had the church my patients would never see me in the office. I would keep my minnows in the baptistery and be on the river fishing. I have taken all of these witticisms in stride and never resented any remark made about my office.

The spare rooms are good for storage and one rather large room in the back has been a good conference room. In addition to my office in the church, I have opened up part of it for a dental office, the basement for the town kindergarten and a beauty shop. I let the Women's Club store clothing for the needy in the auditorium. For a few years the County Health Department operated twice a month out of the basement.

After finishing the insurance exam and seeing other patients, I closed the office a little before noon to go to the ABC Store where we were having our monthly board meeting.

Here is where the trouble began lasting nearly four years. The ABC stands for Alcoholic Beverage Control. It is a state controlled store for selling alcohol or liquor if you like. It operates under state supervision and regulations. The town Board of Commissioners appoint directors to run the store. Two directors and a chairman are appointed; one for three years, one for two and one for one year in the beginning.

When Bert Huffman won the election in 1971 for mayor, he asked me to serve as chairman of the ABC board. I asked Jim and another friend to serve as directors. They are both Democrats. At the time I didn't think politics made any difference. On the old board there had been two Democrats and one Republican.

They all resigned when Bert was elected mayor. I had been a registered Democrat until after we won the election for the ABC Store. The town board was made up of Democrats. I wasn't offered a position in anything in town so I changed my registration to Republican. Bert was a registered Democrat.

We were finishing up the meeting when Reece, our store manager, brought up the gas bill for our ABC officer's car. He had been patrolling the county for bootleggers until a month ago when we received a directive from the state that our officer had no business outside of our town. On this account he had been helping in the store. He had presented a gas bill for $54.62 for the month. Jim thought this was too much to be just driving from his house to the store, a distance of two miles a day. After the meeting I called the officer to come by my office to discuss the bill.

Shortly before two o'clock he came in the office obviously disturbed, his face was flushed and a tremor in his voice.

"The keys are in the damn car down at the ABC store," he said as he handed me the registration card for the car. He told me that he didn't want to get more than other employees at the store.

I didn't understand this or the other statement he made about his political activity as he slammed the door on the way out. It seemed like he said he had always worked for the Democratic Party, the sheriff and the local police chief in every election. I hadn't expected this degree of reaction. He didn't give me a chance to discuss the gas bill. I called Bert and told him what had happened. I thought our ABC officer had resigned. He said I should try talking to him again in the morning.

The rest of the day went along uneventful, though I frequently recalled our ABC officer's remarks about working for the sheriff and police chief. Why had he made this remark? I thought they had nothing to do with the operation of the ABC store. The board was due to be nonpartisan and operated under state control. The State attorney general said the local board was one autonomous body and not under the control of the town board. I found out different a year or two later.

After closing the office I went by the theater to see how Larry was doing with the boxers. From the theater I went to the Rotary Club meeting. I was in charge of the program. I had asked the son of one of the members to give the program. He is a young student studying religion. He selected for his subject Religious Beliefs of Arabs and Jews. He made an interesting talk and concluded his subject by saying the Jews and Arabs would always be fighting because God had promised each of them the land of Palestine.

3

ABC officer range

2-23-1978 √

After my usual breakfast of coffee, toast and some jelly furnished by one of my patients, I went to the front door to call for Jack to get the paper. He brought it to me this time without any trouble, though he limped badly in his left hip with rheumatism. On the way to the office I stopped to check on Melvin. He was sick with the flu. He is better now.

I stopped at the library to find a book on arrowheads, but the building was closed.

When I arrived at the office there were a few patients waiting. I think most patients stayed home due to the cold. Dorothy left the office around eleven-thirty to go prepare our lunch. I closed the office at noon and stopped at the hardware store to get some light sockets for the theater. The clerk waiting on me said the pain in his neck wasn't any better. I had seen him ten days ago and told him he had some kind of muscle spasm in his neck. I gave him some muscle relaxers and told him to check with me again in a few days if it wasn't better. I told him to come by after lunch and I would check on it again. He said no, he couldn't come; he couldn't afford it. I asked him why. I knew I hadn't charged him over five dollars for the visit and the medication. He said after seeing me he had gone to see an orthopedist and he had charged him seventy-four dollars without the medicine. The orthopedist had diagnosed the condition the same as I had.

"Come by after lunch and pay me when you can," I said.

After lunch, Dorothy reminded me of a bank meeting in Hickory I was due to attend. By two o'clock I had seen all the patients waiting so I went back to the library. I found the books and was leaving when librarian said I was wanted on the phone

When I answered the person on the other end said, "It's me, I am sending a man over to your office to get the ABC bill changed. It will save our ABC officer's job." Until this last phrase I didn't recognize who was calling. It was Jim, a member of our ABC board. He said a man from the Lenoir ABC board wanted to talk to me about sharing an ABC officer in the county and the two towns. When Lenoir voted in its ABC store it took half of our business so now we don't have enough money to pay our ABC officer the same as we had been paying. Hugh, the chairman of the ABC board was waiting when I returned to the office.

"For openers, he said I am the head alcoholic in Lenoir and you are the head alcoholic in Granite, at least that is what Jim's brother Jack calls us," he said.

Hugh was a very pleasant fellow. We agreed one officer for the two towns and county would be a good idea. When he left I called Jim to tell him of our agreement. Jim thought the officer had full range of the county. I believed he should be restricted to the town and ABC store. To get a legal opinion I called the town attorney. He asked me to read the reference matter in our bill. After hearing it his opinion was that the officer could range throughout the county.

Now since I had the town attorney's opinion that it was legal for our ABC officer to range throughout the county, I called Hugh to tell him the arrangement might work. Then I called Reece, our store manager to tell him to call our ABC officer to come back to work. In a few minutes the officer was in my office to get the keys to the police car. He was glad to be let loose again. But when I called Mayor Bert to tell him the ABC officer was back at work, he didn't agree with the town attorney's decision. He believed we should have kept the officer in the store.

Time had moved on to three-thirty, time to go to the bank meeting. During the meeting, I worried about our ABC officer ranging about the county arresting anyone he caught selling homemade liquor or liquor they had bought from the store. I decided Bert didn't have any confidence in the attorney who is chairman of the Democratic Party in the county. The attorney is liked by four of the town commissioners and the city manager. They all work together supporting each other. They are all Democrats. I am the only Republican on the ABC Board. Now I believe I know what our ABC officer meant when he said he worked in every election. He meant he worked in every election for the Democrats. The more I thought about it the more I decided my tranquil days were coming to an end.

When we returned from the meeting I went by the theater to see how Larry's boxers were doing. I watched some of the other boxers practicing. Two boxers were in the ring. One was knocking the other about pretty badly.

At the conclusion of a round I heard Larry ask if this was the first time in the ring. I moved closer to the ring so I could hear better. To my surprise the hefty boxer was a girl. I asked Larry if he intended to use her in future bouts. He said no, he was just using her to train some of the boys.

I went back by the office. There were no patients so I closed for the evening. On the way home I felt very depressed about my future as ABC chairman.

4

An insulin reaction

2-4-1978 ✓

I spent a restless night worrying whether we were right letting our ABC officer range throughout the county. When the phone rang at 6:30 a.m. it was Ned calling.

"I can't do a thing with her. Will you come see her?" He was calling about his wife, Hilda. She is about thirty years old and has had sugar diabetes since birth. Ten days ago she went into a diabetic coma after returning from the hospital for regulation of her diabetes. Ned was able to get some sweetened orange juice in her and she soon came out of the coma.

This time he said he couldn't get her to take any juice; he didn't know what was wrong. She hadn't taken any insulin either. I told him I would be at his house in a few minutes.

On the way to Ned's house I stopped at the office to get another 50 cc syringe and two bottles of dextrose, the essentials to combat a diabetic coma from too much insulin. When I arrived, Ned was standing in the doorway and directed me into the bedroom. It must have been the bedroom of one of his daughters judging from all of the posters of Elvis Presley on the walls and stuffed teddy bears on the bed and chairs.

Hilda was lying on her right side in bed, breathing like she was asleep with her eyes open, pupils dilated and mouth slightly open. Calling her by name she would not respond, but a hand motion toward her eyes as if she were going to get hit caused slight blinking. My inquiry regarding insulin taken this morning was not productive of any facts. Ned didn't know if she had taken any, his daughter said

12

Hilda had taken some yesterday and her son thought she might have taken some last night before retiring. If Hilda was in a coma from lack of insulin I would need to send her back to the hospital; if she had taken too much insulin I could pull her out of the coma with my dextrose.

I questioned the family again about insulin. Ned thought she might have taken an overdose last night. I asked him to bring me all of Hilda's medicine. None of it was medicine for sleep or sedation. After observing Hilda for about ten minutes I decided her condition was getting worse. I told Ned we could give her dextrose and if her condition were due to an overdose of insulin she would improve; if it were not from insulin she wouldn't respond and we would need to send her back to the hospital again. Ned had never seen Hilda this bad and wanted me to try the dextrose.

To give the dextrose intravenously I needed a good vein. I called for some scissors to cut the cuff of her gown to raise her sleeve to inspect her arm for a good vein. I found one in the left arm. I put a towel under her arm to keep blood from getting on the bed and applied a tourniquet while Ned held her arm. I slowly injected the dextrose. After a minute Ned asked how soon would she respond if we were right. I looked up to answer. He was sweating and rather pale.

"If we are right she will respond in a few minutes," I replied.

After I had injected about thirty cc of dextrose it seemed like she was responding, but in a minute she stopped blinking her eyes when I moved my hand toward them. I gave her ten more cc of dextrose. Nothing happened. I told Ned it didn't seem to be working and withdrew the needle. I put a Band-Aid over the needle puncture and was about to discuss calling an ambulance to take her to the hospital when I noticed her open and close her eyelids. In a minute or two she moved her head and responded to her name. Ned saw her reaction and began to smile. I called for sweetened orange juice I had requested Ned to always keep in the refrigerator for occasions like this. Her son ran from the room and was soon back with a glass of sweetened water.

He said they drank all the orange juice last night. Hilda was now able to sit up and drink the sweetened water. Everybody was smiling now. Ned agreed to stay out of work with Hilda until the children came home from school.

After leaving Hilda there was just enough time at home for a cup of coffee and toast before opening the office. Sometime around ten o'clock Reece, our ABC store manager, called to ask me what I thought about him calling the lawyer employed by the state ABC Board to find out if we were right to let our ABC officer range about the county. I thought it would be a good idea to get another legal opinion.

Later in the morning I checked on the mail. I had a letter from an insurance company regarding compensation for a patient I had seen with an injury to her right ring finger. She had injured her finger in a most unusual way. She said she was reaching into a bag of socks and something seemed to tickle her finger. She jerked her hand out of the bag thinking there might have been a mouse in the bag. She jerked her hand out so fast she hurt her finger in some bizarre manner. Her foreman at the plant had attended her finger for about a month before he sent her to me. When I first saw her finger it was swollen as if it had arthritis in it. The end of the finger was swollen. I applied a splint hoping that immobilization would improve it. There was no improvement after a week so I took an x-ray of it. To my surprise there was an old fracture of the end of the finger. When I told her what I had found she asked about going to an orthopedic surgeon because her finger was swollen and slightly bent down toward the palm of her hand. I told her I thought wearing the splint would get the finger better. She missed her next appointment. Her plant foreman called me to tell me she had gone to another doctor. I realized then that she probably wanted me to refer her to the orthopedist when she first came to see me.

Now the insurance company was wanting to know just how reaching into a bag of socks could have broken her finger. I had to reply that I was at a loss of words to come up with an explanation. I could agree with the patient that a string might have caught her finger, but it wasn't sufficient to break the bone. I wondered if she hadn't injured her finger before she stuck her hand into the bag of socks and was telling me she hurt it to get the insurance company to pay for it. The tendency of people now seems to be to get what they can however they can from their employer or insurance companies. An example of this was a patient I saw a few days ago with a swollen testicle. When I asked what had happened, he said he was lifting in a bent position and his hand slipped off of what he was lifting and his right elbow struck his left testicle.

Examination revealed a red-hot swollen left testicle very painful to the touch. When I asked him to assume the position he was in when his hand slipped he said his back was too sore for him to bend over. I gave him some antibiotics and asked him to come back the next day. Before retiring the next night I tried reaching my left testicle with my right elbow. I was not able to get my elbow within six inches of my left testicle.

I didn't hear from Reece about the ABC lawyer's opinion. Perhaps he will call me tomorrow.

5

Elderly people

Sunday was a delightful day with a clear blue sky and a light warm wind. On the way to the office I stopped at Ken's garage to see what was wrong with my Torino, my practice car. He said the trouble was the spark plugs and points. He had put the car on a machine to find the trouble. I offered to pay him but he would not take the money since I had not taken any money from him for looking after his diabetes.

At the office I had two patients waiting. One was a man with a sore throat. The other was the wife of a good friend of mine. She was complaining of everything today, no energy, no friends, her house was a mess and her husband was no help at all. About all I could do for her was to listen and suggest that things would be better in a few days. She seemed to feel a little better after having someone to just listen to her complaints.

At church the preacher is recovering from a recent knee operation. He is the first patient I ever had that I filed compensation papers on because he couldn't pray. It was because kneeling to pray is part of his work; if he couldn't kneel with people, he wasn't doing all of his business.

Dorothy and I sit in the back of the church on the right-hand side where my family has always sat. Years ago our family gave a stained glass window for the church and it is located in the back on the right-hand side. The preacher was perched on a high stool at the end of the isle. When the organist began a little soft music he crawled off his stool and came limping up the isle, greeting members on our side. When he got even with my pew I accused him of separating the sheep from the goats. I think this is in the Bible someplace. He grinned a bit and went on to the back to speak to some of the ushers. The probable explanation for greeting the people on the right side was that he couldn't turn to the left without pain in his knee.

Today, Monday, has been another very nice day with things going well at the office. My first patient was Berle, an old classmate of mine in the first grade. He won our class art contest with a picture of a Billy goat eating grass on a green hill. Now he has some hypertension. I have been treating him for about ten years. For some reason Berle always wants to be seen in the same examining room. When Lorie, his wife, came in sometime ago I asked her about this. She said it was because he wanted to be sure I used the same blood pressure machine each time. He has a machine at home and is checking up on me.

My last patient said she had stuck a splinter three inches long in her left thigh. It was about an inch long. After seeing her I went to Hickory to see Elsie, a patient in the hospital. She is an old friend of the family. She lived across the street from us and I sold her apples for fifteen cents a bucket when I was eight or ten years old. She is now suffering from congestive heart failure. None of my treatments are working.

I am afraid she is going to die.

When I returned from Hickory I went to the theater to see Scott, a boxer with an abscess in his nose, a very serious condition. He is disappointed that he will have to give up boxing. To keep him around I asked him to help clean the theater on Saturday afternoons. Larry is working hard with the boxers for a bout in Lavonia next Saturday night.

Last night I was called to one of the rest homes, a new thing for elderly people. When I arrived I recognized the patient as the first patient I had when I first started practicing here. Violet was glad to see me. She was complaining with abdominal pain. After examining her, I believed her trouble was gas pains and left her some tablets for gas. The director was to call me in two hours if she wasn't better. Violet was in the rest home because none of her children are at home to look after her. Our industrialization is hard on elderly people.

They must be placed somewhere while the children work. If their children have babies or preschool-age children, these too must be placed someplace so the parents can work. It takes the paycheck of both parents to pay for all the material things—automobiles, televisions and house payments—that people need today. I think even the schools are acting as babysitters for the children. The schools promote children whether they can pass the work or not. The law requires all children to attend school until they are sixteen years old. Some children don't want to attend and are very bad disciplinary problems for the teacher. Today, children don't have the cow pasture I had to play in. Now they must be enrolled in some kind of controlled supervised play.

3-4-1978 √

The night passed without any disturbance, no phone calls or ringing doorbell. After breakfast I left for the office.

Most of my patients had improved. At ten-thirty I decided to go to the hospital to see Elsie. She was much weaker. I couldn't find any specific reason for her weakness. I increased her digitalis and left word that I would check on her again in the afternoon.

When I returned to the office I had one or two patients waiting. One was an elderly lady about sixty-five years old. Sometime ago she had fallen, breaking her left humerus near the shoulder. She slipped on the wet floor while working in a restaurant. The first four weeks after the fall she complained a great deal, then suddenly stopped complaining and decided to return to work. Saturday she was complaining of bad pain in her arm so I arranged for a repeat x-ray of her arm. The report said her arm was healing, but rather slow. This is characteristic for people her age.

About noon today she called for me to wait, she had some papers for me to sign. She had quit her job ten days ago. Now she wanted papers to the effect that she couldn't work since the x-ray report said her arm wasn't healed. Dorothy thinks she is up to getting more money from the insurance company. She is probably right, especially with the x-ray report supporting her claim. I suppose there will be more to this case for quite a while.

After lunch the hospital called for me to come back to see Elsie. Before I could leave, another patient came in. It was about thirty minutes until I could get to Elsie's room. Her door was open with a curtain pulled between her and her roommate. This was the beginning of bad signs. Beyond the curtain were three or four figures clad in white bending over Elsie. I eased my way between them so I could see Elsie. She looked bad. She would hardly respond to her name. She was lying on her right side, her left thigh pulled up at right angle to her body, her head dropped down to her chest like her neck was broken. She was elevated at the head about thirty degrees. Her pulse was weak, blood pressure about sixty over thirty. There was some rattling in her chest. At times her hands would turn white as if blanching, then blue and pink. Every minute or two her face turned ashen. I believed she would die. Elsie was eighty-two years old. In a few minutes she died. I will miss Elsie.

On the way home I thought of the words of William Hazlitt: "We do not die wholly at our deaths: we smolder away gradually long before. Death only consigns the last fragment of what we were to the grave."

To myself I said as I drove to the office, "Goodbye, Elsie. I will miss you."

6

Saturday night boxing match

3-4-1978

When dawn broke today it delivered a very cold day. At the office things went well. Larry came to the theater around ten o'clock to prepare for his boxing event. We held the match at eight o'clock, the first one of the year. His boxers were all excited and had their parents along for support. Beyond their support there were few people there. I was very disappointed. Larry and the boys had worked for weeks. I think my biggest disappointment was the conduct of the people who did come.

It was a mixed crowd of all ages. Some threw things from the balcony onto the ones below, others spilt their drinks and popcorn on the floor and seats when they weren't throwing it at each other. In checking the dressing rooms a little boy told me two of the boys had climbed out a window onto the marquee and were throwing things onto the people on the street. I found one boy in the upstairs hallway throwing ice at the people with a paper cup when they came upstairs to the restrooms. There was a lot of pot smoking in the restrooms. On one occasion when I checked on the restrooms a little person wearing blue jeans was going into the ladies room. I called to say that was the ladies restroom. The person answered "Oh, that's all right because I am a girl." I gave up. The children were having a better time running around in the theater than watching the boxing match. It gives me a lot of worry thinking one will get injured. I suppose the insurance company is thinking of this too. That is probably why they charged me four hundred dollars for the evening.

After last night I am having second thoughts about the future of the theater. I don't think I would be any better off with more people attending, just more to look after and I don't think I can operate a program without children. It took a lot of time and patience to keep it going last night. It was about one-thirty Sunday morning when we closed.

Dorothy is going to Charlotte to play bridge this morning so I will be here alone. The days seem quite lonely when she is not here.

3-5-1978

We arose about eight-thirty Sunday morning after there had been two phone calls for me to come to the office. When I arrived at the office I had left my set of keys that turned the burglar alarm off. I had to go back after them. When I returned my first patient was Orville, a man I have seen several times. He is a very likable person about 56 years old, very intelligent, well built and could have been most anything in life he wanted. Now his greatest achievement is sobriety. His last drunk about a month ago was not so bad, but the one a year ago was so bad I recommended commitment in the alcoholic center. Today Orville wanted something for his nerves; he was drinking again.

After seeing him I went over to the theater and busied myself fixing some of the broken letters for the marquee. Then I hung some mirrors for the boxers to use for shadow boxing.

All the time I was working I was feeling very downhearted about the theater. Instead of going to church I cleaned up the place. I justified not going to church because none of the church people came to the boxing match. You can find a good excuse for just about anything. I think, though, my most disappointing feeling comes from the conduct of the children running all over the theater last night.

About one o'clock I came home for lunch. After all the popcorn and hot dogs I had last night I didn't want much. I went back to the office, but there weren't any patients. I sat around a while and then remembered the pan on the popcorn machine wasn't heating and there was a light switch out upstairs in the hallway at the theater. I closed the office and went back home to change clothes. While I was taking off my coat I felt a bulge in my inside coat pocket. I recognized it to be the billfold one of the boys found while we were cleaning the theater Saturday night. It had an I.D. card with telephone number inside. I called and the owner was glad to meet me at the theater again to claim his billfold He was very appreciative, but didn't leave the boy a reward.

After he left I went inside to repair the popcorn machine and light switch. The pan on the popcorn machine had come unplugged. The wires in the light switch had been twisted together so that the switch would not work, probably fixed this way on purpose by the last owner. I can guess why. Children were running upstairs flipping the switch off and on so people couldn't find the bathrooms. He had tied the switch off.

When I came downstairs someone was knocking on the door. It was a man I had seen in the office six months ago. Today he had a woman with him. She is about thirty-five, very thin and always wears men's clothes. They wanted something for their colds. Two months ago she had come to the office by herself.

She said the man was her boyfriend and a plumber. We went over to the office for treatment of the colds; then I asked him about helping me with some plumbing. He said yes he would be glad to. I then asked him did he know someone to put some Celotex back on the ceiling. The ceiling is about twenty-five feet high and I had no way of getting it up. He said to let him see it. After looking at the ceiling and commode he said he would take his friend home and be back in a few minutes.

When he returned he ran a long wire down the commode. It flushed like new. For the ceiling he used an A-frame ladder about twenty or so feet tall, climbed up it and nailed the Celotex to the ceiling. You never know who can do what.

I returned home around five o'clock. It was pretty warm outside so I walked about in the snow. After a short stroll, I came in and sat by the dining room window. Long shadows were beginning to fall on the snow from the tree. My thoughts soon turned to approaching night. The night is just the darkness like the shadows from the trees due to the earth turning us away from the sun. Why does this light and dark affect me so? Why does the daylight seem like something new each morning, the evening like something ending, like a life gasping its last. With each new day I feel like I have a new chance.

A little way from the window a chickadee was pecking on a pinecone; the first chickadee I have seen this year. I have seen robins for the last eight or ten days. Maple twigs are turning red. Spring is coming again though it is not apparent from the snow. It is now about eight o'clock and the night stillness has settled in. I can't say I have accomplished much today except returning the billfold and seeing an A-frame ladder.

Tomorrow is Monday. Living through the night I will arise when the sun dispels the darkness and go to the office to wait for patients to come in. It is a little like being by a stream waiting to see what will come down. I wonder what will happen tomorrow.

7

The effect of snow

3-2-1978

There were no calls during the night. After breakfast I looked out the window toward the street. Jack, our dog was looking back for me to request him to bring me the paper. This is done by a sort of ritual of shouting accompanied by vigorous hand gestures towards the top corner of the street where the paper carrier generally throws it. My activity soon gets him to barking whereupon two hundred yards down the street my neighbors' eighteen dogs join in. If there are two papers, the morning and evening, he has a problem deciding which paper to bring.

He will first try getting both papers in his mouth, but finding this cumbersome he will drop the lightest one and bring the heaviest. With the same urging he may go back after the other one. He uses this same weighing process whenever he eats. If there are two portions of food out, one for Blossum, our other dog, he will not start eating until he has inspected both portions, then he selects the heaviest one.

At the office things started off badly. It might have just seemed this way due to my apprehension about the gas heaters in the theater. After the last practice session one failed to respond to the thermostat. It continued to burn so that it had to be turned off at the switch. If it should fail during the night it might set the theater on fire. I checked on it on my way to the office this morning. It was responding to the thermostat again. I have called the gas company to check on it anyway.

A second disappointment happened at nine o'clock this morning when the father of a boy I had seen yesterday came in for some medicine for the boy. He said his finger was hurting and wanted something for pain. I had sutured his finger two days ago. His finger started bleeding and he couldn't find me so he took him to the hospital where they had sutured it again. I agreed to give some pain medicine but I wanted to see the boy first. He didn't believe he could bring the boy in because the dressing on his hand was too big to go through his coat sleeve. Finally he said he would bring him in this afternoon.

I stayed upset all afternoon wondering what had gone wrong with my suturing. I had put three small sutures in his finger. When he left the office there was no bleeding.

During the morning I saw my other patients. At eleven o'clock there was a lot of commotion inside the lobby proceeding toward the reception room. I went to the doorway to see what was happening. The reception room door flew open. My eyes were aimed at where someone's head should be if it came through the door normally. Their aim was quickly changed to half this height as a head and long waving arms brushing the floor pushed through supported by a small woman with a round brownish face with a black eye. She was helping a large tall man stumble through the door into the reception room. Behind her a young man wearing a black leather jacket and a brown taxi cap on his round head was grinning from ear to ear, suggesting he was giving me something.

I didn't want them to wait in the reception room with my other patients. I helped them bring him back to the examining room ahead of my other patients. He flopped into the chair. I stood back to see his face. I had seen him about six months ago with jaundice. At that time I thought his jaundice was due to a cancer of the head of the pancreas. After questioning him he finally admitted he had been drinking for six weeks. I gave him some medicine and his jaundice cleared up. I had not seen him again until today.

When I asked what his trouble was today he said he was drunk again. After examining him I told him he was all right except for being drunk. Then to my surprise he said this was all he wanted to know and motioned for the woman and cab driver to help him up. I was relieved when I heard the outside door close. In a few minutes Sarah, my assistant, came back to summon me to the front window real quick. I thought he might have fallen so I hurried to the window. She pointed to my car and said, "Look out there."

Standing between my car and the cab was my drunk patient urinating on the rear wheel of my car. Sarah wanted me to call the police. I said I was just glad he made it outside to my car rather than on my floor in the office. The round-headed taxi driver was leaning on the hood of his cab looking back at us with his big grin as if saying, "I told you so."

It was now about noon, time to go to a meeting at the ABC Store. I arrived a little early. Our ABC officer was already there with Reece. Reece said he had heard from the state regarding our ABC Officer. They said each ABC bill allowing a town to sell liquor was different and we would have to operate the store according to our interpretation of our bill.

I called the meeting to order. We told the officer we might work out an agreement with Lenoir so it would not be necessary to cut his salary. He seemed satisfied. We dismissed him and discussed the details of sharing him with Lenoir. We are in agreement that this might be a good solution to our problem.

When I returned to the office it had started snowing. Most of the afternoon I was cold and shivering. I had a few patients and planned to close early. I was about to close when Bernie came in for some medicine for his wife. She lost her left leg several years ago following an attack of flu. Something caused the arteries in her leg to collapse so it had to be amputated.

A year ago she fell getting out of bed and still has pain in her hip especially in bad weather. I gave him the medicine and he was about to leave when he said it had begun to snow and he remembered he wanted to go by the feed store to get some cracked corn to go in his bird feeder. Since he was interested in birds, I showed him the jugs I had cut holes in to make birdhouses. He said the holes were too little and would have to be as big as a quarter. He pulled out his knife to make them bigger, but saw how deep the snow was getting and headed for home without the cracked corn. I closed the office after him and went home too.

At home after supper, Dorothy watched the ball game on the television while I did some reading and watched the snow coming down. Around ten o'clock I heard the weather report. It called for clearing and cold. The snow was now about six inches deep.

I have great fascination for snow. I feel some apprehension associated with snow that I can't explain. For some people this apprehension might be due to restricting their mobility, giving a sense of insecurity. In other people it might be due to inactivity, the plants and stores closed, children home from school. For the young there is the excitement of playing in the snow. Sometimes due to this excitement there are fatalities.

Dorothy says that I delight in making my car slide in the snow just for the fun of it. Frequently elderly people suffer heart attacks when there is snow on the ground. They overexert themselves shoveling snow, carrying in wood or pushing on stalled automobiles. The cold air breathed into the lungs may cause the blood to chill in the lungs leading to a heart attack.

Of course there are other things.

I recall a night several years ago when the snow was about ten inches deep. I received a phone call around eleven o'clock from a young widow to please come to her house to see her boyfriend. She thought he was having a heart attack. She said he was having severe chest pains. I left my house as soon as I could but due to the depth of the snow it took about ten minutes to get there. When I arrived at her house and examined her boyfriend he was dead. He was lying on his back on the bed nude and covered with a blanket. This is a pretty difficult situation. I can't leave the dead man in her house until morning. I don't know anything about his medical history. I will need to call his wife to tell her where her husband is and that he is dead. After this a second question is what undertaker does she want me to call to come pick up the body. If his doctor won't sign the death certificate the undertaker will need to call the coroner.

His wife gave me the name of the undertaker to call. It was a very cold conversation. I don't know what part snow played in this man's death. It could have been worry about getting home in ten inches of snow. But if he were thinking about getting home he would have had his clothes on.

8

What the Bible says

3-6-1978 ✓

This has been a very pleasant pre-spring day, a blue sky, a little wind, a warm sun and a sloppy wet ground from melting snow. My day began at three-thirty in the morning when the phone rang.

"I have a fellow who has cut his hand. Will you meet me at the office to fix it?" It was the foreman from one of the plants.

"Yes," I said. "I'll meet you in about ten minutes."

While I was suturing his hand the foreman was trying to keep the patient's mind off of the operation. The patient was a man thirty-five years old, rather gaunt with a twangy southern drawl. Once his color turned rather white. We had him lower his head for a minute or two. George, the foreman kept talking to him and asking questions. I was rather interested in the last one. He asked him where he lived so he could fill out a report. He told George he lived in the last house on Rural Retreat Road. I think this is what got my attention. I hadn't thought of rural people retreating. While thinking of this the next statement was more interesting. I was wrapping the final dressing on his hand when George said to me, "I guess you get tired of the phone ringing?"

"No," I said, "sometimes if it doesn't ring I pick it up to see if I have a dial tone."

The patient then spoke up. "I had a phone installed in my house six months ago and nobody ever called me. I called out to my friends, but nobody called me. Last week I called the operator to ask her if she had told people in the community I had a phone."

Later in the morning things were going well for about thirty minutes when the power went off, leaving us in the dark. I asked Bobbie to call city hall to see what the trouble was. I buy my electrical power from the town. She said it was part of a conservation measure. The coal miners are on strike and the country is running out of coal.

When the lights came on I went into the second examining room where a mother and child were waiting. I recognized the mother. Murial is a big woman in all proportions, weighing about 160 pounds, mostly muscle and red hair. In other ways she is an exceptional person with some difficulty understanding the law. Probably for this reason she frequently takes the law into her own hands.

The most recent occasion was at Larry's last boxing match. About the middle of the event while one of her sons was boxing Larry came to me and said we had better call the police; things were getting out of hand down front. One of the boxers told him a man and woman were getting into a fight. I called the police station for a policeman. They said one was already in the theater. I found him in the balcony watching the boxers. He hadn't seen any trouble. I watched a while with him and then returned to the front of the theater where Dorothy was selling hot dogs. As far as I could tell the event went along without any trouble.

I found out what the trouble was when it was over while Larry and I were cleaning up. One of the young boxers about twelve years old helping us said, "Say, did you all see the fight?"

"No," we said. "What happened?" He pointed to the middle of the left isle and said, "This big man was sitting right out there and reached over and pinched this big red headed woman right on the tit. She slapped his face real hard. He drew back to hit her and she screamed, 'You bastard, you son of a bitch. You touch me again and I'll slit your damn throat.' She would have done it too. She had a knife with a big blade already pulled back in her left hand,"

Larry and I had no comment to make. We were real glad the event was over. Today she wanted something for her sore throat.

My next patient was Hub, a friend who has frequent tension headaches. Today he had been at the lake just resting. While at the lake he said Rev. Gray came down with his dog. Rev Gray is a young minister in town with a lot of energy to spend. He likes fishing and duck hunting. I recently gave him my decoys and duck caller.

Today he was training his new Labrador retriever. There was a gang of ducks up in the head of the neck and the dog flushed them. On the way out one of them hit the power line crossing the lake. His dog caught it and brought it in. Hub wondered if the game warden would get the preacher for taking ducks out of season.

"I don't know about ducks," I said, "but I can tell you about a man who got caught with a trout that was not the legal size. He and a friend were fishing on opening day. His friend caught a trout nine inches long. He didn't have a creel so he put it in Fred's creel until he could go to the car for his. While he was gone the game warden appeared and checked Fred's creel. The trout was one inch short so he demanded Fred to ride with him and another warden to appear before a magistrate. They put Fred in the back seat with his trout and drove to the magistrate's office about ten miles away. When Fred showed the trout to the magistrate it was ten and a half inches long."

The rest of the day went along well. I closed at five for supper and a pleasant evening at home. I was about finished eating when the telephone rang. A lady said her father was threatening people with his shotgun, rambling at night and talking to women and men having a party in his trailer and nobody was there. I told her I would take out commitment papers for him to go to a mental hospital tomorrow. I had hardly hung up the phone when it rang again. Another lady was calling about her husband. He is the chief of police and had stepped on a nail. She wanted me to see him tonight. I asked her to have him come to the office at seven o'clock tonight.

I was getting ready to leave for the office when a small car pulled up in front of the house. A large man got out holding the left side of his head and came to the front door. When I opened the door I recognized him to be Karl, one of the supervisors from one of the plants. He is about forty years old and was wearing a white dress shirt and pants. His face was pretty red and his shirt looked like he had spilled mercurochrome on it. He wanted something for his headache.

"Yes," I said. "Go to the office and I will follow you out."

It was now about six-thirty. With better light at the office I could see he was bleeding above his left ear. "What happened?" I asked. With some hesitancy he said "I lost my temper. Someone cold-cocked me with a pop bottle from behind." His wife had stopped at a convenience store on the edge of town. While she was in the store two boys jumped in her car and got the keys. Before they could make off with the car she ran out screaming to them. They jumped out and ran down the road to a used car lot. She ran back into the store and called Karl. He rushed to the store and they both drove down the road to the used car lot. He spotted two boys and jumped out and grabbed one. He requested the keys to his wife's car. When the boy didn't give the desired response he grabbed him around the neck aiming to choke it out of him. While he was engaged in choking, the second boy cold-cocked him with a pop bottle from behind. He didn't understand why his wife had not alerted him of the coming blow.

I had him bend over the sink so I could wash the blood off his head. He had a large bruise and a small laceration above the left ear. It didn't need any sutures. I was about through when there was a great commotion out front in the waiting room.

I left him to go see what was taking place. A rather tall man about twenty-six years old and a deputy sheriff about a foot shorter were trying to come through the door together. Both were bloody from shoulders to hips. They were a bit comical both trying to get through the door at the same time. I couldn't tell who was leading, the short or the tall. The young man was calling for Karl. I didn't know how he knew him. When they cleared the door I saw they were handcuffed together.

One of the tall man's hands was bleeding. He was trying to hold his bleeding hand with the handcuffed hand. This was getting him and the sheriff's deputy covered in blood. His voice was strong and forceful. He had a wild expression on his face. I said he could talk to Karl outside whenever I had finished with him.

"No," he insisted. "I want to talk now."

Again I said no. After a few more times I told the deputy to take him outside until I finished. He took him outside. As soon as they were out Chief Barlow who had stepped on a nail came in. He saw I was busy and sat in the waiting room. I was through with Karl and he was ready to leave when his wife rushed in to check on him. Chief Barlow had come back and was sitting in the examining chair with his shoe off so I could see his foot. Before she could speak Karl said," Honey why didn't you warn me about the boy behind me with the pop bottle?"

She said, "I did, but you were so busy choking him you didn't hear me." When she saw he wasn't seriously hurt she left to go to the police station to make out a report.

While I checked on the chief's foot Karl asked him what to do about the boy outside. He was still screaming for Karl to come out. Karl first wanted to know if he should talk with him outside, handcuffed to the deputy, or go to the police station where his wife was. Chief Barlow asked, "Who struck the first blow?" Karl said, "I jumped out of the car and grabbed one of the boys by the neck first."

Chief Barlow said, "In that case I don't know what to do"

I finished with Chief Barlow's foot and they had not made a decision on where to talk, outside or in the police station. Recalling the expression on the face of the man handcuffed when he came through the door, I told him the best thing to do was to talk in the police station. I didn't want another fight in my office. Chief Barlow agreed. He knew the boy and said he was under a suspended sentence of twenty years for car theft. If he had any more trouble with the law he would go to prison for twenty years.

I said if it is a case of mistaken identity, meaning he had grabbed the wrong boy, they might settle it tonight. To support my opinion I said the Bible says to settle with your adversary quickly.

"I want to do what the Bible says," Karl replied. "I will go to the police station to talk now."

We went outside where the deputy and boy were waiting. Karl said he would talk to them in the police station and left. The deputy brought the boy in for me to see his wounds. He removed the handcuffs so I could wash his hand. He had several small lacerations on the right ring finger. The pop bottle had probably broken and a piece of glass had cut his finger.

I dressed it and then the sheriff handcuffed him again to take him to the police station. I went home around ten-thirty. That was the end of my pleasant evening.

9

A bleeding leg

3-9-1978 ✓

My first patient of the day was Hester, the elderly lady I had seen with the flu. She is much better. Her husband Henry said he was glad she was better. They had been married fifty years and Hester was the only woman he had ever thought of. When he saw her sitting on her father's front porch fifty years ago he knew she was for him. Until that time people called him a woman hater.

Hearing this Hester smiled a bit at him and said it took her to change him. Henry said, "No, I waited till I saw what I wanted. I am not like some folks, just jump in the first puddle they come to. I believe if people would wait there would not be any divorces. I believe what God put together let no man put asunder."

I was about to make some reply when Hester said, "Feel here on my stomach where it hurts." With this I turned my attention to the job at hand. I explained that I thought her pain was due to so much coughing with the flu. I said, "Now that the flu is better your stomach will be better in a day or two."

Later in the day there was more discussion about marriage with another patient. This was a man about sixty years old. He was in the office in regard to his driving license. About four years ago he had been arrested for drunk driving. The state requires a medical examination on these people about once a year to see if they are drinking again. Toward the end of the examination I asked him if he was still drinking. He replied, "No, my wife won't let me. She won't stand for it." I asked him then how did the patrolman catch him for drunk driving. He said it is his second wife that doesn't allow drinking. He and his first wife had five children while they lived in Washington, D.C. They moved back here four years ago to her parents' town. Each time there was trouble she went over to her parents house and stayed three or four days. The fourth time she took off he told her three times is out in baseball and four times is out with him. "If you leave this time don't come back." She didn't come back. He lived the next two years in a cabin on the lake. Things were pleasant until one day he decided he was getting old. He might have a stroke or something and there was no one to help him. He started courting a woman and soon married her. She had money, a house, a car and good friends. He is happier now than he has ever been.

One patient asked me did I know a man named Rick who is interested in Indian artifacts. I said yes, I know him well. He was in the office about a month ago and I gave him a very hard piece of black flint a Cherokee Indian had brought me from Cherokee. It was so hard I was not able to make anything like an arrowhead out of it.

At four-thirty a patient called me to come to her house. She said her leg was bleeding and she couldn't get it stopped. At the house the front door was unlocked. I went into the living room and called out, "Hello, hello!" No one answered. I went to the bedroom off from the living room. There was some blood beside the bed. I called out again and someone said to come on back to the porch. The floor was smeared with big clots of blood. To the left of the kitchen on the back porch were two elderly people holding the patient up on a kitchen stool.

I sat my medical bag down on a chair and pushed between them to get a look at the patient. It was Virginia, a patient I had been seeing for ten years. She was pale, but conscious.

"Look at my foot," she said. "It's been bleeding for an hour and I can't get it stopped." Her right foot was covered in blood up to her knee. We were all standing in blood on the floor. She said she was taking her hose off and caught one of her varicose veins with her fingernail. I unwrapped the towels she had around her ankle. Her ankle and foot was a dark brown color as if it had been cooked. I looked real close and saw that this brown color was coming from a sock she had pulled up to her knee to try to stop the flow of blood. After removing the sock I wiped the blood away and found the bleeding was coming from a small varicose vein. I wrapped a dry towel around it and we moved her to the bedroom. She had some old ace bandages in the drawer that I used to make a compression bandage. This controlled the bleeding. I told her to come by tomorrow for me to see it again.

After closing the office Rick, the man interested in Indian lore, came to the house. He wanted to show me the arrowhead he had made from the piece of flint I had given him. It was a very good one. I told him I would have to take lessons from him. He also brought an Indian bonnet he is making. He has his wife stand on a stool in the living room to model it for him. His greatest ambition now is to complete his attire of full headdress and tail feathers. Then he wants to ride about like Chief Crazy Horse in someone's pasture chasing cows.

He wants me to find him a picture of Crazy Horse. I am wondering if there isn't some disturbance in his head since he also says with assurance he was an Indian in a life before now, probably Chief Crazy Horse.

10

Harold and Richard

3-10-1978 ✓

It rained all night. Water running off the house made a lot of noise going through the gutters that I had cleaned out a few days ago. At the breakfast table Dorothy and I discussed people who always visit the homes of dying patients and then visit in the home of the deceased. This might be to make a visual inventory of the possessions and later attend the auction when they are auctioned off. They might just steal something while they are visiting.

At the office my first patient was Walter, whom I have known for about ten years. I was a little surprised when he told me he needed an examination to retain his driving license. He is a very nice looking man about forty years old and rather quiet except when he is drinking. Then he is argumentative and difficult to handle. The state record indicated he had been arrested for drunk driving about four years ago. This is about the time he and some friends were fishing at night with set hooks for catfish. The next morning he called me because of pain in his hip. I ordered an x-ray, which showed a fracture of the left hip. He stayed at home in bed for six weeks until he recovered.

While examining him for the driver's license I asked him if he had been drinking any more. He said no, he hadn't touched a drop since that night he fell down a bank and fractured his hip. He didn't remember falling or driving home. This was so frightening he had not drank since. He was afraid it might happen again and he could be accused of anything. Last fall he was about to break over. He and two friends were fishing late in the evening. He was sitting in the middle of the boat and

38

he passed the liquor from one end to the other for his companions. It smelt awfully good but he didn't drink a drop.

Around ten o'clock I saw a patient with a bad cut on the knuckle of the little finger of the right hand. He was a young man about forty years old. His hand was swollen and the wound looked like it was three days old. When he came back to the examining room he walked with a limp. All I could do for his hand was dress it, give antibiotics and tetanus toxoid. He was a bit reluctant to tell me how he had hurt his finger. It looked like he had hit something. To fill out the insurance forms I needed to know how the accident happened. He said it was no accident. He got mad with his horse and hit it in the mouth with his fist. The teeth had cut his hand. When he saw his cut hand he kicked the horse in the flank and hurt his foot. I told him anytime he cut himself on a tooth or a bone it was a bad wound and he should get medical attention. He would need to soak it in warm water and come back in the morning.

I didn't tell him I had a butcher a few years ago who stuck a piece of bone in his thumb. He died two years later from complications from this wound.

In the afternoon Harold came into the office. He is about thirty-five and has five children. He is a well-developed man, about six feet tall weighing about two hundred pounds. He has trouble accepting responsibilities. He says he is always nervous. I had not seen him for two years. The last time I saw him he had cut his wrist in a suicide attempt. This was his third attempt at suicide. Two times before this he had cut both wrists and I sent him home. His father called me and said if Harold wasn't committed to the insane asylum I would be responsible for his death. I told him I didn't see any reason to send him because he didn't want to go and I had sent him before and it didn't do any good. This time he wanted to go because he was due to go to court. If he was in confinement he would get out of court. On this last visit we had some disagreement. I think it was that if I sewed up his wrist he would go home and cut them again. I answered I didn't want to waste my time. He told his driver, "Let's go," and they left. I heard later another doctor sewed his wrist up.

Today was the first time I had seen him since that night. He said he had been studying nerves. He had been in several hospitals for his nerves without any improvement. I told him he was built with the nervous system he had and must live with it. I asked where he was working. He had not worked in two years. I told him he must work to get better of his nerves. He must work all the time and nothing else would help him. He had always sought something to make his life easier, alcohol, drugs and rest. None of these would help him. His only way was to work. I told him nerve medicine would keep him like a zombie. To this he replied, "I don't want to go through life like a zombie."

He promised to get a job and left without nerve medicine. I hope he does well.

Richard was my next patient. He wanted some medicine for his arthritis. He is a self-taught philosopher and mechanic. We talk together a great deal when I am not busy. He has an old steam engine he uses to grind sugar cane to make molasses. I visited his engine last summer. He fires it with wood. He has it rigged up with a saw to cut the wood it burns and a pump so it will draw water out of the creek for the boiler.

Today he was nearly run over at a filling station. Someone pulled out in front of him.

My next patient was a man about forty-five years old. He had been drinking and wanted something for his nerves. I asked him why he had gotten drunk. He said his girlfriend had left him because he didn't go to his daughter's birthday party. His story goes like this. He had been living with a woman thirty-six years old. They have been living together for ten years. He had one child by her who is six years old. The mother had rented a community center to give a birthday party for their daughter. When he didn't attend she took the daughter and moved out of his apartment. They have been separated three weeks. He started drinking the day she left. He didn't go to the party because her brothers and sisters would be there and they don't like him. He figured all along this would happen because of the age difference. He had refused to marry her because he always believed she would leave him for a younger man.

Around five o'clock a young man came in the office with a piece of yellow paper in his pocket. I thought it might be an insurance form. It was so near closing time I was about to tell him to come back in the morning, but decided I should look at the paper first. It was a form for wrestling. After completing it I asked him if he would like to wrestle in the theater. He said he had wrestled in barns and tents. He would like to try a theater. He agreed to call me about a date on Monday.

11

My 60ᵗʰ birthday

3-12-1978 ✓

Today began with a clear sky and a warm spring breeze. Before breakfast I had a call from a patient who said she was broken out with red spots and her lips were swelling. I told her to come to the office and I would meet her there in five minutes. When I arrived there was a card stuck in the door from Jim and his wife Dot wishing me a happy birthday. I recalled then that I had thought of Jim when I saw a red bird in one of the trees this morning. Jim said several years ago just after a snow that the prettiest sight he ever did see was a red bird among the blooms on his Japanese cherry tree and snow on the ground.

My patient, Savannah, followed me in the door. Her face was swollen and her lips were twice as large as normal. There were red spots on her hands and arms. Some medicine she was taking was giving her an allergic reaction. This is an example of the treachery of medicine and why it is necessary to be very careful about giving people medicine. Sometimes it works smoothly; sometimes it works like a deadly snakebite. This was the second time she has had trouble. This time, she had a slight sore throat and wanted a few penicillin tablets. Penicillin had always worked well for her. It was about ten o'clock in the morning. She left the office and I was seeing another patient.

The phone rang at ten minutes later. It was Savannah's husband calling. He said she took one tablet a few minutes ago and now her lips are swollen and she feels funny all over. I told him to bring her back to the office. When she returned in about five minutes she was almost in a

42

state of shock. I worked with her for an hour before she was well enough to return home. This is a daily apprehension when administering medicine. It seems so easy until something goes wrong. Sometimes the patient develops the sensitivity gradually in which case the medicine can be withdrawn before there is a severe reaction. But there are times when the sensitivity develops almost at once and there is a severe reaction. This is an example of a sever reaction.

My next patient was Jerry who suffers with cancer of the bladder. He is about 70 years old. His father delivered mail to my grandfather in a buggy. My first meeting with the patient was about twenty years ago shortly after I began practice here. Dorothy and I and our children were at a lake swimming and Jerry and his wife were there along with a lot of other people having a picnic. They invited us to share in their picnic though we didn't have any food. I have been treating him for his blood pressure. Another doctor is treating him for his bladder.

Today Jerry is complaining of pain in his shoulder. I suspect it is cancer metastasized to his shoulder. When he left, the man who had hit the horse with his fist was waiting. His hand and foot are much better. He is to return Thursday. When patients do not return, I don't know whether they have gotten better or gone to another doctor. This adds to the frustration of my practice.

In addition to the difficulty with my patients, I am either taking a cold or having a terrific spell of hay fever. My nose is dripping so bad I didn't go to church. All the remedies I have tried have failed. The things I have thought of that I might be allergic to like peanuts, milk, eggs and cheese do not appear to be the cause. If I do not find something successful soon I will have to see a nose doctor.

I closed the office around eleven-thirty. Dorothy had prepared a big birthday dinner for me. All my children called me wishing me a happy birthday.

During the day I had three more calls to make. One to see a lady recovering from a stroke. Her catheter had stopped up. I removed it hoping she was well enough to know when she needed to void. My second patient was a seventy-five-year-old lady with pleurisy. I have been giving her injections of penicillin. The third and final patient was a drunken man.

When the phone rang at nine that night asking me to see the patient, I became uneasy about the call. I could not recall the patient's name. I didn't recognize the caller either. Sometimes if I can recognize the caller I can place the patient with the right people. When I asked what was the trouble the caller said he had stomach trouble. When I asked if he had been drinking he said no so I agreed to meet them at the office. I called the police to meet me there too. They will come whenever I think I have a call I don't know about. As I approached the office my headlights reflected on the tail light of the car. There were three men in the front seat. One got out of the front on the passenger side and opened the back door of the car. Seems like he was checking on something in the back seat. I moved closer and saw a man lying on the seat. I got into the back to examine him. His pulse and blood pressure were normal. There was a strong odor of alcohol. When I asked if he had been drinking an elder man who had got out of the car said yes. With this I was upset because I believed someone had lied to me to get me to see the patient, but since I was here now I would have to do the best I could do with it.

I soon remembered the patient. I had seen him several times for the same thing. The last time he developed jaundice and I thought he must have died since he never returned to the office. I told the elder man I thought he was drunk again and if he would take him home and look after him he would be better in a few days. The man said the patient didn't have a home to go to, but he would take him to his home. He was his brother-in-law. When I heard this I was more sympathetic, realizing that these people were going to have to look after this man all night and my part would soon be over. They promised to bring him back tomorrow if he wasn't any better.

This was the last call and the last of my sixtieth birthday.

12

Too weak to work

3-14-1978

I left home for the office around eight in the morning finding many robins in the churchyard and some blackbirds whistling on the power line. At the office a big blue pigeon was walking about on the church tower. I flipped a rock up toward it with my slingshot. It flew before the rock got near it. I keep the pigeons scared off because their droppings cause the roof to leak. I am surprised at their sensitivity. When I first began observing them I thought they had to be looking straight at me to tell the rock was coming. I have now concluded they are looking at me when they have their head turned so one eye is turned toward me. Even if they haven't seen me they can detect the rock coming shortly after it leaves the slingshot. They detect the vibration the rock makes coming through the air.

When they leave the church they fly over to the town water tank about a block away where their droppings have turned the roof a dark red color. Sometimes after a big rain when the water tastes bad people call city hall and ask why they haven't fixed the roof. They say, "Those droppings from the pigeons are washing into the water and making it taste bad."

My first patient today was Minnie, a woman thirty-four years old accompanied by her husband. I have been treating her for about ten years and this was the first time I had seen her husband. Most of her complaints have been of weakness, tiredness and mild arthritic pains. Recently she had the flu and recovered in six days. Today for some reason I believed this was an unusual call for her. I asked them to come back to the examining room for examination and consultation. In the examining room I have three chairs in addition to other equipment. Most of the time I use all the chairs and desk. Minnie sat in the green chair at the end of the desk so she was facing me sitting at the desk. Her husband pulled up the third chair so that he was almost between us. I asked my patient what was the trouble today. She said she was tired and weak and couldn't work any longer. Before she could say anything else her husband said she was disabled. With this remark his wife began to cry.

I could see her husband was quite tense. He repeated how weak she was and that she couldn't work any longer. His remarks soon confirmed what I thought was the reason for their visit.

"We have paid the damn money into the government and now we want it back," he said.

I agreed that they had paid in social security and to get it back they would need to go to the social security office in Hickory. What he would like is for the social security office to pay her so she could stay at home. I didn't tell him but social security will not pay unless the applicant is disabled to the extent she can't work.

Harold, my elderly man I saw about a week ago for commitment to a mental institution, was my next patient. He has been staying with one of his sons. He was smiling and seemed happy. His blond hair was combed and parted on the side. He had a new brown jacket and a bright red shirt on. I was glad he had recovered. He will spend the next week with his other son. After this he will go back to his cabin on the lake. By then the weather may be warm enough he can fish and work his garden. A little love and company is often better than any medicine.

When he left there were no more patients waiting so I went up to Jim's store to exchange a jacket someone had given me for my birthday. I wanted to swap it for some pants. When I walked in Jim was in a little corner in the back of the store and almost under the stairs. When he heard me speak to the two young male clerks he came out to ask what was the trouble. His left cheek was much larger than the right. He was chewing tobacco. He held two round white things about the size of pecans in his left hand.

"Think they'll work," he said and threw them on the counter for me to see. They were floats he had made out of Styrofoam to use for crappy fishing. I said they were too big.

"Wait till they are sanded. Then they'll be just right," he said spitting into a little cup. I told him I wanted to swap the jacket for some pants. He went around the counter and was back in a minute and threw some gray pants onto the counter. He found a tape measure and measured me from my belt to a little above my shoe heels. I think he just did this as a matter of habit. He knew how long to make the pants from past years. Anyway he had a little piece of paper and made some notes and said. "You are getting too damn fat just like me." One of the clerks took the pants upstairs and Jim pulled a puzzle out of his pocket. "Bet you can't work this," he said. He knows I don't like puzzles. When I couldn't work it he was delighted to show me how it works. We discussed crappy fishing a bit and I returned to the office.

A mother and grandmother were waiting with a boy six years old. The mother said he had a piece of apple stuck up his nose. He was crying and I figured he would be difficult to hold. I told them it would take some good holding or they could take him to the hospital where they might put the child to sleep. They said they could hold him. By now the grandfather had also joined the group. The grandfather held the child on his lap with the child's legs between his thighs, the mother held his hands and grandmother held his head. I think he felt secure and stopped crying. He held still and with a pair of tweezers I pulled a small piece of red plastic out of his right nostril.

When the mother saw it she said, "Oh, yes he tore one of the plastic buttons off of his teddy bear before eating the apple."

One of the foremen from the mill was my next patient. He complained of nerve trouble. I ask him what the trouble was.

"I work with my wife too much," he said.

You can take this a lot of ways, but his story goes like this. He is a fixer in the mill and keeps the machines running for all the employees on the floor. His wife works on the same floor. The other workers complained because he always keeps his wife's machines running and neglects theirs. He was afraid they would get him fired. I thought the best thing for him to do was to get transferred to another floor, but not at his request. My reason for him to get transferred without asking was so his wife couldn't say he did it to move off of her floor.

Around four o'clock Willie came in. Willie is a big boy twenty years old, married, six feet tall, well developed, a little freckle faced, blue eyes and unkempt light brown hair. He has mostly a round face with no wrinkles and almost a permanent smile. I like to see him because he always looks happy and curious about everything. He is at a dangerous age, seldom sick or tired, lots of energy. He was wearing a short sleeve red shirt and a pair of well-worn blue jeans and tennis shoes. He has an inner restlessness driving him to challenge any movement like fast cars and motorcycles. It is a peculiar thing in man's development to desire to do physical activities that don't add anything to the family income. It is probably a natural instinct in man that is now suppressed by society.

If Willie were an Indian 400 years ago there would be nothing wrong with his activities. He would be excited to join in the tribal hunt every day until exhausted, rest a bit at night and lead the hunt in the morning. Since Willie is not an Indian, but a member of society that lives by going to work every day and spending a lot of time in front of a desk, this drive must be satisfied in some other way than in a hunt. Now Willie satisfies his drive in sports and riding a big motorcycle.

About five days ago I filled out insurance papers for an accident he had on his motorcycle. He injured his left leg and was out of work three weeks. Today he was back with another accident to his right leg from another motorcycle accident. If he can survive until he is about fifty he will be content to do deskwork.

13

A spring day

3-20-1978 ✓

Today was beautiful day, temperature around seventy degrees. The grass is a little greener and the maple trees have started blooming. Birds were adding their voices to the traffic sounds. As I drove to the office, blue jays were calling "Thief, thief, thief." In the mill yard robins had one eye cocked toward the ground checking for worms.

My first patient was a very friendly man, but very rough looking. He does some farming and trades in cows. He is about six feet tall dark complexioned and weighs about two hundred and fifty pounds. Jim says he is a pin hooker, a person who buys cows, takes them home, fattens them up and resells them in the farmers market. Today he was complaining of pain and numbness in his right leg. He had been splitting blocks of wood about two feet long.

He said, "They split awfully good while they were frozen. I speck I strained my leg on one of them. I feel just like I did ten years ago when my bull knocked me on its back. I rode it into the barn before I could get off for fear it would gore me."

His leg was swollen some and had a bruised place on it just above the ankle. His blood pressure was 190–100. I gave him medication for his blood pressure and some pain medication. He is due to return tomorrow morning.

My next patient wanted to get married. She was 17 years old and three months pregnant. She said she knew it and her boyfriend with her knew it too. I gave her the marriage certificate and they left happy.

Reece came by before noon to discuss the ABC store. Our business is improving. He believes we are getting a lot of our customers back that moved to Lenoir. This is because we have a wider selection of liquor than Lenoir. Some people have very special ideas about where they buy their liquor. Some don't prefer to be seen buying it in their hometown. Too, Reece gives everyone very special attention whenever possible.

In the afternoon I had three drunken patients. Of course you think like some people did when we voted in the liquor store. They said I just wanted the store so I could treat the drunks. I supported the ABC store because I had drunks buying liquor in other places and we were not getting any money for our town.

The first drunk was the woman who came four or five days ago in the yellow cab. She still had the black eye and was drunker than before. I asked what she wanted me to do for her. She said to see if her blood pressure was all right. I said it was fine, she opened her pocketbook to pay me and it was full of large bills. As far as I could tell she left happy.

The second was the one I saw on Sunday. The small woman who had brought him a few days ago was with him. Her cheek was pushed out. I think she was dipping snuff. He agreed to go to a detox center.

My third man was Ira, the old man threatening people with his shotgun. He was a very pleasant man about 75 years old in good health. He could joke a little and didn't seem too disturbed today. After examining him I decided what he needed was to be looked after. He was living by himself, doing his own cooking and cleaning. Two men brought him in. When I asked him who they were he said they were his sons, the oldest by his first wife, the youngest by his second wife.

"Both of my wives are dead," Ira said. "I thought that was enough. I haven't looked for nary 'nothern."

He agreed to stop drinking and live with his eldest son. It makes me sad to see old people end up this way.

I was closing the office when two young men helped another man seventy-eight years old into the reception room. I saw him about a month ago for the flu. Today I hardly recognized him. He had a four- or five-day-old beard stained with brownish material from mouth to ears. His face was reddish with fiery blue eyes. His clothes were like he had been sleeping in them. When he came back to the examining room he stumbled along with his hands outstretched feeling the wall. In the examining chair he sat with his head almost between his knees. While examining him I thought I smelt rotten apples.

"What medicine are you taking?" I asked him.

"Everything," he replied. "Asperines, bufferins, your medicine and whatever anybody else told me."

"What about whiskey?"

"Yes," he said, "with lemons."

I gave him some medicine for his nausea and requested one of the young men to stay with him and see that he didn't drink any more whiskey.

After supper I went to the executive club meeting of the Republican Party. I have accepted the position of co-chairman of the finance committee. I can't belong to the party and expect other people to do all the work. I don't believe Democrat members of the town board will like it with me being chairman of the town ABC Board. They want their people in all positions.

14

Dorothy's trip

3-26-1978 ✓

This has been a day of apprehension. My daughter Susie is due to fly back to school in Maryland at two o'clock today. This morning the sky was covered with one big gray cloud. At the office I watched the cloud from the window. Around ten-thirty there was an opening in it in the southwest. Soon there were other openings in the same area. If the clouds continue to break up there may not be any difficulty with her flight to Maryland.

Last night I worried a lot about a child a mother called about. When she called around eight o'clock she said the child had been sick two days and was running a fever of one hundred and one degrees. Her voice was trembling, indicating her concern. Last winter the child had a convulsion with a temperature of one hundred and three. At present the child was not retaining any medicine due to an upset stomach.

She wondered about using a suppository for nausea another doctor had prescribed for another child. I agreed to this. She was to call me back in an hour to let me know how the child was doing. During the hour that passed I kept wondering what I should do if the suppository didn't work. I resolved if she called to have her bring the child to the office and I would meet her there if the child wasn't any better. After three hours the phone rang. It was the mother with the sick child.

She seemed happy; the child's temperature was normal and it had gone to sleep without vomiting any more. She called again this morning to say the child seemed well now.

During the Polio epidemic in the fifties a mother would call about a child like this and on the third day or fourth the child would have lost the use of an arm or leg.

Most of my patients are doing well. A patient who had fallen on the hand truck is getting better. Harold, the old man living with his son is doing well. Another patient got drunk because he got disgusted with his work. Now he is still disgusted with his work and has got to get over his drunk.

I closed the office around eleven to go home for lunch and get ready to take Susie to the airport. The weather is still rainy and foggy. I am worried about the plane flying in weather like this. After lunch the weather cleared and Susie had no trouble at the airport.

A few months ago it was weather like this when Dorothy was scheduled to come back from Maryland after visiting with Susie at the University of Maryland. She had gone up to help her get a room. Susie was transferring from Virginia to Maryland. Dorothy was due to arrive at the airport in Hickory at one-thirty on Saturday afternoon. I closed the office at twelve-thirty. At this time it was raining and foggy. When I came by the house for a sandwich, I didn't believe a plane could land in this kind of weather. Driving to the airport, I kept looking at the sky for a sign of clearing. All I could see was fog, rain and gray sky.

At the airport people were walking about from door to window. They were quite anxious too. At one-thirty it was announced over the loudspeaker that the plane would be late. I sat down on the couch facing the window watching the fog roll over the airfield. I wondered how scared Dorothy was somewhere up there in the plane. My anxiety drove me to move to the window again.

While standing there the airport announced that the plane couldn't land in Hickory. Plans had been made for it to land in Atlanta, Ga. We were told to leave our phone number and the airport would call us when the plane had landed in Atlanta.

Driving home through the fog and rain I felt very lonely. I guessed Dorothy was scared and lonely too. The airport had my telephone number so I decided to make the office my operation headquarters. One or two patients came in while I waited.

At four-thirty I thought the plane would have landed in Atlanta. Someone should have called me by now. I dialed the airport number and got a recorder that said something like they were too busy to talk now. I should call back later. I felt sure the plane had crashed. After waiting a few minutes I decided to call the Hickory airfreight number believing they might not be busy. The phone rang once or twice and someone answered.

I inquired about the flight to Atlanta. It was a great relief to know the plane had landed safely. I waited for Dorothy to call me. Frequently I lifted the phone off of the hook to see if it still had a dial tone. After about an hour I called back to the airfreight department telling them I had not heard from my wife. I asked him if he would please check and see if she was on the plane that had landed in Atlanta. Perhaps she had missed the flight in Maryland. He said he would find out.

In a few minutes he called back and said she was in Atlanta.

By now it was six-thirty, dark and rainy. I closed the office to come to the house. As I opened the front door the phone rang. It was Dorothy calling to say she was all right and was planning to take a seven-thirty flight back to Hickory. She didn't have her bags and wanted to come home. I insisted that she stay in Atlanta over night because the weather was still bad here. She agreed and promised to call me whenever she was in a hotel room. In about thirty minutes she called to tell me she was in the Hilton Inn in Atlanta, Room 224. With this call I felt like I could relax now for the night. Hopefully the weather would be better in the morning and she could fly to Hickory.

There was no relaxing during the night. I listened to the wind and rain all night. Sleeping was impossible. At daybreak there was a little thunder soon followed by a loud bang of lightning. I thought it had struck the house. This was the first lightning I had seen in January and the first storm of the year. I was worried again about Dorothy. With this weather I didn't think she could land in Hickory. Sometimes though, I have seen the sky clear following a thunderstorm.

Around eight-thirty the rain stopped and visibility seemed pretty good. My spirits began to rise with improving weather. Dorothy would probably be getting ready to leave the hotel room to go to the airport. She would be glad to hear from me. I decided to call her to see how she fared without her baggage and to give her the weather report. When she had called from Atlanta I did not ask for the phone number of the hotel so to call her I made the call person to person. The operator placed the call to the Hilton Inn and reported the line in her room was busy. Who could she be calling in Atlanta, the airport or possibly her sister? After fifteen minutes I placed the call again. The operator gave the same report: the phone is busy.

With this second report my apprehension began to rise. I tried calling her again in thirty minutes and got the same report, line busy. Now I was sure something dreadful was wrong. I asked the hotel operator if she could check the line and see who was talking. She said she couldn't do that. Then I asked the operator to see if Dorothy Jones was registered in this room. She replied that Dorothy Jones was not who was registered in Room 224. I asked her what hotel was this. She said the Holiday Inn. I told her I was sorry this was the wrong hotel. I felt sure each time I had asked for the Hilton Inn, but the operator had given me the Holiday Inn each time. I dialed the operator again and said very emphatically I wanted the Hilton Inn near the airport. This time the call went through to Dorothy's room. She answered. She was glad to hear from me and that the weather here looked promising for the plane to land in Hickory. It was now around ten-thirty. She asked about the flight she wanted to take last night to Hickory. I told her it had to land in Asheville. The passengers had been bussed to Hickory and arrived around midnight. She was glad she waited. She was due to leave Atlanta at noon and would be in Hickory at one-fifteen.

I went to the airport in Hickory around twelve-thirty. The weather was getting worse, fogy and raining. In the airport there were some of the people who were there Saturday afternoon.

While standing at the window looking over the airfield a man standing beside me said, "If you can see the legs on the water tank over there across the runway the plane can land." Looking in the direction he indicated, I could see a water tank and make out four legs. Fifteen minutes later I could just see the tank. At one-fifteen the clerk announced that the plane from Atlanta could not land. It was going to land in Winston-Salem and the passengers would be bussed to Hickory arriving in Hickory around five o'clock. Again I drove home wondering how scared Dorothy might be.

Around four-thirty I drove back to Hickory and arrived just as the bus arrived from Winston Salem. It pulled around to where passengers unload from planes. My anxiety began to mount until I saw Dorothy get off the bus. We were both delighted for her to be home again.

15

Bird dawn

3-30-1978 ✓

Today began with the phone ringing. Caroline was calling for me to come help her breathe. She is seventy-four years old and one of a set of twins. She's a retired schoolteacher and a heavy cigarette smoker.

When I hung up the phone it was four-thirty in the morning. I dressed, putting my pants on over my long handles and my coat over my flannel nightshirt. Going out the basement door I glanced up at the stars. They were shining bright in a dark sky. The big dipper was in about nine o'clock position. I couldn't see what I call the square of Pegasus. To me it looks more like a kite than a square or a belt buckle." Sometime I will show it to someone who has studied the stars more and find the right name for it. My friend Pinkney, an electrician, says he can tell the time of night by the stars.

Remembering my call, I started out for Caroline's house a few minutes away down Lakeside Avenue. As I walked across the porch I wondered who would come to the door. If Caroline came I felt like she wasn't too bad with her breathing; if someone else came it could mean Caroline was very sick. After ringing the door bell three or four times I heard footsteps approaching and the latch turn in the door. The door was opened slowly. In the dim light of the living room I saw Caroline shuffling slowly in her slippers to her bedroom where she flopped in a large green reclining chair. Standing over her I could hear her wheezing with each breath. To see her face a little I pulled on the string fastened to the back of the chair. She was pale and sweating, pulse rate a hundred and ten per minute. I thought she was having circulatory problems from the flu. I gave her medication I thought would help and then called her sister living next door to come sit with her. I waited with her for twenty minutes until she was breathing better. When I went out on the porch again, there was enough light now to make out the shrubs and flowers. In the east the sky was beginning to turn pink. In some of the shrubs and trees birds were softly chirping something that sounded like "tweetlee, tweetlee tee." I translated it in English to be "Are you awake; did you sleep?" I seemed to remember that I had read somewhere that this time of morning is called "Bird Dawn."

On the way to the office I met a young boy about fourteen years old riding a bicycle. He was moving swiftly along, his hair waving in the wind and his mouth open like he was laughing. He might have been so pleased with himself that he could ride so well without holding the handlebars; just feeling great. I thought what a contrast between this happy boy and Caroline struggling for breath.

At the office I had two patients with urethral drainage. The first one was married. I made a smear and under the microscope looked for the gonorrhea germ. I could not find any. I told him he had an infection but I couldn't tell him what germ was causing the trouble. He has had relations with his wife so she will need to have treatment too. If she isn't treated they will continue to reinfect each other.

I found the gonorrhea germ on the slide in the second case. I told him he had gonorrhea and would need to tell his wife. He said he didn't mind telling his wife, but he didn't know how he would tell his girlfriend. Without thinking I asked if he had had relations with her also. He said he had so he would need to bring both partners in for treatment.

After lunch I had a call to come to see a ninety-eight-year-old woman living six miles out in the country. Some of the relatives were visiting her and wanted me to come to see her. This is a frequent request when relatives are visiting in the home after a long spell of absence. Perhaps it is a way of showing their affection. I agreed to come.

It was a pleasant drive past green pastures, yards with jonquils and yellow bells, new plowed fields of red clay with an occasional crow flying across it under a clear blue sky. When I drove into the yard I noticed several out-of-state cars. As I approached the house the front door opened. A very small woman wearing a brown apron led me into a large living room/bedroom combination with seven or eight people scattered about. Three or four were sitting around an oil stove in the left corner of the room. Some others were on a couch against the wall. I was introduced to one of the visitors and his wife. He was a nephew of the patient. He was well dressed, wearing a coat, vest and tie. I thought he was about fifty years old and well built. Three women were sitting on another couch in the right corner of the room. The little woman with the apron led me to the left corner in the back of the room to a small cot. A very small woman was lying on the cot on her left side with her head on a pillow. Her eyes were closed, her mouth open, tongue drawn back in her mouth and covered with a brownish secretion, legs pulled up near her chest and held there with her arms.

While I was looking to see if she was breathing the nephew came over to express his concern about hospitalizing her and giving her glucose. He said she might be dehydrated and have pneumonia. Because her mouth was open she might have a sore throat. Because of all these conditions that might be wrong he wanted a professional opinion of her condition. It seemed like he was working up to telling me he wanted me to call in a specialist for further examination though I had not yet given my opinion.

I was thinking if he wanted someone else he should have called someone else. Before I said anything I thought to myself that my thirty years of seeing people should entitle me to some professional opinion. Before examining her I asked if he wanted me to call in some other doctor. He said no, he just wanted to know about her. Now I thought we were getting somewhere. I told him I could tell him after I examined her. After examining her I could find nothing specifically wrong.

Her heart was beating regularly seventy-four per minute. Her blood pressure normal.

Turning to him I said it was amazing that her heart had beat seventy-four beats per minute for ninety-eight years. I could find nothing wrong except that she was worn out. Glucose in the hospital might buy her another day or two and it might make her worse. I suggested they give her the best nursing care they could. I didn't have anything that would make any difference in her condition. When I closed my medical bag to leave they were all very grateful for my visit. This is an instance in which it pays to be as patient as possible. I was about to misjudge the nephew who just wanted to know what was best to do.

Later at the office, things went along very well. My patient with the swollen testicle is about well. I had one or two other patients with the flu. One elderly man with pain in his right shoulder was sent back for more x-rays. His previous pictures made me suspect a lung tumor. Around five o'clock a man came by to make arrangements for a wrestling match in the theater. We have agreed to try a match in May. I closed the office after he left.

Caroline called again. She is a little better. I was called again to see Donna, a lady in her eighties. She had a weak spell of some kind, possibly a light stroke. She was stable when I arrived.

16

Jim's Catch

This morning there were three young men waiting in the reception room. One was holding a piece of white paper up to his right cheek. As a I walked past him he lowered the paper to show a small treble hook buried in his cheek. He wanted me to hurry up and remove it. He was anxious to get back to the lake.

I asked him to sit in the chair next to the sink. With a sharp pointed scalpel, I followed the track of the hook to the barb and extracted it. Thanking me, he took, it back with him to attach to the line his partner was using. While fishing, his partner had made a wild cast, striking him in the face with the lure. Each year, I get one or two patients who have been foul-hooked about the face.

This reminded me of the time Jim came in with Kerry, a friend of ours. They were fishing below the dam for stripers using a heavy buck tail. This is a hook with a lead head weighing one or two ounces. Ten to twenty-five pound stripers had been running for the last three days. To a fisherman, this is very exciting. It's enough to get him to leave his wife, jump out of bed at four-thirty in the morning, climb down a hundred-foot rock wall, then crawl along a narrow rock ledge for another hundred feet. At the base of the powerhouse there are twenty or so other fishermen standing shoulder to shoulder, casting into the turbulent water boiling out from under the powerhouse. If he fell in, there would be little chance of getting out, because the water would have him downstream in a second.

On the opposite shore, 100 yards away, fishermen are in boats anchored close to shore. They are casting their lures toward the men on the rock ledge. Lines from opposite sides are frequently tangled with each other and there is a great thrill for each one until they discover their line has caught another line and not a big fish. Because of the rocky bottom, lures frequently get hung between the rocks and must be broken off. When this happens, the fisherman ties another one on as quickly as possible so as not to miss a strike. The fish don't run but a few hours so one must not lose time. Too, if he moves out of his spot someone else may take it.

Any experienced angler knows not to turn around when he needs to tie on another lure. If he does, he is apt to get snagged with one of the lures as other fishermen swing their lures back over their shoulders to make a cast.

Fishing was good this particular morning and several twenty-five pounders had been landed. In all this excitement, our friend Kerry, who had lost his lure to a big fish, forgot and turned around to tie another lure on his line. There was a sharp yell from our friend. Jim's cast was fouled. Reflexively turning around, you can imagine how shocked Jim was to see his lure hanging from Kerry's eyebrow.

When they got to the office they didn't wait to see if it was their turn to see me, they just called out for me.

"Of all the mornings you have been down there, this was the morning you were needed," Jim said. "Did it get in his eye?" Though he likes to hide it, Jim was quire shaken seeing his lure hanging down from this man's eye.

With the patient sitting in the examining chair beside the sink, I was glad to see that the hook had entered just below the right eyebrow and no permanent damage should occur. I pushed the barb through the skin and with some wire cutters cut the hook at the shank. The barb end then easily slid through the skin and out. Jim and Kerry returned to the rock wall to continue fishing, just like young boys.

Due to my limited time for fishing, some years ago I asked the operator of the power house if he would call me whenever the stripers were running, allowing me to save time from the office. One day, he called while I was at home raking leaves. My young daughter Gail took the message. She had no idea about fishing or what the man at the powerhouse was calling about. She called to me and said, "The man at the firehouse called and said to tell you the stompers are striking and for you to come."

It is possible that all this activity got my mind off of my business a bit. After Jim left, my next patient wanted an examination to play ball at school. All children now must have a physical. The patient was a young person about fourteen years old with medium-long brown hair wearing a T-shirt and blue jeans. My patient was seated in the examining chair when I came into the room.

"Are you going to play ball?" I asked. The answer was "yes."

I checked the throat, ears and nose and then asked the patient to "stand up and pull your pants down." It seems like there was more reluctance than usual, so I repeated the instruction. "Stand up and pull your pants down." This time my attention was diverted to my desk for a moment. When I turned to the patient who was just straightening up from pushing pants and shorts to the floor my eyes followed the ascending movement from the knees stopping for a brief moment at the crotch and revealing something missing. My mind suggested for a brief moment a case of hermaphroditism. Then it registered.

"This is a girl."

With this revelation, I checked the chest and said pull up your pants and shorts. As the patient left, I requested from my female staff that from now on, one of them stay with any patient of their kind.

17

A home death

4-13-1978 ✓

During the night I was awake frequently with pain in my throat. While I was examining a little girl on Monday she coughed in my face just as I was about to examine her throat, spraying me with droplets from her throat. She had a temperature of one hundred and one degrees. I think I have caught whatever she had.

This is one of the occupational hazards of being a doctor. You sometimes get what your patients have. My throat is still painful this morning, making me feel pretty bad. I thought there would be a lot of people needing my help so I came to the office. I was caught by the stoplight at the square as I was coming to the office. Before the light changed two or three cars with boats and trailers passed through. Noticing these people going to the lake for a day of relaxation caused me to wonder just what is my position in life. A patient I saw yesterday had just returned from a week of golfing. He is one year younger than I am. Life to him must be a system of "druthers," meaning a process of selecting the most appealing option of what to do today. But one can't be or do everything. I could spend the day fishing but then I couldn't accept the responsibility of looking after my patients. I had rather be seeing them than fishing.

There were two patients waiting when I arrived. After seeing them I went to check on Donna. I felt sure she would be feeling better. It was about nine-thirty when I arrived at her house.

I opened the front door and gave a few loud "Hello, hello" without getting an answer. I walked through the living room, past all the family portraits hanging on the wall and on the mantle. I knew which room Donna had been staying in. I was about there when a neighbor woman stepped out of Donna's room and asked, "Doctor, did you ring the door bell?"

"No. I didn't see one," I answered.

She said she guessed they must be having spooks. I think she was referring to my "hellos" instead of ringing the doorbell. Donna was lying slightly turned to her right with her head turned to the window away from the door. I thought she was asleep until I greeted her with a "Good morning." She said she was going to fire me if I didn't get her better soon. I thought she was teasing, but there was a lot of truth in her statement. Yesterday she was feeling better. This morning her breathing was like an asthmatic. Her temperature was one hundred and one; blood pressure and pulse were normal.

She had a restless night and didn't want any breakfast this morning. She was very tired with some numbness in her left hand and left ankle. I thought this might be the beginning of a stroke. My best judgment told me it was time to move her to a hospital. She was agreeable and I called the ambulance.

From Donna's house I went home where Dorothy had prepared our lunch. She wanted to know what took place at the Board of Health meeting last night. I told her the only thing I remembered coming up was that Laney wanted to know how long it was legal for him to keep a body without burying it if it is not embalmed. We are due to get the answer at the next meeting. He doesn't have a refrigeration unit at his funeral home so I think it wouldn't be long, but I didn't give my opinion about it.

After lunch I saw my first patient coming across the lawn. Reeves was about seventy years old, medium size and using a walking cane. Ten days ago he was in the office for heart trouble. The times before this he has always been drunk. Something must have happened in the last month. He has not been drinking.

I greeted him in the reception room and asked him to come back to the examining room. He was wearing a dirty brown cap pulled down on his head so that it seemed to make his lower lip stick out so far you would think it was his tongue. He had on a dirty gray coat and brown pants to match his cap. Shortly after he had settled in the chair I noticed the smell of kerosene. I think he must live alone and uses kerosene for heating and cooking.

A lot of papers were scattered on my desk from the morning requiring my attention so I turned to arrange them before starting my examination. During this time of two or three minutes, Reeves pushed his cap back off his eyes a bit and squinted at my diploma hanging on the wall a few feet in front of him. He raised his right hand as if to point to my diploma. Before he could say anything I noticed his hand was missing some fingers. I hadn't noticed this before so I asked him how he had lost his fingers.

"Electricity," he said "A man didn't ground the transformer." Then turning to my diploma he asked, "You go to Duke?"

"Yes," I said

"You know who turned the lights on down there?" he asked

"No," I said. "Who did?"

"I did," he said squirming a little to look closer at my diploma. "I did in 1931. I helped put the line in and I am the man that pushed in the switch at the substation that turned the lights on."

I examined him again and found that he was doing much better. I cautioned him about taking up drinking again and for him to return in two weeks.

My next patient was a very pretty eighteen-year-old girl. She was neatly dressed. I sensed something was unusual about this case. I asked her to have a seat in the green chair.

She sat down and said, "Thank you."

This was a bit unusual, I wondered if she was here to ask about a job. When I asked her what her trouble was she said she wanted birth control tablets. I asked if she was married. She said "no." She was going to college in the fall and wanted to be safe rather than sorry. I tried to discourage her by telling her there were side effects from the tablets but she still insisted on the tablets. I asked her who was going to pay for her while she was in college. She said her parents were. With this I told her to bring her mother and I would check on her. She agreed to this and said she would be back soon.

The plant nurse was my next patient. The ophthalmologist had not given any report to help solve her eye problem. She said he said she was okay. I mentioned a brain scan again but she said she had rather wait.

Though the ophthalmologist couldn't find any trouble, I am suspicious of metastasis of breast tissue to the brain. We were just closing the office at five o'clock when the phone rang. A woman called for me to come back over in the country to see the woman I had seen about a month ago. She said she thought she was dead and they wanted me to come check on her.

I asked Dorothy to ride with me. We could stop at a fish camp on the way back for dinner. We didn't talk much on the way over. I think we were enjoying the fresh green fields, woods with snow-white dogwood blooms, and houses surrounded with all shades of red azaleas and apple blossoms.

This time when I arrived at the house there was only one car in the yard. I parked near the road so if other cars came I would not be blocked in. Going into the room I met the little woman with the brown apron. There were a few a elderly women in the room and one young girl. I followed the little woman to the cot in the back of the room. It was pretty dark at first but after a few minutes my eyes got accustomed to the dark and I could make out a sheet lying on the cot with a few bulges here and there. I lifted it up at the head of the cot. The body was lying on the cot with the head on a pillow, eyes open, mouth open and arms folded over her chest. I listened to her chest for a while without hearing any sounds. I pulled the sheet up to her chin, and closed her mouth and eyelids for the last time. Then I pulled the sheet over her head and pillow.

Turning to the little woman beside me I said, "She's gone."

There was an outburst of sobbing from the women in the distant corner of the room. The little woman with the apron, daughter of the deceased, began to sob softly. She had been looking after her mother for the last twenty years. She walked with me to the door and thanked me for coming. It made me feel good inside to be appreciated so much.

Dorothy and I drove away without saying anything.

18

No understanding women

When I came into the kitchen for breakfast Dorothy reviewed her missionary meeting she went to last night. There was some discussion about next year's church bazaar. While she was talking she had the television on and I was listening to Barry Goldwater's discussion on the vote in Congress. He was talking about giving the Panama Canal away when she suddenly accused me of listening to the television rather than to her. I can't understand why she had the television going and didn't expect me to listen to it. When she is telling about some of her activities I am due to mentally tune out the television. If I say "Turn it off while we are having a discussion," she will say, "Leave it on; something may come on I want to hear."

I tuned Barry out of my mind and began to listen to her discussion of last night's meeting. If I didn't she might give my office away sometime and we would both be in trouble. She is unhappy about the bazaar. The trouble seemed to be getting along with Rev. Oliver. If she could correct this she was willing to put on the bazaar for the church again next year.

As things are now she didn't want to fight with Rev Oliver just to run the bazaar. She said if they had a fight she couldn't go to church as long as he was her minister. She asked me why it is that some people can get along well and others can't. I couldn't tell her why because I have the same problem, especially with the town commissioners. I said some people get along by agreeing to everything and do whatever they are asked to do without any question.

My first patient today was a young man wanting an excuse for being out of work yesterday. My first thought was not to excuse him because I had not seen him. When I asked why I should excuse him he said because of an ingrown toenail. For this I certainly wasn't going to give an excuse, but I remembered that quick decisions are often costly. I asked to see his toe.

It was his left big toe, swollen and painful. I gave him an excuse. Harold was my next patient. I was surprised that he came back. You remember he is the man I told to work every day and leave off nerve medicine. It was his only way to live.

From the way he walked into the examining room I could tell he had pain in his back. His opening remarks were that he had taken my advice and worked every day since his last visit.

Today he had developed a catch in his back while stretching in his car to get his hand in his pocket to give his wife some money to buy groceries. I gave him some muscle relaxer medication. I hope he isn't pulling something to start drinking again.

My next patient was Ralph wanting his medicine refilled. When I gave him the medicine he wanted to know what could be done for a crazy woman with a headache. He was speaking of his wife Rennie. When she gets upset she has migraine headaches.

I said, "Ralph, the Lord knew exactly what He was doing when he made a woman. He planned her so it would keep you and me busy for a lifetime trying to understand her."

He laughed and said, "That's about right."

My next patient was Don, a man who raises azaleas. I called Dorothy to see if she wanted any. She said eight red ones to go in front of the house would be nice. When I came home from fishing there were eight pretty red azalea plants on the curb.

About mid morning Rev. Gray came in. He seems to be bothered with pollen from the pine trees. I have been giving him some antihistamines for it. On the way out he said he would bring me a stuffed duck tomorrow. I wondered if it was the one his dog had retrieved at the lake sometime ago. He said he was taking a course in taxidermy at the college and this was his first specimen. When I told him I would put it up in the office with his name on it I detected some reluctance to this display. I suspected some of his church members might object to him having killed the duck. He confirmed my suspicion when he said some of his members would fuss at him for killing it so if I didn't mind just take it home with me.

Before closing the office at noon Dorothy needed to talk to the plant nurse about an insurance claim. The plant nurse was in the hospital having a brain scan for her headaches. I wasn't surprised at this. Yesterday she had called and asked me if it were possible for some of the cancer cells from her breast to have broken off and lodged in her brain. The best I could answer was to say that anything is possible in cancer cases. I was sure she was fearful now that her cancer has gone to her brain and was causing her headaches.

After this call I called Hugh, the chairman of the ABC board in Lenoir to tell him that we were planning to change our ABC bill so we didn't have to give our ABC money to our ABC officer any more. We were planning to give it to the town police department. Reece has told his employees at the store we will have to let one go because we are not taking in enough money to pay all of them. We discussed our position again at the ABC meeting today at noon. Reece said our auditor had figured there was no way we can maintain our ABC officer. Our bill will not allow us to give more than 10 percent of our profits for his salary. We decided we could carry him until the first of October when he is due to retire. When I told Ted he said he knew it was coming, but he didn't understand why he couldn't have one of the clerk's jobs. I told him I thought it would look pretty bad for the store to have the man who had been going out arresting people for purchasing liquor now selling it to them in the store.

Our profits for this quarter were about twenty thousand dollars. We agreed to give all of this to the town and county. Reece said we had given the town more money this year than any previous year. Our concluding decision at the meeting was to go to the National Alcoholic Control meeting in San Francisco. Jim declined to go because his daughter is graduating from high school. We had four bottles of damaged whiskey that we poured down the sink.

After the ABC meeting Jim and I went fishing. The weather was cold and threatening to rain. Sometimes the wind blew the boat near the shore and sometimes out in the middle of the neck.

We were fishing near the dam where a large group of sea gulls flying high overhead looked like a whirlwind of white leaves. Another group of about equal number were content to sit on the water flying only when necessary to escape our boat. I guessed they couldn't get along with the group in the air. About dark we were in the head of a neck where a large water snake swam across. I have heard that there is a snake called a "thunder snake" that comes out only when a storm is coming up. It was the first snake I have seen this season.

Right at sundown a few raindrops fell, followed by a rumble of thunder. We decided to go back to the dock. I already had my raincoat on and was reaching for my umbrella when there was a vivid flash of lightning. Observing the bright metal tip of the umbrella and remembering lightning's affinity for it, I gently laid it back under the seat. We arrived at the dock just before it began to rain.

19

Marriages

4-22-1978 ✓

Caroline called me at one-thirty this morning to come to her house. She had pain in her chest and shortness of breath.

When I arrived the front door was unlocked allowing me to go into the back room. Caroline was sitting up on her bed. Her sister in the other bed returned home from the hospital yesterday with a heart condition. She felt pretty strong, though not strong enough to get out of bed to help Caroline. She told me Caroline's troubles and what I should do for her. I should tell Caroline to stop smoking, but Caroline said cigarettes were so good she couldn't give them up.

After examining her I thought she was weaker than the last time I saw her. Her pulse was around a hundred and irregular. She was wheezing and her feet were swollen. I moved her from the bed to her recliner and gave her an injection for her breathing and to relieve fluid. I wrapped her in some blankets from the bed and asked her sister to call me in two hours if she didn't feel better.

The phone rang again at five-thirty. A man wanted me to come see his wife. She was vomiting and had diarrhea. I left home wearing my flannel nightshirt under my coat. Going out the basement door I paused to observe the morning. In the west the sky was a light blue, in the east it was a faint pink. The morning air was fresh and cool. Birds were beginning to sing their morning songs. Blue jays "Thief, thief, thief" and robins "Are you awake, did you sleep." A crow flying, waking others of the group up with "Caw, caw, caw," and a dove in a pine tree "Who, who, who are you, who, who?"

Driving to the house through the morning stillness by yards with flowers in full bloom was a wonderful sight of nature. At the house I found the woman holding her head and retching from her nausea. She was having an attack of inner ear trouble, labrynthitis. I gave her an injection and left some capsules. Her husband was to call me if she wasn't improved in two hours.

At home Dorothy and I started breakfast at seven-thirty. When I came into the kitchen I told her I found out yesterday why Terry, one of our patients, is not living with that pretty blond he married. It is because of a child she had by a previous marriage. Terry was in the office yesterday because of a urethral discharge. He and the child don't get along and this starts a fight between him and his wife. They have been seeing a marriage councilor, but they still can't agree on discipline for the child. They couldn't send the child to live with the father because he has married again and doesn't want the child. On account of the child, Terry is living alone.

Dorothy said he wasn't treating her right. A woman is different from a man. Men can't expect to treat a woman just any way. Women are independent working people equal to men. If a man expects to live with one he must treat her equal to men. Marriage must be a partnership with both partners contributing to make the marriage work. There can't be one set of rules for men and one for women. A man can't run around and come home expecting his wife to be there like some domestic animal.

She believed marriages are going to last longer now because people are marrying for love. I disagreed, saying there will be fewer marriages because workingmen and women are putting their children aside in day care centers and nurseries. Their marriage means nothing except an excuse to sleep together. The demands of their work keep them in continual temptation to make other partnerships.

I said a woman's place was in the home and took off for the office. I will hear the disagreement about this soon.

My first patient was the electrician who turned on the electricity at Duke. He is doing well.

When he left I took some medicine to Caroline. She was resting in the recliner chair. On the bedside table was an ashtray with the butts of eight cigarettes. Her twin sister was propped up on her elbows giving instructions. I said I thought Caroline should go to the hospital but she wanted to wait until Monday morning.

"You can never get anything done on Saturday morning in a hospital and I had rather wait if I can," she said.

While Dorothy and I were eating lunch she said I was right about women. I asked why she had changed her mind. She said did I remember the little girl with the boy that came into the office about ten o'clock this morning carrying a little baby. That girl is only sixteen years old and he is the father. Men can go out for a one-night stand but women can't. That sixteen-year-old girl has that baby to care for.

I asked her did she still believe that men and women were equal? She said women must be treated as women, special from men. When society comes back to this belief it will be wrong for men to leave women with children to care for. Even other men will reject men who mistreat women. She concluded her argument by referring to the Bible and the Ten Commandments.

Before I could make a reply the phone rang again. Caroline had changed her mind and wanted to go to the hospital. I was glad she was making this decision. I went to her house to check on her and tell the ambulance people what medication she was on.

While driving back to my house I thought how strange it is that as our lives wind down things occur that are not thought of during our active life. Here are two sisters now helpless with no able-bodied person to call for help. During their active life they had the strength of each other for support. They had their pride and independence. Now for some reason close relatives living nearby don't give them much help. This is no exception. I have seen it in many families in time of sorrow and illness. Laney says he has had relatives to fight in his funeral home over who was the best to a member of a family or who is going to get this or that now that the person is dead It is rather strange that in their time of need people sometimes have no one nearby willing to help.

20

Night of the prowler

5-3-1978

At the office things went well again. Caroline is in the hospital. Donna is doing well again at home. Part of the time this morning was spent worrying about a man I had let park an old car on my front office lot. He wanted to park it there to sell it but he didn't keep a "for sale" sign on it. This is the third day I have called him to move his car. I think this has taught me a good lesson about helping people. I will not be too hasty next time to console people who are having trouble with someone else. When he approached me he was angry with the town about having to move the car off of their parking lot so I let him park it on my lot. Now, after two months he has abandoned the old thing on my lot. I believe the man is not such a good character. The town probably had requested him to move it after he had left it with them for four or five months like he planned to do for me. I will not be so agreeable next time to help someone who has not treated the first party fair.

When Dorothy returned from the beach Thursday night she said she had a good time. She left with another group today to go to a play in New York on Friday. I went to Lenoir Saturday night to see Larry in a boxing match. His opponent had been in forty professional bouts, Larry had been in twelve. During the first round I thought they were about even. Neither one won the round. Though they were evenly matched in weight, I thought Larry would lose the fight. His opponent was about six feet tall; Larry is about five foot five inches. His opponent had longer arms that would allow him to easily hit Larry.

In the second round he pinned Larry in the far corner for about a half-minute. Larry kept his face covered and someway broke out and gave his opponent several severe body punches knocking him out. I was sitting beside his little girl about six years old. She stood up in her seat and cheered, "Daddy, daddy, daddy, that's my daddy."

Sunday morning Laney, the funeral director, came in the office. He was feeling very bad. His pulse was irregular and he felt faint. I felt like he was having a heart attack. He had been up most of the last three nights embalming bodies. With this history there was a good possibility that he was exhausted. I gave him a mild sedative and asked him to return Monday morning. On the return visit he was much better. His pulse was regular again but he didn't feel well enough to come to the Rotary Club meeting.

Bert was there and I told him the ABC Board was going to the National ABC Meeting in San Francisco. He didn't express any objections. Tonight Dorothy and I began laying out the clothes we plan to take. She called Mary in Los Angeles to make arrangements to fly up to San Francisco to spend a few days with us. Mary was thrilled with the idea.

Dorothy and I retired for the evening around ten o'clock. I think she was pretty tired from her trips and from the excitement about going to San Francisco. I wasn't sleeping well and awoke around eleven-thirty. I couldn't go back to sleep and in about thirty minutes I thought I heard something downstairs. I was real concerned and frightened.

After listing again for about ten minutes I dismissed it thinking it might be the house cracking from temperature change with colder air, but I couldn't go back to sleep. I recalled that some people broke into my neighbor's house at the bottom of the hill about three months ago. Troy and Mae work at night and all of the children have moved away. There was no one at home but Sarah, Mae's mother who is seventy years old. It was about ten o'clock and Sarah was planning to go to bed. When she came out of the bathroom she heard the back door being knocked open.

She started screaming loud as she could "Frank, John, Tom, you boys get up, get up and come down here quick. Someone is breaking in the back door!" She screamed this three or four times like there was a house full of people, though there was no one in the house but her. The burglars got frightened and ran away.

I remember my dogs barking that night for a long time. I was about to go to sleep when I heard something very definitely scratching on a screen as if they might be slashing it with a knife. Our dogs, Blossum, a female, and Jack, a male, barked a few times and seemed to run off down toward the creek away from the house. I got up and slid my rifle out from under the bed. It is a twenty-two automatic. It was loaded, but there wasn't a shell in the firing chamber. I pulled back on the mechanism that loaded the shell.

I lifted the phone off the hook for a moment to see if the telephone wires had been cut. The phone was still working. Dorothy was awake and had heard the noise on the screen. She wanted me to call the police, but I whispered that before the police could get here we could be dead. The furnace came on again blowing air into the room so I couldn't hear anything else. I sat on the bed until it stopped running. I was about to go to sleep again when there was definite thump like a ball might have been dropped somewhere downstairs.

I turned on the hall light from outside the bedroom door so I could see down to the hall near the kitchen. Again I waited and didn't hear anything. I eased down the stairs and reached into the kitchen from the hall and turned on the kitchen lights. I waited a few minutes and peeped in with my rifle at hip level, my right index finger on the trigger. I couldn't hear or see anything. I looked in the living room with the same results, nothing in there. The noise must have been in the basement.

Our kitchen is over the basement so I stomped around in the kitchen so anyone in the basement could hear me in the kitchen and would know I was up and they could leave. I waited a few minutes and then eased toward the basement door just across from the kitchen door. Everything was very still. I wondered if someone would be waiting for me at the bottom of the basement stairs. The basement now was the only place someone could be.

Suddenly behind me there was a scratching noise near the broom closet followed by a thump on the floor. I wheeled around with my rifle at hip level to see a half-grown squirrel run to the kitchen window and climb up the screen to hide behind the draperies.

This was our night prowler.

Using a towel, I finally cornered it in the bookshelf. All this time Dorothy was wondering what was going on downstairs. She might have thought I left the house when I opened the front door to put the squirrel outside. When I went upstairs to tell her what had gone on, she was upset because I had not called the police. I don't think that would have worked because I would have had to go down to let them into the house to look around.

Probably no one is sure what to do when they hear something in their house in the middle of the night. I was real glad it was a squirrel rather than a person.

21

First rift

5-8-1978

My practice is going well now, but my practice car is giving me trouble and I may have to get another one. It is about five years old now.

At the theater I have put a notice on the marquee that the theater is for rent or lease. Yesterday a young woman wanted to know how much the rent was. Her husband is a band director and wants a place for his band to practice. Before agreeing to rent it I called Glenn to see if he was still interested in the Disco idea. I was pleasantly surprised when he said he was and would come by Saturday to talk over the arrangements.

There seems to be a lot of political activity taking place in town and a lot of talk about the ABC store. I think it started after a visit to the store by the new city manager, Sam Noble, and Mayor Bert several days ago. Bert called me and said some of the town commissioners were asking questions about our operation at the store. He brought Noble down to find out how we were managing the store. Reece and I answered all the questions he had and showed him around the store. When he left we thought he would tell the commissioners and end whatever complaint the commissioners had. Within a few hours after they left Bert called me to say the commissioners wanted to meet with the ABC Board; they weren't satisfied with Noble's report.

We agreed on eleven o'clock. At ten forty-five Reece called me. The meeting had been changed to one o'clock.

When Bert called to set up the meeting he thought none of the commissioners would come. He felt they were more interested in harassing us than anything that went on in the store. If they could make it look like we were doing a bad job we might decide to resign and then they could put their friends in the store. I couldn't agree with this. I didn't believe there was any way they could say we were not operating the store according to the law. Any liquor that isn't sold or picked up by the supplier is poured down the sink at the end of each month. We send the state a financial report every quarter. We keep accurate records of everything. One member of the board was a first cousin to our ABC officer. We asked him to resign at the end of his term because it was a conflict of interest, according to the state policy to have someone working in the store kin to someone else.

A letter on the ABC policy also implies that the State ABC board makes the rules for us to operate the store by. The ABC Board is a part of the town too. To harass us to make us resign would not help the town any.

I believe all the commissioners came except two. They did not seem interested in helping us run the store. I have a picture with three of the Democrat commissioners that came. Sam Noble and Mayor Bert Huffman are also in the picture. One Republican Gene Johnson is shown. Commissioner Simmons, the other Republican on the town board is absent. We held the meeting in the warehouse part of the building since it was the only place big enough to accommodate the group. Pete, our other board member and secretary read the minutes of our last meeting and then we opened the meeting for questioning. Commissioner Chapman seemed to be spokesman for the group. He first wanted to know the number of employees we had and how much we were paying them, their insurance, their retirement benefits and the number of hours they worked each day. Reece reported all of this to him, but while Reece was reporting I was observing Chapman very closely. I didn't believe he was paying any attention at all to the report.

As soon as Reece concluded the statistics about the store, he asked about our trip to San Francisco, who authorized it and why we went. I told him the ABC Board authorized it just the same as the board did before we were appointed. We went to keep up with the ABC business.

If we didn't go we would not know what went on in the liquor industry.

Commissioner Tucker could hardly wait for me to conclude my answer before he said, "Who gave permission to take your wives?" I replied, "The board gave permission. If we couldn't take our wives we would not go."

His reply was that schools didn't give permission for schoolteachers to take their wives. I sensed that this didn't satisfy him, but he didn't ask anything else. He had moved here about five years ago to take a position in one of the schools. About a year ago he ran for a seat on the town council and won.

There were some questions about our inventory being so large. Someone said it wasn't necessary to carry so much, but Reece said with Lenoir opening up we needed a large inventory of all brands of liquor to keep our business. A final statement from Chapman was that we had too many employees for this size store.

In concluding the meeting I said the more people talked about the store on the street the worse the talk would be for the store. We won the right to sell liquor by eighteen votes and then had to go to court to get the election declared legal. I have a copy of the headlines of the suit filed against the commissioners by the Christian Action League. According to the paper we didn't follow the state statutes in conducting the election. The Christian Action League believed if the state statutes had been followed the ABC store would have been defeated. Voting was so close the ballots were counted six times. In concluding the meeting, I said it wouldn't be hard to get the Christian Action League to vote the store out of town.

I don't think this remark made any difference. I believe they were not acquainted with the league. Something was said about Bert that made me think they were not going to be cooperative with him. A few hours after the meeting Jim called me to tell me that Ted had brought his badge by his store and said he was quitting again. Jim said he talked to him about his work in the Democratic Party for the sheriff and chief of police. I think he went to talk to Jim because Jim and his family are all Democrats. Jim might do more for him than I would. I said I would call Ted and talk with him. Before I could find him, Reece called and confirmed what Jim had said.

In addition, Ted told Reece he was going to work for the town police Monday morning. Until now it made no difference whether you were Republican or Democrat; we worked together for the good of the town. That's how we won the state trophy for the best United Fund drive, how we put up the recreation center and voted in the ABC store. I am proud of the United Fund award. Our motto then was pretty much like the Bank of Granite says, "When we all work together, there's no end to what we can do to make Granite Falls a finer community."

When Bert came by the office I told him how the meeting went. He believed the city manager and the town attorney have joined forces with the four commissioners against him and would like control of the ABC Store. He thinks they want control of the store to give jobs to some of their political workers.

I reminded him then that there was a piece in the paper about the town attorney's political policy. It is to the effect that the political party that wins the election should put their people in office. It is an honorable process. I told Bert that the city of Brevard had made inquiry from the state attorney general about the power of the town commissioners over the ABC board. According to his letter, "It would appear," it says, "once the Board of Aldermen has appointed a local Board of Alcoholic Control it is not then further empowered to direct how matters will be conducted by that Board." There is also something about flagrant violations for which a member or members can be removed. From this letter I felt like the commissioners couldn't direct how we ran the store unless we committed some flagrant violations.

To make the store look bad Bert said someone had called the state ABC Board this morning to find out how to get our store closed. The state people told him the excuse they gave for wanting the store closed was that our sales had declined so we would not be able to pay our ABC officer as our bill required. I told Bert we were doing all we could to maintain our profits. We were running the store according to a letter to Sam Noble from Michael Crowell, Assistant Director of the Institute of Government in which he said in conclusion, "Neither local nor state law give the ABC board authority to do anything more than is necessary to operate the local ABC system. Profits may be retained, money may be invested, and property purchased as needed for the sound financial administration of the local ABC system, but not for other purposes, no matter how worthwhile they may be." Bert said he wasn't aware of this letter. Before leaving he said we should keep Ted on the payroll until he could get a job with the town police.

When Bert left I went to visit my brother Melvin and to talk with chief Barlow if he was visiting with Melvin. Sometimes Melvin hears about things in town that I don't know about. Too, he has some friends who tell him things they don't tell me. He and Chief Barlow are good friends and are frequently in his office having some discussion about the town. I wanted to find out what Chief Barlow knew about Ted our ABC officer.

Chief Barlow was in Melvin's office and I told him Ted had stopped working for the ABC Store and was going to work for the town. Chief Barlow is a short stocky man about sixty years old and has been police chief for the last fifteen years. He and Ted have been good friends so I asked him to talk to Ted about coming back to work. He believed Ted had quit because we might ask him to work in the store again. He said the town attorney told him it was legal for Ted to range in the county and we should not confine him to the store. I wondered how he knew what the attorney had said. In addition he said people were getting upset about us planning to operate without an ABC officer.

I didn't think I was getting anywhere talking to him so I returned to my office. On the way I wished I hadn't gone. He is a strong Democrat and probably against Bert.

Reece came by in a few minutes with some checks for me to sign. I gave him a letter to take to city hall to get our bill changed so we can give the money we have been giving for our ABC officer to the town police. Reece said he would also find Ted and talk to him about coming back to work. After supper I rode up to Commissioner Chapman's store to inform him about Ted. He might be wanting to know whether we had fired Ted or Ted had quit. Before I could close the office Hub came by to tell me he heard we had fired Ted so I thought it would be best for me to tell Chapman what I knew about it.

His response was a complete surprise. He said, "I knew Hub was coming to see you. He just told you that to get you to tell him the facts about Ted." Then he said he expected he would be getting a lot of calls about the ABC Store. He looked like he knew a lot more, but wasn't going to tell me anything else. I recalled that he was the chief spokesman at our meeting in the ABC store and a Democrat. I left him to go home to review our ABC bill.

I have never been fired from a job and I wanted to know my position. Who was my boss, the town commissioners, or the state ABC board? What were the rights of our ABC Board? Could the commissioners harass the ABC Board so that we would resign?

22

Laney's Road

5-21-1978 ✓

A mild thunderstorm is just finishing up. All day the temperature has been around ninety degrees. Right now a pleasant cool breeze is blowing. Arnold, my painter has just come in the office to tell me he will be back tomorrow to finish painting the theater. Due to the storm he thinks it will be too damp for the paint to dry if he works on.

Our gardens are green and will soon be producing vegetables. From what I hear from my patients, town politics is growing too. The commissioners are divided politically into two groups, two Republicans and four Democrats. Bert has more support from the two Republicans than from the four Democrats, though he is a registered Democrat. The town manager and the town attorney are working with the four Democrats.

On Monday the school principals had a meeting with Bert to find out about the money they are getting from the ABC store. They wanted to know if they are going to get the same amount each quarter. Bert told them it depended on the amount of business we did and that we averaged it out over the year. He said they seemed satisfied with this. He believes someone has been talking to them and urging them to request more money.

Two years ago when Jim's appointment to the ABC Board came up for renewal, Bert had to break a tie vote. When Jim first came on the ABC Board he was accepted unanimously. He is a Democrat and from a large family of Democrats. At this last meeting three Democrats voted against Jim's return to the board. Two Republicans and one special Democrat friend of Jim's voted for him. I have a feeling that the votes against Jim were cast to put in a replacement of their own in place of Jim. I think the Democrat commissioners want to get Bert out too since he doesn't join with them and still supports the ABC Board.

Probably to show the people they are doing something, the town commissioners plan to take a strip of land two hundred feet long and one hundred feet wide off the front of Laney's parking lot in front of his funeral home. Laney made the funeral home from one of the oldest and nicest red brick homes in town. It is a three-story house located on a slight knoll surrounded with large oak trees. The road coming from Rhodhiss curves around the base of the knoll.

Their excuse for changing the road is that trucks coming into town have trouble negotiating the curve. Their proposal would take about all of Laney's front parking lot and most of the oak trees. Now if work on the road was delayed after it is started, the inconvenience would ruin Laney's funeral business. People couldn't get in to view the bodies. Laney couldn't get in or out with his funeral cars.

Sure, it would look good on the city manager's resume to show he straightened a road and had secured a grant for the project. But it isn't the best place for the road and I haven't heard any truck drivers complaining about the road as it is. If roadwork is started and then delayed a lot of the funerals would go to the new funeral director. Now it just so happens one of the town commissioners is secretary and treasurer of the new funeral home. It would help the new funeral home's business if Laney's home was shut down due to road construction.

I told Bert what I thought about it this morning. He believes the roadwork is unnecessary and we should do what we can to support Laney to block straightening the road.

At the theater I am trying a disco program for teenagers. Murphy is due to move the boxing ring out on Monday, and then Glenn will begin the disco. He is letting a band group practice in the theater and in return they are to play for the disco dance on Saturday nights. But before he can get started playing, his band group is building up into a large group of teen-age boys and girls. Last night the parking lot was full of cars filled with young people partying. I called Glenn because I believed they were not associated with the band. He said he had stopped by earlier and saw them. He called Steve, the band director, to see that no one but the band people were in the theater or on the parking lot. Because of all the people milling around in the theater Dorothy has insisted I take all of Mary's paintings out of the lobby. She is afraid they will steal them or tear them up. We are real proud of her paintings.

Tonight we have a meeting at the Board of Health. Laney is coming by for me at seven o'clock. He is about seventy years old and fishes with Jim and me when we go to the coast. Jim tells other fishermen on the pier they needn't have any worry, he has brought a doctor and an undertaker with him to take care of any emergencies that might occur.

23

A hectic day

Today things were pretty hectic at the office. It started off with a day someone backed into in the Cone Mill parking lot sometime toward the last of February. The plant nurse brought her to the office for treatment. I have done the best I know for her, and each time she has gone somewhere else for further treatment. At the last visit, I returned her to work about the first of June.

Today, she was in the office wearing a neck collar. When I questioned her about it, she said I had recommended it. I don't remember this. There were a few other patients ahead of her. When it was her time, I inquired from Dorothy where she was. She said she had left the office. Dorothy said she thought I had some money from the insurance company for her and also that I had overcharged her ten dollars in the bill. We checked the record and it seems she owes me ten dollars for the last visit.

During the day, I was worried that she may not be working. I called the mill office and they told me she had worked only one to two days when I sent her back to work. I think she is seeing another doctor and is planning to sue the mill and me for more money.

Another disturbing incident was a patient about eighty years old visiting another lady here in town of about the same age. She was from Wilmington, a major port city on the North Carolina coast. She had begun to cough during the night and was sick this morning with a fever. The lady she was visiting uses another doctor in neighboring Hickory, but she couldn't find him this morning and called for me.

The patient's temperature was one hundred and two degrees. At first, they wanted me to find their doctor in Hickory and ask him to put the visitor in the hospital. This was agreeable, but when I called I found that he was out on vacation. I suggested another doctor in Lenoir who I knew the family used, but they didn't want to go to the hospital in Lenoir. I told them then they would be no worse off if they gave my medicine a try until morning. This was agreeable.

I gave her an injection of penicillin and another type of antibiotic and some cough syrup for her cough. They left the office fairly content, I thought. Around two o'clock, Hannah called to tell me that they wanted me to call them. When I called it seemed that they had called their doctor on vacation and if I would call him and discuss the case, he would have his assistant admit the visitor. This made me quite displeased as I asked her that if they wanted another doctor why did she bring her friend out to see me anyway? After a few other factual statements, reminding her that I was a doctor and if she wanted another physician it was not my business to find her one, she agreed to wait until morning. After hanging up the phone I decided that I had better go check on the patient myself. When I got there, she seemed already doing better. I will check on her tomorrow before I call anyone else to see her.

One bright thing today was that Donna, the woman suspected of having had a light stroke, was much better. She has returned from the hospital, probably for the last time. Fannie called Saturday night, saying that she didn't want her mother to go to the hospital again. But if she gets bad again, I will insist on her returning. I can't do what can be done in the hospital. I went by to see her this evening. She was sitting in a chair. Her eyes were closed, her breathing very rapid, her skin cold and clammy. Her pulse was steady and blood pressure normal. The chair she was sitting in was a toilet chair. She didn't respond to her name. She may improve for a while.

Tom, the man who has helped me some at the theater, developed a high fever Friday night. He seemed to respond to treatment until

Monday afternoon. He became confused, and his temperature elevated again. He insisted there was snow outside, two feet deep, and that the roof of his house would fall in. I have referred him to the hospital for treatment. I haven't found out what is causing his fever.

Glenn is still excited about the theater. Last night, he changed the marquee to "You Wanna Dance?" We think Steve and his band have broken up. They didn't practice yesterday or today. I think they do not like the theater because the acoustics are so much different than in the places they play. I discussed with Glenn that we might be better off to hire a band when we get ready to open than to have one in the theater each night. I think it would be hard to develop our disco decorations with the band practicing.

The wrestling matches we held at the theater last month were a big disappointment. The turnout was very light. I had expected a large audience. A lot of people had said what the community needed was a good wrestling match.

The participants were a lot like the people that put on the country music show, not very talented. Even before the activities began, I became uneasy. It seemed to be a family affair with a lot of children running throughout the theater.

While the event was taking place, the wrestler taunted back and forth with some of the audience. Several times one or two people stood up in their chairs and challenged the wrestlers to come out and fight. I knew some of these people to be very bad characters and they intended to make it a fight with knives. I think I was lucky I didn't have a free-for-all in the audience.

At the conclusion, the manager suggested setting a date for another match. He was not real pleased with the turnout, but thought we might do better with a return engagement. I suggested waiting until the last of the week because I was going to the beach. He agreed, promising to call me Thursday. While at the beach, I decided not to have anymore wrestling. So far, the manager has not called to set a date.

24

New funeral director

7-8-1978 ✓

This is a hot Saturday afternoon in July with the temperature in the nineties. It is so hot and dry the grass is beginning to turn brown. To combat the dry weather I made a hydraulic ram and put it in the creek at the bottom of the hill. It pumps about a gallon of water every five minutes, not enough to do much good. It has a good rhythm, a little like a heartbeat, just as regular as a clock. I use it to water my tomatoes.

Dorothy and I have just returned from Topsail beach. I might have stayed longer even though the fish were not biting if there had not been a dredge working in the sound. It was pumping sand out of the channel onto the beach to control beach erosion. I didn't notice it during the day, but at night it sounded like a giant helicopter flying around the house. I couldn't sleep with it going. I suspect other people left too because of the noise.

Wednesday I worked at the office seeing several patients. Bert came in around ten o'clock to tell me Ted was working for the town police. He still believes the commissioners want to harass the ABC Board so that we will resign. He asked if Ted had talked to me about working for the police department. I said I had not heard from him since I came back from the beach.

Our discussion soon drifted to Laney's road. As far as Bert knew the state was going through with the town manager's request. He thought Laney should have handled his objections to the road differently. Instead of ordering the surveyors off of his property when they first came on it to put up stakes, he thought Laney should have let them drive up the stakes and then made known his objections to the newspapers. I agreed with Laney. I would have ordered them off at the very start. Anyone having designs on someone else's property should contact the owner first as politely as possible.

I think Dorothy and I would have a sewer line into our house now if the surveyors had talked to our neighbor first rather than going into his cow pasture and putting up stakes for him to find when he came home for lunch. As long as he lived he would never talk to me again about a sewer line across his property.

During the afternoon I had a few patients. One was a boy about twelve years old with a fishhook in his left cheek. I used a pointed scalpel to remove it. Sometime I am going to make a good fish hook remover.

Donna is improving. For eighty-eight years old she is very good. She can walk a little and her breathing is much better. There is some pain around her tenth rib on the left side. I think it is coming from arthritis in the spine. I will check on her again Monday.

After supper Dorothy and I took a walk around town and then to Laney's funeral home. Laney and Annie were sitting on the front porch where there is usually a little breeze. We discussed the road proposal again. It seems everyone agrees that it is not going to help anything to widen the intersection and straighten out the road. The best we could figure is it is being done for some political reason. Laney has been calling various political leaders trying to get them to stop the project. He has got some support from them and believes the state people have dropped the project for now.

Friday morning Bert called to find out when the ABC Board is going to make a quarterly distribution. They need more money to buy some equipment for the town. He said again Ted is working for the town police. When I called Jim to tell him what Bert had said he said we should get the title for the car Ted had been driving turned over to the town. If someone had an accident with it the ABC Board would be liable. When I called Bert he said he would take it up at the town meeting Monday night.

Around eleven o'clock I received a call from the manager of the new funeral home where Commissioner Chatman is secretary and treasurer. He wanted to know how he could get a death certificate signed by the county coroner. He said the coroner would not answer his call anymore. He had been calling him all morning. I questioned him about his difficulty and asked if he would like for me to see if I could help him. The coroner and I are pretty good friends. He was real glad to hear that I might be able to help him. I called the coroner to find out what was his trouble. The reason the funeral director was having trouble was that he had taken the body from the hospital morgue without anyone's permission and without having obtained a death certificate from one of the doctors who had seen the patient. He had brought the body to his funeral home, embalmed it, held a funeral service and buried it in the town cemetery without a death certificate. This procedure is pretty much against the law. He must have a death certificate before he can move a body. The coroner was threatening to have the body exhumed for autopsy. Members of the family were in his office wanting to collect on the insurance the man had, but without a death certificate the insurance company wouldn't pay off.

I checked on my records. As a favor to a friend I had seen the man on June 22nd. My friend said the man was his wife's son and was in pain from phlebitis. He was going to take him to the veteran's hospital the next day, but was out of pain medicine now. It was about five o'clock. Dorothy and I were ready to close the office, but I agreed to wait to see him.

He arrived around six o'clock. He was about sixty years old and very thin. He walked with a bad limp. His left ankle was swollen and he had his right arm in a sling. Two years ago he had a stroke that left his left arm and left leg partially paralyzed. I examined him and gave him enough pain tablets to do until he could get to the veterans hospital. I thought this would be the last I would ever hear of him. On June 28th around six o'clock in the morning the ambulance crew called me at home and said they were at his trailer and he was dead. They asked if I would sign the death certificate. I declined, saying that the doctors in the veterans hospital had seen him last. The ambulance must have taken him to the local hospital where, after pronouncing him dead, they put him in the morgue for the coroner to examine.

When I called the county coroner to find out what he knew about the case, he said he told that son of a bitch funeral director not take the body out of the hospital until he had examined him. Someway he had taken it out anyway. Now he was going to hold his damn feet to the fire and have him exhume the body.

I told him the director's feet were getting pretty hot now. Members of the family were in his office wanting insurance forms filled out. I told him I had seen the man about two weeks ago and felt like he died from another stroke. He had high blood pressure when I examined him. Since I was the last doctor that might have seen him he agreed for me to sign the death certificate.

There were quite a few patients waiting when I finished the call so I didn't get to call the undertaker. I didn't need to; he called me again in a few minutes to know if I could help him. Members of the family were in his office threatening to sue him if he had to exhume their father. I told him the coroner had agreed for me to sign the certificate.

He brought the certificate to me in a few minutes, but it was the wrong form. He used my phone to call back for the right form. One of his attendants had it in the office almost before he hung up the phone. I wish now I had him to have Commissioner Chapman call me. Perhaps if he knew how helpful I was to his director he wouldn't be so critical of the ABC Board.

The only other unusual event of the day happened just before closing time. A patient I had been seeing for high blood pressure rushed in for me to take his blood pressure. He wasn't due to return for two weeks. When I asked him why I had to take it now he said his wife had just called him to come home to kill a large snake she found in her closet. He wanted to see if the excitement had run his blood pressure up. It was about the same as on the last visit.

My last patient for the day was a drunken man with a cut on his head. He is about thirty years old and weighing about 250 pounds. At first I didn't intend to accept him, as I didn't think I could do much good wrestling with a fellow that big and sew up his head. When I told him I wanted him to go to the hospital he agreed to be good and hold still for me to sew him up. He and his wife had some kind of altercation and she had hit him with something giving him a cut about two inches long on the right side of his forehead. He held still like he promised and I sowed up his head. He seemed rather grateful.

25

A Sunday morning drive

7-15-1978 ✓

Sunday morning was a beautiful morning with a light blue sky and no clouds. The temperature was in the nineties again. I like hot weather better than cold. While Dorothy and I were eating breakfast the jaybirds were flying about in the oak trees trying to find cool places. In the back yard a bobwhite was whistling.

At the office I had one or two patients waiting. While I was seeing them a mockingbird bird was just outside the window making all the sounds a mockingbird bird can make on a hot dry July morning. Just before church time I received a call to come to see Wanda, a woman in North Catawba, a distance of about six miles out in the country. I promised to come after church.

When I came by the house for Dorothy to go to church with me she said she didn't feel like going. Since she was not going with me I told her I had a house call to make out in the country and would be back around noon. I had been to Wanda's house about a month ago and felt like I could find it again but just in case I didn't remember I carried the notes I made the last time I was there. The general direction was southwest past Dry Ponds to Cajah's Mountain then right to Baton School Road, then left to a creek and just across the creek take a right again at the second road with four mailboxes on the corner. Go up this road about a mile to the first unpainted house on the left. There were two apple trees in the front yard.

It was a nice summer Sunday morning for a drive into the country where I had a lot of fond memories. About a mile out of town I passed the farm where my mother's people lived. On the left of the road leading into the farm there were a lot of apple trees. When Jim and I rode our bicycles out this way going fishing we would fill our pockets with apples.

A little farther down on the left is a small pond surrounded with bamboo. If you look close, a narrow road leads off across the dam to a small brick house surrounded with large white pines. One of my distant cousins on my mother's side lived in this house by himself. He was a retired Methodist minister and we became good friends after he moved here from the mountains. He was pretty high up in the church organization, maybe a Bishop.

I never heard him preach but one or two times. One of these times was when race relations was a hot issue during the Civil Rights movement. He was to be the visiting minister and preach at our Methodist Church on race relations. I knew he was pretty much of an old southern gentleman holding to a lot of old traditions so I was anxious to hear how he would handle his sermon. Well, he was pretty smart too. He never did give his opinion about race relations. He took his text from somewhere in the Bible where it tells of Gamelia, the young prophet.

The conclusion of his sermon was that if a thing is the truth it will stand and if it is wrong the thing will soon fall. After the sermon when we gathered outside the church everyone I talked to was satisfied with his sermon.

The last time I saw him was when the sheriff called me to come over to his house. Some people noticed a fowl odor coming from the house and called the sheriff to investigate. He found him dead in the bathroom. I think he had a stroke while straining with a bowel movement. He had been dead about a week when we found him.

Since I mentioned odor there was another time some years later when people noticed an odor again emanating from this house especially at night. To some people it was a very pleasant odor, something like fresh corn in contrast to the last odor. They soon figured out what it was and called the sheriff again.

This time the sheriff found a liquor still in the front room with the smoke going up the chimney. I never did hear whose still it was.

A little farther down the road on the left a friend of mine lives in a small brick house with his front yard extending down to the creek. He and I flew radio controlled model airplanes together several years ago. It was quite a thrill to get them up in a clear blue sky, push a button on a little box and see them turn this way and that. Sometimes they didn't respond to the signal. I had one with a strip of aluminum on the leading edge of the wings get out of control and hit a power line. It disintegrated in a blue flame.

The last time we flew together he had a nice new cub plane. It was doing well, about five hundred feet up and flying level. Something went wrong, maybe the wing slipped a bit and sent it into a tailspin. When it hit the ground pieces flew like feathers from a bird. I think this was our last time flying. It still is pretty difficult to pass a nice field without thinking of flying a model plane.

When I crossed the bridge over the creek I remembered the times my father would meet Jim and me here. We would ride our bicycles to the head of the lake. There was a big hickory tree beside the creek there where we parked our bicycles. We had a minnow seine and bucket hid under a brush pile. We would seine for minnows all the way back to the bridge. By the time we reached the bridge we generally had three or four-dozen minnows. They were different kinds. One was very pretty, a light pink with white fins. Some were horny heads and a little brown one that looked a lot like a miniature sturgeon. My father would come by soon and take us back to the lake where we caught many a good bass.

On the other side of the creek and going up a hill the road goes through a forest of loblolly pines set out by the power company. They are about twenty-five feet tall now. At the end of the pines the road runs by pastures with grass turned brown from the dry weather. All the cows were in the shade along the creeks. Along the terraces near the creeks are patches of daises and Queen Ann Lace blooming among the blackberry bushes.

Just over the second ridge a brown ford pickup was parked on the side of the road. A family of four children was climbing over the fence with buckets going to pick blackberries. Farther on, fields of corn had yellow tassels with bees flying about. Below the tassels the ears were putting out silk. Beside the houses there were gardens with tomatoes, beans, corn and potatoes. Here and there were small churches with cars parked around them. The houses were of three types. Some of the houses were the old type house like the one I was going to, never been painted, a brownish gray showing growth streaks in the wood. They had a front porch, a door in the center and two windows on the front. On the back was the kitchen and dining room.

The second type and more recent is a small brick house with a car-port on the side. These are in rows in the fields where Jim and I hunted birds and rabbits. Jim says the state should not have let them build houses in the best farm fields.

The third type is the mobile home or trailer. Sometimes these are in a group called a trailer park, others are in the back yard or side yard of an old house. They are a complete unit making it easy for young peo-ple to get started house keeping.

Close to the third bridge was an old service station with the hand operated gasoline pump still standing outside. My father had one of these out front at his garage. I pumped many a gallon of gas for ten or fifteen cents a gallon. And sometimes the customer only wanted one or two gallons. These stations were built of wood with a tin roof. The roof extended out to the edge of the road so you could put gas in without getting wet.

The front of the building had two large windows with a door in the center. Beneath each window there was a long bench making a good place to sit in the shade. A fellow could sit there and drink a Nehi or R.C., whittle, play checkers, tell yarns, or just scratch his feet in the dirt and wait for cars to come by. Things moved a lot slower then.

Thinking of all this caused me to miss my next turn to my patient's house and I had to turn around. I knocked on the door and Wanda called for me to come in. She is about sixty years old and very thin. Her complaint consisted of trouble with every organ left in her body. Mostly she complained of her heart. While I was listening to her complaints she held one hand on her wrist checking her pulse.

After examining her I couldn't find any specific trouble except her fear of dying. I encouraged her to live one day at a time. I told her one day she would be in a lot worse shape than she was now. She again said she was afraid to die. I told her it was going to happen sometime and she had better try living as best she could every day.

We talked for about an hour. I think she was encouraged some and told me she was very glad I had come to see her.

When I returned home Dorothy had lunch ready. She had peaches we had brought back from the beach, some tomatoes a patient had given us, an apple pie made from some of the apples Jim had given and a barbecued chicken bought at the food store.

I think I could have gotten a chicken from one of my patients, but Dorothy doesn't like picking off the feathers. When we were first married my aunt Kate brought us a young pullet.

Dorothy started preparing it one Saturday morning around nine o'clock. About ten-thirty she came into the office with a few feathers on her head and others here and there. She had been working on the chicken and said if I wanted it I had better come to the house and fix it. She was not going to work on it anymore.

I went to the house, which at that time was back of the office. I pulled off some more feathers. We had feathers all over the house and the chicken still had plenty of feathers left on it. I finally skinned it. That was our last live chicken.

During the week things have gone well. Glenn is still interested in the disco dance for the theater. We may get the floor in front of the stage slick enough for dancing. I called a man to come check on it Tuesday.

The town commissioners are still concerned about the ABC Store. Reece called Thursday and said from now on they want us to furnish them a quarterly audit like we do for the state.

Most of my patients are doing well. I still have the lady that got hit in the parking lot in April. She is going to sue the insurance company for more money. She has not been happy with anything I have done for her. I think from now on I will be more selective of the patients I treat. I would have been better off if I had referred her to the hospital.

Monta continues to do well. She can walk a little better. One patient died of cancer of the bladder.

Another wanted his medicine filled. I told him he was not my patient since I had not seen him in a year. I recalled that I went to see him early one morning for a light stroke. He was due to see me the next day. In about a week I found he had been going to see another doctor. I didn't mind this so much as I minded just supplying his medicine without seeing him. When something happens he will call me and I won't know anything about his case.

Another patient came in Tuesday with a spider bite on his leg. It was a pretty black place and made his leg swell a lot. He is much better now.

26

Skiing accident

It is still hot and dry. Even with the dry weather most gardens are producing anyway. Patients have been bringing me green beans, tomatoes, cucumbers, squash and yellow corn. Today I brought in three ripe tomatoes from my garden.

At the office things have gone along well. Donna is doing more walking. Tom, the man who helped me about the theater died sometime Sunday morning. I noticed the funeral sign outside his house Monday night. I stopped to inquire about him. One of his sons said his gall bladder had ruptured causing an infection in his stomach that finally killed him. I don't think I ever saw a patient with gall bladder attack that didn't complain of pain. Tom complained of some pain in the abdomen when I sent him to the hospital Wednesday morning. That afternoon he was operated on for acute gall bladder infection. He died Saturday morning.

Around ten o'clock a young man came in with a cut on his elbow. He had been using a chain saw. He was lucky it didn't cut his arm off.

Another patient I saw was a young girl about sixteen years old. There was nothing remarkable about her except her color. She was the color of a corpse four or five days old, a purple plumb color. She said she had just come from the food store where they had the air conditioner on. Cold temperature' makes her turn blue even to the ends of her fingers. She had come by for some antibiotics for a sore throat, not for her color.

I am still involved with the town commissioners and the ABC store. When Ted, our ABC police officer left the store we decided to give the car he was driving to the town because we were not taking in enough money to pay him and maintain a patrol car. Monday night at the town board meeting the town attorney pointed out there were some legal matters about turning over the car. There was also some concern that we were not following the law in that we were no longer maintaining an ABC officer as directed in the original bill. We will have to leave all this to Mayor Bert to work out with the city attorney.

Sunday afternoon around four o'clock a car pulled up in front of the house. It was a group of young folks about twenty years old. One came to the door to ask if I would see one of them that had a cut. I agreed and told them to go to the office where I would meet them. When I arrived two of them, a boy and a girl wearing bathing suits, were standing against the front of the car drinking beer. I thought I might be in for some trouble. I asked that only the patient and one other person come into the office. This was agreeable, though two others wanted to come in too. They said they wanted to call their parents to tell them why they would be late getting home. I thought this would be all right. I recalled how many times I have worried about my children when they were late. These children had been out with a speedboat for the first time and I felt sure their parents were worried about them.

My patient was a young boy wearing a pair of cutoff blue jeans and a blood stained brown towel around his right knee. He had been water skiing and fell off. When he fell off, the driver of the boat lost control and put the boat into a spin, then straightened it out heading straight for the boy in the water. He saw it coming and tried to dive but with his life jacket on he couldn't get under the water. The propeller had cut three gashes in his right leg. They were not very deep and I sewed them up.

Not long ago a person was killed this same way. When he attempted to dive he didn't get under the water far enough and the propeller cut him to pieces.

My theater business is going pretty bad. Glenn isn't sure he wants to do the teen disco. Another man wants to hold country music shows but he doesn't like the idea of working with Glenn for use of the theater. After discussing it more with Glenn he and I decided to finish up with the disco idea before trying country music shows. Time will tell what was the best thing to do.

27

The bicycle and the train

8-9-1978 ✓

A few days ago it was rainy and I didn't have many patients. In the afternoon I saw a man with a sore throat. Another patient was a little girl about ten-years-old. She fell under a moving railroad box car. During the morning, I called the railroad company to tell them about the track being loose at the crossing in front of the office where the road from the town of Rhodhiss joins U.S. Highway 321. Around one o'clock I saw a man come up the track on a little three-wheel cart. He looked at the track and then left, going back the way he came.

Around two-thirty it stopped raining and the sky began to clear. I was sitting in the front office looking out the window watching the train switch cars near the crossing. The engine had made the switch and was pushing a car loaded with coal along the track into the Shuford Mill lot. The engineer was sounding his whistle intermittently, loud enough to deafen anyone near the track. Some men were standing in the road where the train crosses the highway with flares flagging down all the vehicles till the train crossed the road.

When the coal car was about across the road I saw a small boy on a bicycle coming up the sidewalk peddling as fast as he could aiming to beat the train across the crossing. He beat the train by a few feet and went on up the sidewalk toward the Western Auto store. Men in the road and beside the track began waving their flares and shouting at him as he went by. They were watching the first rider and didn't see the second bicycle coming up the sidewalk the same way with the rider again standing up on the pedals and straining for dear life. By now the coal car was across the sidewalk cutting off the second rider.

Instead of stopping, the rider turned up the track going just in front of the car. Suddenly the bicycle must have hit a cross tie and the rider went down on the left side in front of the moving car. The wheels of the car were now where I last saw the bicycle. I couldn't see any more of the bicycle or rider.

The engineer must have seen the second rider and slid the wheels of the coal car, stopping it about ten feet past where I last saw the bicycle.

I stood up and told Dorothy sitting behind me the train had just run over a little boy. She looked out the window. All she could see was the engine and the black coal car resting on the track. Men ran to the front wheels of the coal car looking under it for the bicycle and rider. One pulled out a twisted bicycle. He motioned for the engineer to back up the car. Now all the men began looking under the car. They didn't see anything and began to look up and down the street. They were thinking the rider might have scrambled out from under the car. A policeman stopped with the blue lights flashing on his car and inspected the bicycle. While they were looking, another policeman came down the street from the Western Auto store leading two children. From their size and dress I recognized them to be the two riders. When the crowd dispersed some the policeman brought the children for me to see. The one that had fallen under the car was a little girl about ten years old. She was muddy all over and even had some mud in her mouth. She was pale and shaking. She had skinned her elbow and left knee. I couldn't find any other injuries. The policeman asked them why they didn't stop for the train. He had heard the whistle blowing all over town. Her brother said the bicycles didn't have any brakes on them so they couldn't stop. I think he was trying to show his sister he could beat the train across the crossing and she was following him.

The policeman told him it had almost cost his sister's life. He asked where they lived and took them home. I learned sometime later the railroad company bought her a new bicycle with brakes.

28

A cut finger

9-7-1978

There is definitely a touch of fall in the air now, though the days are still hot with the temperature in the eighties during the day. During the night it drops down to fifty, making good sleeping conditions. Some of the trees are beginning to show their fall colors, especially the sycamore and poplar. Their leaves are beginning to turn yellow; those on the sourwood are already a deep red. We call these trees sourwood rather than sour gum. Before long all the hardwood trees will have all their colors, yellow, orange, red, purple and brown. Even the nights are different in the fall. On a still night, especially after a rain, all the bugs that make noises are having a symphony. I think they cease around midnight when the temperature drops below a certain level.

At the office I have not been very happy. I have a girl about fourteen years old with a cut finger. It was about an inch long requiring four sutures. Her mother is unhappy, thinking I am charging too much. I charged thirty dollars the first time and ten dollars the second time. This is the third visit. She has grumbled with each visit. I would like to tell her to get another doctor, but I will have to wait now until the finger is better. Today her father brought her in. I was seeing another patient and she had to wait in the reception room. Her father stood at the desk looking back toward me.

While he was standing there Beckey came in for me to check on her.

She is about fifty-years-old and has an artificial left leg and this man knew about it. Beckey stood beside him at the desk while Dorothy pulled her record. In a few minutes Dorothy came back and told me I should see Beckey right away. I was quite alarmed. Beckey had a severe heart attack three years ago. I thought she might be having another heart attack.

Dorothy brought her to the first examining room and closed the door. When I spoke to Beckey I saw her eyes well up with tears. I asked her what the trouble was and she started to cry.

"I would like to kill that son of a bitch out there," she said.

"Why?" I asked.

"He said, 'Say anything to me and I will break your other leg.' I had not said a thing to him."

I suggested he might have been trying to make a joke.

She replied, "That is a damn poor way of making a joke. I wonder how he would feel if he had a peg leg and I said that to him?"

I thought of telling her I had trouble with this family too, but kept my mouth shut.

Today at noon we had a meeting at the ABC store. Members of the town board were due to attend, but only Mayor Bert, Jean and the city manager attended. None of the commissioners doing the most complaining came. Dorothy says they are just harassing us to get us to resign. It was a general meeting with no particular purpose.

Earlier that day I had called my insurance agent to find out about my insurance on the theater. He had called earlier in the week implying that the insurance company was unhappy with the theater. They want to increase the premium. I am certain that times have changed to the extent that people are expecting someone else to take care of them if something happens to them while they are on your property. The mill is having to pay for people if they faint and bump their head or lift and strain a muscle. I am beginning to wonder if developing the theater is worth the possibility of a lawsuit from someone getting hurt. Calvin said my policy was good until the last of October and since I was not having wrestling or boxing they may not increase the premium.

Thursday Glenn came to the office to call off our disco program. He had not been able to find anyone to help him. I was a little reluctant to quit, but thinking more about it I think it was best. He had lost his enthusiasm and it is not good to try pushing someone into something they are not enthused about. I didn't see that the disco as we planned it, the band of teenagers and all the other people would add much to developing a better character for the participants.

I called Dudley and we agreed on a partnership for him to run the theater. He has been by every day since to check on something in the theater. Today he came by to let me know he had put an ad in the paper and that he was getting a piano. He seems real happy and has plans for coming events. His first event is to be a talent hunt for the best dancers among teen-age children.

29

Our new bank

9-15-1978 ✓

The day began with a hazy morning and light fog that gradually cleared. There was a slight breeze with the temperature around seventy. During the day the sky cleared and now at nine o'clock it is clear outside with a full moon. Crickets and all other insects that can make a noise are busy doing it. My plans for the day consisted of seeing my patients, fixing a light over the theater stage for Dudley and attending a political meeting in Lenoir about raising money for the party.

Today is the day the bank is having the birthday party. It was nine years ago that the banking commission granted permission for the Northwestern Bank to open in Granite Falls.

At the office it was a rather routine morning. Some of my regular patients came in for examination and treatment.

Later, on the way to Lenoir, I began to wonder why I was leaving my office to go to a political meeting. I should stay in my office seeing my patients and leave running the country to politicians. Then I told myself that at these meetings people are being appointed that will make the laws that I must operate my office by and live by. Somewhere it is written if good people don't serve, bad ones will. I don't feel like I am particularly good but I believe I should learn about the process of electing people and do what I can to make this a better place to live in.

When I returned to the office Dorothy was still at the bank anniversary celebration. My first patient was a lady with a sore throat. When I went across the hall to get her some medicine I noticed the mother of the girl whose finger I had sewed up about three weeks ago. There were plenty of seats in the reception room but she preferred to stand beside her daughter. She wanted me to make three copies of her daughter's record. I made the copies and inquired how her daughter was doing. She said she had taken her to a doctor in Hickory who said she had gas on her stomach.

I hadn't been asked to treat her stomach. Then she said there was a big hole in her daughter's finger where I had sewed it up. I asked her to bring her daughter back so I could see it. She said if I wouldn't charge for it she would bring her in this afternoon. I said there would be no charge. I wondered why she wouldn't let me see her then.

Sometime later in the afternoon she brought the girl in. I looked at the finger and couldn't see a hole. I asked her to stick her finger in it so I could see it. The mother overheard me and said she couldn't see good. The girl pointed to a little speck where a stitch had been. I took some tweezers and pulled it out. I said, "It's off now." The mother heard me and screamed, "What's off?"

I said, "The speck. Did you think it was the finger?"

As she left Sarah brought another patient to the room. Sarah had a big grin on her face. She had predicted I would have trouble with this patient. I don't remember just why she thought I would have trouble. I think we got along all right. Dorothy returned from the bank and said I should go over now. When I entered the bank there were a lot people there who had gone to Raleigh with us to get permission for the bank to come to Granite. We were serving cake and punch. Lamont was there too. He had made a speech in Raleigh along with Mayor Bert and me. It was the first time I had ever been involved in a fight to get a bank in a community. In this case it involved getting people to write letters to the banking commission in Raleigh stating why we needed another bank. At the same time other people were writing letters telling why we didn't need another bank.

One of the most interesting things about the letter writing was that about a week before we were to go to Raleigh, someone sent back copies of all the letters that had been written against having a new bank.

We were surprised that so many of our friends had written against having a new bank. I think all the school teachers wrote against the bank. Even my preacher wrote against it on our church stationary, implying that our church was against it.

But when the time came to go to Raleigh we had about a hundred people up at two o'clock in the morning ready to go. The opposition had about ten. At the meeting, each side was allowed three speakers. I was selected to speak first, then Bert and then Lamont. Whether or not the speeches helped or not, I don't know, but in about a month it was announced in the paper that the banking commission had granted permission for the Northwestern Bank to open a branch in Granite Falls.

Shortly after returning to the office Dudley called for me to come to the theater. He had engaged a soft drink company to put a drink machine in the theater and didn't have the money to cover the cost of it. It was around sixty dollars. He agreed to refund me later, but after thinking it over I thought the fairest thing to do would be to pay half the cost. While I was there the man he had bought the piano from brought it in.

It is a tremendous one and real heavy. We finally got eight men together to put it on the stage. Dudley's wife was there and played some hymns. I was amazed at the tone and quality of the sound. You could hear it in the balcony as well as in the front. The man he got it from said he didn't have room for the bench, and that he would bring it tomorrow. Dudley is just beaming about his show for Saturday night. I hope he isn't disappointed.

I was proud of my bank speech so I have saved it for the last. You can see what you think of it. After a few preliminary remarks expressing my appreciation for allowing us to appear, I began my speech as follows:

"I am Dr Martin Jones from Granite Falls North Carolina. Granite Falls is my hometown. I am here to express my opinion on banking in our town. First I want to mention some civic activities I have been engaged in. They are the Review Board for the Boy Scouts, Chairman of the committee for the Recreation Tax to support our recreation department, Chairman of the Citizens Committee for the Legal Control of Alcoholic Beverages in our town, A member of the Recreation Commission from its beginning in 1957 until 1969, president of the Granite Falls Rotary Club twice, Vice President of the Granite Falls Development Corporation since its beginning, three times president of the Granite Falls United Fund and won the trophy for the year the last time, served on the Board of Stewards of The First United Methodist Church where I am still a member.

"I am one of the four practicing physicians in our town. I have named these positions to let you know I am an active member of my community. However, at this moment I am in need of being a great orator, a Patrick Henry, a Douglass or a Winston Churchill. Instead I am by profession a medical doctor, a general practitioner. My business is helping the sick and injured. What I have to say therefore is not in figures or dollars, but in terms of my understanding of human nature and my community. People like a choice of doctors so why should they not have a choice of banks in their community? I have read somewhere that in the course of the affairs of men there comes a time like a high tide which if recognized and seized they may be carried to greatness. Likewise are the affairs of our community. Some people in the community must encourage expansion or else the community will be left to dry up. At this moment the tide is high for expansion in my community. Our hopes are on you to weigh the anchor.

"Being a member of the community, I add my voice to those you have already heard from by mail for a new bank. Our community, a small community in western North Carolina, is made up of old and young people. The old are content; the young are restless—all proud and sensitive. Due to our closeness we know each other very well and we know our local bank and its personnel. Due to human nature we have differences with each other and our bank. This affects our trade with each other. As a result of differences, accounts are moved to another bank, thus affecting all our business because people going out of town to trade in another town. Therefore as long as we have only one bank this trend will continue due to differences in people.

"With another bank there would be a checking of this trend as people could shift their accounts to a new bank for a 'cooling off spell.' With a new bank an applicant could shop for competitive interest rates. With a new bank some loans might be made that are not made by the other bank due to individual interest in the object of the loan and faith in the borrower by the lender. With only one bank in town this bank may have no fear of becoming strong politically as the people of a different faith have no choice but to go out of town. This may result in a deadlock of all community efforts for self betterment. With a new bank in the community the competitive spirit would be revived resulting in faster and kinder service to the patron. It is more difficult for people to establish credit reference out of town. A new bank in the community might help establish credit here, tending to keep people shopping in this community.

"Finally, due to the present bank having extended itself out of town into Lenoir where there are several banks and is now making application for permission to move into Hickory, I hardly see how the Bank of Granite is now, nor has been for sometime except by location, our local bank as it claims to be. By you granting permission for The Northwestern Bank to come to our community we will set sail on this high tide to a full service community with two banks. Thank you."

30

Dudley's first event

9-17-1978 √

I attribute my despondency tonight to two things.

The first is I would like to go fishing on Topsail Island. A patient was in the office this morning and reported that two schools of blue fish came by Myrtle Beach last week. The schools were about one hundred yards wide running close to shore and around the pier. They were so thick the bait would not sink in the water for the fish. They would not hit bait or any type of lure. He finally snagged two little ones with treble hooks to confirm that they were really blue fish. He saw some jumping that were three feet long. Nobody caught any.

I feel sure some are at Topsail and would hit my Salty Dogs. He might have just made this up to get me excited. Sometimes a fisherman has done this and I get so excited I forget to charge him for the call.

The second thing and more acute cause of my despondency is the poor attendance at the theater for Dudley's talent show last night.

Dudley and I began planning for it Saturday morning. I went to the theater early and checked on the lights and the seats. Everything seemed ready for the big night. I spent the rest of the morning in the office until about eleven o'clock. Suddenly there was a lot of horn blowing outside similar to a wedding party except this was louder and involving more cars.

In a minute or two I recalled that at the last Republican meeting in Lenoir our party had agreed to have a motor caravan tour the county and gather at the headquarters building in Lenoir for a grand opening to begin our campaign. This must be it. I didn't think at the time it could be arranged. The man that volunteered for the job was a tall full-bearded individual that I hadn't counted on for anything. I had seen him at meetings, spoke to him as friendly as I could and that is about as close as I ever got to him. He seldom spoke at the meetings. Now he was the lead man in our campaign. At noon I called for Therman to go to Lenoir with me, but he didn't answer the phone so I went by myself. After greeting everybody out front I went into the building for a pep talk by our county chairman. After his speech each candidate gave thanks again for our support and to the man who had arranged the caravan. I don't believe I could have arranged such a show. It is a thing I am not good at. I began to realize that success of a project involving people is directly related to the proper selection of people capable to do certain things. My bearded friend probably has no inhibition among people and is good at leading people. If I were as big and strong as he is I think I wouldn't have many fears among people either.

Driving home I wondered how much the caravan meant to winning an election. It let people know that the party still existed and was active. I think they would be pleased about that. I doubt that seeing the candidates drive by in their new cars was enough to change anyone's vote. Probably most people vote for one candidate or the other according to how their parents voted. Some may change their vote because they believe their party isn't doing anything for them. Others vote because they are members of the party or have positions gained through the party.

When I returned to the theater Dudley was already there. As I entered the lobby he came out of the bathroom. He smelt like a bottle of after-shave lotion. He is a pretty big man, about sixty years old, well developed, about six feet six inches tall and has a soft southern voice. He lost his left eye some time ago in a fight when someone hit him across the forehead with a tire tool. He had his white hair neatly combed and parted so that some of it shaded his bad eye. He was wearing a neat pink shirt fastened around his neck with a little black bow tie. He had on clean light pink pants and clean white shoes. He looked like a showman.

I told him he looked nice. He still showed excitement in his face. He continually smiled and hummed a little tune. He was restless, pacing back and forth down the aisles to see if the seats and floor were clean. He checked on the supplies in the concession stand and decided we needed something else from the Winn-Dixie store.

While he was gone Tommie his young assistant came in. He is about twenty years old, five and a half feet tall and rather thin. He was dressed like Dudley except for a white shirt with a little red bow tie. He went down to the stage and unpacked various musical instruments and set up three microphones.

Dudley returned without any supplies. I think he went over to tell the manager of the store he was having a talent show in the theater and ask for prizes to give out. He said they didn't have what he wanted. Soon some other members of Dudley's group arrived along with Dudley's wife and grandchildren. His wife, Mom, had brought two boxes of doughnuts. I said they would be pretty sticky. She said people would want them with their coffee. She planed to sell them out front in the concession stand.

The time was now about five o'clock so I popped the popcorn. The first stick of seasoning I picked up for the corn was very soft giving me quite a fright thinking it had spoiled. On closer inspection I saw that it was different than what I had been using. Mom said it was margarine and she had brought it for popping the corn. She used it all the time. It was now bubbling in the kettle so I poured in the popcorn. Tommie tasted it and said it was as good as any he had ever had.

Though it was not yet dark, Dudley wanted me to turn on the marquee lights. We were all getting pretty anxious. Dudley's smile had now turned into a real serious expression, forehead wrinkled and lips drawn tight across his mouth. His big red nose seemed to be leading him around. Until now I hadn't noticed it being so big. The time had moved on to seven o'clock, the time Dudley had put in the paper for the contest to start.

This was to be our big night.

All the participants we had at this time were his grandchildren, about eight, ranging in age from eight to thirteen. No paying customers. Around seven-thirty a young girl appeared wearing leotards and tap dancing shoes. She had come to compete in the talent show. Following her there was a tall heavy man carrying a guitar, then two girls about twelve years old wearing little black caps, shirts and blue jeans with red disco signs on their shirts.

These were the last contestants we had. Dudley was standing out front waiting for more people. I didn't believe any more people would come. The girl dressed in the leotard suit forgot her phonograph. I went to the office for one. The girls wanting to do the disco act were sitting on the front row holding their records and swinging their feet. I went to the front and suggested they start practicing their act before the crowd gathered. They came over to the phonograph and began dancing. Dudley heard the music and brought his group to the stage and began the show. He was very upset, but made the best of it.

The girl with the leotard and tap dancing shoes was voted the best of the contestants, winning a clock. The man with the guitar was second, winning an ax, and the two disco girls each got a cushion to use when they needed a rest.

While we were cleaning up the theater Dudley asked me why more people from town had not showed up. I told him in a small community the people are like he is in the song he frequently sings. "You go to your church and I will go to mine." People are going to whatever appeals to them. In the theater we are competing with the movies, the television, ball games and the county fair.

I didn't go to church today, feeling that since none of the church people came to the theater I wouldn't go to their church. Next Saturday Dudley has booked the Happy Mountain Boys, a gospel-singing group.

As we were leaving the theater, one of Dudley's granddaughters asked me if we had lights in the bathrooms upstairs. I told her we had, but I had forgotten to turn them on. Maybe that is why we had poor attendance. I will have to make out a checklist of things to do before the next event.

31

Marriage troubles

We are having early fall weather with foggy mornings, hot afternoons, cool evenings and cooler mornings. All my patients are wearing light jackets in the mornings. There is some similarity in the color of the jackets and the color of the autumn leaves. The leaves are in full color, brown, yellow, orange red and a little purple. Most of the jackets are brown, orange, red, blue and yellow. There are a few green ones, but most are the same color as the leaves. One of the things I missed most when I was interning in the Panama Canal Zone was the change in seasons, bringing with it the change in clothes. There were no season changes and the clothes were the same all year.

My first patient was a nice redheaded lady who came to me on Monday. She was afraid she had contracted something. She had been separated from her husband for the past six months. During this time she had been seeing a truck driver. On Friday night she had relations with him. Saturday night her husband called and she made up with him and had relations. Sunday afternoon the truck driver called to tell her he had a venereal disease, which he had probably given to her. He had been treated by a doctor and he said she should see a doctor. She said the truck driver told her he had the "clap."

I wanted her to go to the health department to be tested, but she wanted treatment now. She said she would go tomorrow. Her next question was what to tell her husband. She said when he drinks he becomes violent and might kill the truck driver, or her and the truck driver. I couldn't tell her what to tell her husband. She went to the health department for examination and treatment.

I have two ladies with large varicose ulcers on their legs and another lady very sick with the flu. Another patient is a man who can't sleep due to worrying about his wife. I guess most every married man has had this trouble. His began when he noticed that the car she was driving to work was using too much gas. He worked on the carburetor for about two weeks, but the gas kept going down. He finally hired someone to follow the car and found out his wife was driving out someplace to meet a man after work. When he confronted her she didn't deny it, just told him she didn't care for him any more.

Another young man was in with a sore throat. His wife generally gets a sore throat if he gets one so I told him to bring her in for some medicine. He said then didn't I know she had left him. Some of the neighbors called his father one day when they saw a moving truck at their home moving out the furniture. He found out that his wife was seeing another man.

Another patient is a big fat lady. She left her husband three weeks ago because he threw a beer bottle at her. She said he always goes crazy like this when he drinks and she couldn't take it any more. She shot at him one time with her pistol just to scare him. I asked if she was a good shot. She said no, this was the first time she had shot at him.

Another patient I have been treating died at home Thursday. I think she died of a heart attack. Most other patients are getting along well.

At the theater things are at a low ebb. At our last event we had about twenty people. Dudley said the group he had engaged for the evening did not show. He and his group sang gospel songs.

We discussed what we should do to get better attendance. A member of Dudley's group asked me if I knew much about gospel singing. I assured him I didn't. Then he said they might sing good but they are also liars. I think he was referring to the group that didn't come.

The only spark of enthusiasm Dudley had was in a girl named Mable, a young lady singer who some of my patients had already told me about. She was at one of Dudley's shows two weeks ago. I thought her singing was very good, certainly better than anything we have had so far. Since my patients had recommended her I thought they might come to hear her on stage as the star performer.

Dudley wasn't too enthused because she sings country music. He prefers gospel singing, but gospel as we are doing it now is not selling. I encouraged Dudley to set up a show for her. She is due to come October the fourteenth. She is booked under the stage name "Cotton Candy" because of her soft white hair.

Dudley is worried about what the people will think since he has advertised his shows for gospel singing. We discussed it again today. We can't expect people to come to things they can see at home. So far his songs have been the same old things, "You go to your church and I'll go to mine" or "If anybody gets to heaven surely I will."

Even Tommie wants to change things by putting in a little comedy act. Dudley didn't like it, saying there is no comedy in gospel. I think he and Tommie have had a falling out. I haven't seen Tommie around since Saturday night.

To try to make the performances more enjoyable I asked Dudley to see if he couldn't keep things quieter. Children running up and down the isle and on the stage during performances should be stopped. The ones running around are his grandchildren. He said he would have them behave.

I called a young man in Hickory who had spoke to me about running another disco program. He thinks we can get some sound equipment and some records for about two thousand dollars and get it going without a band. Dudley is very reluctant to look after the building and concession stand for him on Saturday nights. Mom is more agreeable. She said they needed to be doing something and they would like to help.

On Tuesday, I went with Laney to the executive club in Hickory. On the way he brought up his troubles with preachers. One of the preacher's members had died and Laney wanted another preacher to furnish a choir for the funeral. The preacher thought Laney should pay the choir since he was charging for the funeral. When members of the deceased's family were asked about paying they maintained that the deceased was a member of the preacher's church and since he was performing the funeral he should furnish the choir. The family wouldn't pay Laney for a choir.

The town commissioners must be content with the ABC store. We haven't heard from them in a month.

32

Cotton Candy

10-14-1978 ✓

The fall colors are at their peak. A lot of people have gone to the mountains this weekend to see them. So many people are in the mountains an announcement was just now made on the television that there are no available rooms in Asheville this weekend.

At the office my patients are doing well. I thought they were doing so well Jim and I took off Monday night for Topsail Island with two friends for two days of fishing. We returned late Thursday afternoon. After unpacking I went by the theater to see how Dudley was doing with our next event, a country music show featuring Cotton Candy.

Before I left town Dudley said she would be practicing in the theater each evening until her show on Saturday night. Dudley was cleaning the floor in the lobby when I went in. He said Cotton Candy had not called him or been by to practice, but her brother had been in to see about renting the theater for the Saturday night we had her booked. He didn't know why he wanted it, but he wanted me to call him as soon as I came back to town. Dudley gave me his telephone number. Dudley said he didn't believe Cotton Candy would appear on Saturday night since she had not been practicing. We discussed what we would do.

I said we could do like they do in baseball, give rain checks. He was in favor of his group singing gospel songs again. I thought we should cancel because we had advertised Cotton Candy live on stage. He finally agreed to cancel the show if she didn't appear.

Before I called the number Dudley had given me I recalled that some months ago a man had asked about renting the theater. I wondered if this was the man. I called and he said he wanted to talk about renting the theater for this Saturday night. He said he had mentioned it to me some months ago. I told him we had it booked. He knew that and wanted to rent the show too.

Cotton Candy was his sister and he knew we would fill the theater. He said she had been singing since she was five years old and could play most any musical instrument. He wanted to know how many seats were in the theater including the ones in the balcony. When I told him five hundred, this was not enough, but it would do for the first performance.

I told him it would be up to Dudley if he wanted to negotiate a contract and concluded our discussion.

Now I was excited about the possibilities of Cotton Candy. Perhaps we had discovered a star for our show. Cotton Candy was about twenty-three years old, a brownish blond about five feet six inches tall. When I told a man who had been coming regularly to our shows that Cotton Candy was coming Saturday night he began to smile and seemed pleased, but for the wrong reason. His response was that he had rather be going out with her than listening to her sing. Her brother Lee was so sure that she would be a star he called back and wanted to do the future booking for her. I was glad for his enthusiasm. He took every poster we had of her and posted them throughout the county. We had large ads in three papers and Dudley had the show announced on the radio all week.

On Friday, the day before the show, Lee, Candy's brother who had been putting up posters, came in the office around ten o'clock in the morning asking for a hundred dollars for the band Cotton Candy had hired for Saturday night. He had asked Dudley for the money and Dudley had told him to see me. He also said unless he had the money by noon Cotton Candy was accepting another offer of three hundred dollars to sing in a local night club on Saturday rather than come to the theater.

My spirit began to sink. I sensed a failure. I sent him back to Dudley because Dudley was in charge of the theater. He said he and that old man didn't get along and Cotton Candy didn't like him either. That was the reason she had not been practicing. This didn't seem to be agreeing with what Dudley had told me earlier. He and Cotton Candy had agreed on a certain percentage of the gate receipts.

I told him I thought our best chance now with the show only twenty-four hours away was to work together for this time and we could make some other arrangements later. After the show he would know what Cotton Candy was worth and he could ask his price for her before the next show. We talked to Dudley. He said when he first called her she agreed to accept 25 percent of the ticket sales as her part for the evening show. If she packed the house at three dollars a seat that would be fifteen hundred dollars for all of us. Her part of it would be three hundred and fifty dollars. Lee seemed satisfied and went to work again. He said he knew thirty truck drivers and their wives who would advertise on their CB radios. Cotton Candy's husband, also a truck driver, had been advertising all week on his CB.

With all this my spirits began to rise a little, but I recalled the time I had a wrestling match which was what a lot of people said was just what the town needed. I felt sure with all this support the theater would be full of people wanting to see the wrestling. We had about fifty people. None of the people who came to the boxing event came, and none of the people that came to the gospel singings came. I learned from this that everyone has their thing and they don't cross over very quickly.

Could this event be different? I was hoping so.

Saturday morning started with a bright sun in a clear blue sky and a cool breeze. It had rained a little during the night. I thought this would cause a cool night so the first thing I did before going to the office was to go by the theater and light the furnaces. I went back to the office and frequently looked out to the theater to see if there was any activity.

I had promised Lee that I would have the theater open at one o'clock so Cotton Candy and her band could get set up and begin practicing. Around nine-thirty I saw Dudley go in the back door. I had planned to take over some pictures for the lobby so as soon as I could take a break I went over to the lobby.

When I arrived Dudley had left. He had pinned a note on his office door saying he had come to put a banner across the street announcing the show but no one had come to help him. As I suspected, he is having trouble with his group. Tommie, his primary helper, is mad because Dudley will not give him a key to the theater. When Dudley asked me about it I told him I didn't see any reason to give him one. The only time he needed in the building was when he was with Dudley.

Mickey, another of Dudley's group, a thin blond boy about nineteen years old, is mad because we have not made any money. He is in love with a little redheaded girl about fifteen years old and frequently brings her with him to the practice sessions. Half of the time Dudley can't find him because he is up in the balcony eating snacks and fooling around with his girlfriend.

The best place I found for my picture was on the wall near the door into Dudley's office. There were nails in the wall where I had recently removed a lot of school mascots, bears, wild cats, and some old men. I had taken the animals down thinking they had no place in Dudley's gospel singing. I had left one mascot, an old man with bulging eyes. After hanging my picture of the girl fixing her earring as if she were going out on a date I stood back to view it. I couldn't help grinning and laughing to myself. I had hung it beside and level with the old man with the bulging eyes. Now he seemed to be looking back at her a lot like the man who said about Cotton Candy that he'd rather be going out with her than listening to her songs.

I went back to the office where a few patients were waiting. After taking care of them I went home for lunch, then hurried back to the theater to be sure to be there when Cotton Candy and her band came to practice. There was no one there, not even Dudley. I busied myself checking on the furnaces, then checking on the bathrooms. There was a slight odor in the men's room so I mopped the floor.

Dudley came in just as I was finishing. His hair was neatly combed over his bad eye. He was wearing a new light gray suit and clean white shoes. His nose looked too big and his lips were drawn tight around his mouth. I could see he was worried, no light in his eye today.

He spoke softly saying, "Howdy," and would I get him something for his headache. He had not slept a wink all night worrying about the show. He went outside to look up and down the street as if he were expecting people to already be waiting for the show. I went to the office to get him something for his head.

When I returned he was slouched in one of the chairs rubbing his head. He said he didn't believe Cotton Candy would come. She had not called him nor had she been practicing her show. He didn't know what she would do even if she came. He didn't know what kind of program she had planned for the evening.

I gave him the tablets for his head and we reviewed our previous decision to cancel if she didn't come. His eye was wet and he was about to cry. He got up and went to the outside door. He said Mickey was sitting outside in his car with his girl and wouldn't help him hang the banner. Tommie was not here either.

I told him I thought Tommie was probably upset because he wasn't due to be in the show tonight. He agreed but said he didn't care, he was going to continue with the theater whether they stayed out or not. While we were talking, Mom came in with a load of candy and potato chips for the canteen. She arranged these on a table along the wall. Dudley picked up a pack of potato chips and began pacing the floor again. Suddenly there was a lot of commotion in the back coming from the hall leading to the stage. We all ran to the auditorium.

Cotton Candy had arrived with her band.

They gathered around the piano and began to practice. The time was now about five o'clock. There were four members of the band. The leader was about thirty years old, heavyset slightly bald and about five feet eight inches tall wearing cream-colored slacks and an open pink shirt. A fellow about twenty-five years old, five feet tall and about five feet around dressed in loose fitting blue genes and a light blue shirt was electrician for the band and also banjo picker. The guitar picker was a young, thin fellow about twenty years old wearing a red shirt, blue jeans and tennis shoes. The drummer was a big man, about six feet five weighing about three hundred pounds, a little bald and with a fairly dark complexion. He was wearing a white shirt and blue jeans and a big cowboy hat.

Dudley was happy to see them. His eye was bright again.

Someone played the piano and Cotton Candy sang a few country songs. I didn't get to see her for all the other things going on, moving chairs and plugging in their electrical instruments. Before they had completed their work, Dorothy came for me to go to dinner at Grace Chapel. The church was having a chicken and dumpling dinner.

When I returned I saw Mickey still sitting in the parking lot with his girlfriend. Tommie had also arrived and parked beside Mickey. I asked Tommie why he didn't come in. He said he was waiting for someone. I think his girlfriend had stood him up. I entered the theater through the back door. Candy and her group had left, probably to get something to eat. In the lobby Dudley and his wife were sitting in the front door looking up and down the street. Dudley was smiling now knowing that we were going to have a show.

Soon Mickie and Tommie came in to join us. They were wearing their best suits. Mickie was wearing a sports coat and slacks without a tie. He had a bright red shirt on. Tommie had on white pants and a blue shirt and red tie. Mom began to tease Tommie about being stood up. He kept looking out the door for someone. A few days ago and even an hour ago we were thinking we would be stood up by Cotton Candy. Tommie assured us his date was on the way.

Around seven o'clock Dudley showed me the tickets he would use, pink for adults and blue for children. He wrote the starting number down and gave me a copy so Candy could see where he had started on the roll of tickets. When the last ticket was sold he could subtract the first number from it and tell how many tickets we had sold. He was still pacing around in the lobby. Mom was helping me with the pop-corn. We had popped four poppers full and were on the last one when someone called me to come to the stage. When I returned to the lobby it was full of smoke. The thermostat on the popcorn machine had stuck and set the popper on fire. Mom had dumped the burning corn into the bin of good corn I had already popped trying to get the fire out. I got the smoking kettle loose from the machine and took it out-side. Mom picked out most of the burnt corn from the good. We thought we could stand the smoke, but it began to make our eyes water so we had to open all the windows and doors to get it out before show time.

We had most of it out when Candy and her band returned. She was wearing a light tan pants suit that revealed all her figure. Dudley went up to the stage to greet her and to explain about the tickets. They had a conference lasting about ten minutes.

When Dudley returned he was looking very sad again. He said Cot-ton Candy was real nervous. She had never performed in a theater before and this was the first time she had seen this band. The band she had been using had started drinking Friday night and she had fired them this morning. She engaged this group for a hundred dollars. She didn't have the money to pay them. She wanted Dudley to open and close the show.

Some people were already gathering outside around the ticket office. Dudley began to smile again. The gleam had returned to his eye. It was only seven-fifteen but Dudley thought because of the big crowd com-ing he ought to let them in. I turned on the tape system and began playing country music. By seven-thirty we had about forty people. At seven forty-five, ten more had come. At eight o'clock, show time, we had a total of fifty people.

It was time to begin. Dudley went rapidly down the center isle turned left and came on to the stage from the left side. We had the stage lit up so everything looked good. You could see Dudley's eye was sparkling and his silver hair shining. He smelt again like a bottle of aftershave lotion, but I think it was a good thing with all the excitement he was having.

Cotton Candy began singing one of her songs. Dudley was upset when he returned to the lobby. He said Cotton Candy was crying and he didn't believe she could continue the show. He and Tommie might have to take over. She was crying because all the people who had promised her they would come to the show were not here.

Well, there was no use to cry we were into it now. I was boxing some fresh popcorn when Lee came in from the auditorium. I had not seen him buy a ticket. He wanted a drink and a box of popcorn. His face was about as white as a sheet. His eyes were red and wet. He said thirty truck drivers had promised him they would come to hear his sister sing. When he left I let Mom work the popcorn machine and went into the auditorium to sit with Dorothy and my brother Melvin. Candy's sister always cuts his hair and had threatened to quit if he didn't come to the show.

Candy was singing her best, I thought a bit too loud. I looked over the audience to see if people were enjoying the singing. Most people seemed to be pleased except for one man in the middle seat in front on the right hand side. He was a large man crowding the person on each side of him. He was wearing a black cowboy shirt with little white balls strung from the shoulder down the sleeves. He kept turning in his seat looking back over the audience. Once or twice he almost stood up to see better. I could see his face once in a while. He didn't look a bit happy. Melvin said he was Candy's husband.

The show went along very peaceful. Whenever Candy seemed to be tired the band leader would break in with some comedy songs until she regained her strength. Some of the songs Candy sang were, "Another Time Another Place", "Violets are Blue", "You Ain't Woman Enough To Take My Man Away From Me" and "If You Miss Heaven You Have Missed It all."

When Candy announced she had sung her last song she left the stage for the lobby. The band leader took over on stage.

She and Dudley went over the ticket numbers. Dudley came for me to come back to verify the figures. We had taken in one hundred and fifty dollars. Her part was thirty-seven dollars and fifty cents. She began crying again. We comforted her best we could by telling her of our expenses and that we didn't make anything either. She left us still crying and walked rapidly down the center isle. The band was still playing. At the end of the isle she turned right. The man with the cowboy shirt jumped up and grabbed her. The two of them embraced and started dancing in front of the stage.

It was at this moment I realized we should have been doing this all along.

Tommie in the front row on the left side with his date got up and began dancing too. Mickie joined him with his girl. Soon there were about a dozen people dancing around between the seats and in the aisles. Dudley came down the center isle. He was happy again, eye shining and a big smile. He walked on the stage to conclude the show but no one could hear him. Everyone was either dancing or rocking in their seats to the music. After about five minutes the band director stopped playing and stood up and announced he was having a good time too but they had another engagement at ten-thirty. They would have to leave.

As people were leaving I think the show we should have had was just beginning. The people should have been dancing. Perhaps we can have another show using the same band and Cotton Candy and her truck driving husband as leaders. We could have a great time. Everybody dancing to country music. I'll take my lead from her song, "Another Time Another Place."

33

A news reporter

10-31-1978 ✓

Outside the air is still and warm for this time of year. The noises of Halloween have about ceased since it is now about eleven o'clock. We haven't had any trick-or-treaters. It is a little out of the way for them to come to our house, though it is a nice clear night so walking would not be difficult. The sky is so clear with lots of stars, I think I can make out the constellation called Pegasus.

Most of the day I have been too busy to check on the theater, though I did get over to put some little plastic windmills on the marquee. When the wind blows they might attract attention to Dudley's announcements. He may be doing a little better in the theater. Our last event, The Jones Brothers, was our best show; we had about seventy people.

At the office I had a patient yesterday with pleural effusion. I referred another patient today for repeat x-rays for a mass in her chest. My major accident case is a man who let a tree limb fall on his head. It cut a gash about two inches long in his scalp.

Just when I thought the town commissioners were content about the ABC store they flare up again. Now they want to bring up the last three audits again Monday night. Mayor Bert called me Saturday to tell me they are having a meeting Monday night and were going to go over the past ABC audits. He wondered if it would be a good thing to talk to the principal commissioner causing all the trouble.

I thought the best thing was to let them make whatever charges they had at the meeting. We are running the store the best we know how and according to the state laws as best we could interpret them. He agreed to wait and see what happened at the meeting. We wondered why the commissioners keep looking for something wrong.

Later in the day, I went by the theater to see how Dudley was doing with his show. He had a group of young people doing a dance they called clogging. He had very poor attendance.

Monday morning Bert called me around nine o'clock. A reporter from the Hickory Daily Record was in town and wanted to go over the ABC audits with me. We agreed to meet at my office at five o'clock. When he hung up I called Reece to let him know what was taking place. The reporter arrived at five and had the last three audits from the town hall with her. She wanted to know about our net profits and how they were distributed. I told her that we paid off on the last quarter audit early. We didn't have the report back from our auditor and the town wanted their money early to buy something so we cashed in some of our certificates of deposit and gave them the money. Right away, without looking at the audit, she said this was illegal and that by law we were due to give 100 percent of our net profits out in distribution each quarter. I said that was not the way we interpreted the law. To help satisfy her I called for Reece to come and go over the audits with her. She left around six o'clock. She knew we had purchased the property on the north side of the store and claimed this was illegal too. We didn't satisfy her on any question. I think her mind was made up when she came in that we were not operating according to law and she was going to make it so.

When she left, I called Dale to go to the executive meeting in Lenoir. A pep talk was given urging all precinct workers to get on the phone on election day and call their people to come to vote. The candidates made a plea for support. Without the precinct chairmen doing their jobs they couldn't get elected. Next a candidate running for a judgeship made his plea for support and what to watch for during the election.

He told the precinct chairmen to be sure to check on the conduct of the election and especially the counting of the ballots after the election was over. He urged them not to let the ballot boxes get out of their sight. The first thing they should do in the morning was to check the ballot boxes and see that there were no ballots in them. They must check around the top of the lids on the inside to see that no ballots have been taped or concealed there. The watchers and checkers were to watch to see that no voter took a ballot out of the voting place, that there wasn't any extra paper in the booth and when a voter came out to drop the ballot in the box they didn't have more paper than what the ballot should be.

One thing about taking a ballot out of the voting place was if the ballot ever got out to the driver or hauler he could always be sure he had his voters voting as he wanted. He would mark this ballot like he wanted and give it to his next voter who must bring him the blank ballot given to him in the voting place. This practice is called "chain balloting." During the counting, the watchers were to pay close attention to the fingernails of the people counting the ballots after they are marked. The counters might have long dirty nails so that they can break off the lead of a pencil and stick it part way under their nail. With this they can mark in the square of the ballot and make it a straight ticket or they can mark the ballot so it is voided for the opposite party. Counters are to check each pile of ballots stacked in piles of twenty-five or whatever number. If they were not watchful the counter may put ten more in his pile than the other thus when they are counted again from the pile his party wins.

Then there are irregularities about the man calling out the name of the candidate on the ballot. He may call out A when B is the name on the ballot. The marker gives A a vote. They may intentionally misread the name and put it in their pile of votes. Any irregularities of the election must be challenged.

No one except people connected with the party are to be trusted. If anyone needs to go to the bathroom he must get another member of the party to take his place. If lunch is needed someone must be called in to go get it, preferably a member of the opposite party. Under no circumstances can the voting place be left unattended.

At the next meeting of the Granite Falls Rotary Club the town manager Sam Noble was sitting a few seats down from me and asked me before the meeting started how I got along with the young lady the other day. He was referring to the reporter. I said I thought very well. Outside after the meeting I asked him what he knew about her visit. He said she had come in response to one of the commissioners thinking we had too much money. He must have called her to come check on the store because he thought we should be giving all of our money to the town.

I told him that my interpretation of the law was that we did not have to give all our money each quarter to the town. I quoted again what Michael Crowell said in his letter, "Profits may be retained, money may be invested, and property may be purchased as needed for the sound financial administration of the local ABC system." I also told him that my copy of the State ABC Laws said we could buy property and retain money for ninety days.

He didn't make any reply. I suspect he is working with the commissioners against the ABC board. Perhaps he believes since there are four commissioners they could decide not to retain him if he doesn't cooperate with them.

34

Town attorney meeting

11-17-1978 ✓

It is a rainy night with temperatures in the seventies, unusual for this time of year. Leaves are off most trees. Across the road in front of the house the old apple tree is beginning to put out leaves as if it were springtime. Soon, unless the weather gets cold, it will be blooming. Mary painted a picture of this tree one spring when it was in full bloom, a real pretty picture.

At the theater things have not been going well. Dudley had two people at the last performance. The group that put on the show was very good with country music. I think we are doing something wrong. We have not got the know-how to operate a theater for country music, boxing, wrestling or gospel singing.

We have two events planned that might work. One is a fiddler convention and another is a square dance. Dudley thinks his fiddler convention will go over big. I think the square dance. Our square dance caller came up to check on the theater two weeks ago to see it was suitable for square dancing. He believes it is just right and he can get a lot of people to come. However he had one stipulation to make. He would not call if there were mixed races on the floor. This has reduced my enthusiasm. I haven't told Dudley about it but with this stipulation I think I will cancel the show. In my office I never separated people.

Our plans for a New Year's Eve party are progressing slowly. Steve, the man I have engaged to try a disco program again is having trouble getting the proper equipment. He has a few of the lights, but can't get records to fit the turntable on the record player.

One of Dudley's helpers is planning to quit. He is complaining of headaches and high blood pressure. I checked his blood pressure and it is too high. He is also having emotional problems. He thinks his wife is seeing another man.

My office work is going well. One patient this morning reminded me of an antique clock I bought several years ago. He said he was awake every thirty minutes. I was on a house call and the patient had an antique clock that had beautiful chimes. I decided to get me one. The first night I stayed awake waiting for it to chime. The next night I stayed awake because it did chime. The third night I stopped the clock.

Jim, Laney and I left for the beach Saturday. We returned home around seven Tuesday evening. Dorothy met me at the car and said Reece had been trying to find me. It was something very important, something about the ABC store. I finally found him at a friend's home.

He said Mr. Hester of the state ABC board had called him this morning and said, "Get this damned mess straightened up or they would come up here and do it for us." Reece said he had been trying to call Mayor Bert but he was out of town too. This was a pretty big shock to return to after such a pleasant trip to the beach.

I felt like resigning, but then I thought this was exactly what some of the town commissioners wanted. Reece said Mr. Hester with the state ABC board in Raleigh said our town attorney had called Raleigh about the land we had purchased and the certificates of deposit we were holding. The town attorney was not sure it was legal for us to have purchased the land or to be holding CDs. I wondered why Bert had the town attorney to call Raleigh? What reason did he give the state people to have them start an investigation? Were there some laws we didn't know about?

Why didn't Bert have the town attorney talk it over with the ABC Board first or send us a letter about our trouble? When the ABC Board talked to an independent attorney he didn't find any violations we were committing

I called Bert at his plant before leaving for the office. Dorothy said the commissioners always waited until we were out of town to start something. Bert didn't know anything about the attorney calling nor did he recall requesting the city manager or anyone to call the state ABC people. He said he would go to town hall and find out about it.

On the way to the office I stopped in Jim's store to tell him what was taking place. In a few minutes Reece came in and we reviewed the conversation he had with Mr. Hester. I thought of calling Mr. Hester myself but since Bert was going to check on it I decided to wait. I think this was a big mistake. I should have found out firsthand what the trouble was if there was any. From Reece's conversation it was the town attorney who called Raleigh. He had never talked to us about any trouble.

I called Bert again to see if he knew anything. He said we ought to talk to the town attorney first since he was the one that called the state to find out about the law but he needed a good excuse to start the conversation. I said we could start with the ABC car. The paperwork had not been completed on it. In about five minutes Bert called back and said City Manager Noble had asked the town attorney to call Raleigh and that Noble and the attorney would meet us in the city hall right away. It was now about ten o'clock.

I left the office for city hall a few blocks away. As I turned at the stop light in the center of town I noticed Bert was following me. I parked first in front of the old bank building. Bert parked a few car lengths back of me. I didn't wait for him since I saw the town attorney coming from his office across the street and heading for city hall. I met him on the steps leading to the council room upstairs. I shook hands with him and Bert joined us going up the stairs. Bert didn't speak to the attorney as he followed us up the stairs. Noble must have also been waiting in city hall because he came out of his office when Bert started up the steps. Noble came up behind us. I kept thinking I should have called the other two members of the ABC board. It was too late for that now.

The council room is upstairs over the police and fire department. It is part of a large room, which has been divided by a partition. When I first came to town I made my first speech against socialized medicine in this room. We used this room for United Fund meetings and for many other civic affairs. It was in this room that I met with three friends and began the campaign for the ABC store. Now is it in this room that I am going to be accused of some great violation of the law?

At the west end of the room there was a large beautiful green rug with a table shaped like a horseshoe in the center of it. I asked the city attorney if the horseshoe table was for good luck. He didn't reply. I think his mind was on other things.

Bert and Noble pulled up chairs to the table. The attorney sat next to Bert with Noble sitting to Bert's right. I sat next to the attorney at the end of the table. Bert opened the meeting. As soon as he sat down he turned so he was looking straight at Don, the attorney.

"Don, I don't appreciate you going over my head to make these inquiries," he said. Bert was very upset. His face was fiery red and his voice was trembling.

"I inquired for my own information," the attorney said.

Bert told me earlier in the morning when he called me that Noble had asked the attorney to call. The town attorney made some other remarks as to why he had called. The tension between him and Bert was getting worse. I was thinking Bert was going to physically attack him if something wasn't done. Noble was sitting like a statue. I interrupted the conversation and said that the newspaper article said the title to the car hadn't been transferred. The attorney turned on me then as though I was accusing him of something. His face was red and covered with sweat. I said to Noble the town was using the car and I wanted it parked until the paperwork was done transferring it to the town.

The attorney seemed a bit cool and replied that he had made some special suggestions about the car and no one had followed them. He said it was like taking medicine. I could prescribe it, but I couldn't make the patient take it.

Then I asked him why he had called the state people. He said he had called them about the legality of the land purchase and the CDs we were holding. He concluded it was illegal for us to hold CDs and the purchase of the land was illegal. We could satisfy the part about the CDs by cashing them in and turning all the money into the town. About the land, he didn't know. It was illegal for us to have purchased it and it might turn out that the ABC directors would have to be responsible if when the land was sold it didn't bring what we had paid for it, and we had given too much for it anyway. He said that the attorney general said if we didn't settle this trouble locally the state ABC people would come here to settle it. He was sure we could settle it locally and proceeded to tell how to do it. The best way to settle it was to meet with the town commissioners and the sooner the better.

Noble said we could have a meeting next Thursday and still be within the law requiring notification of a public meeting. He would call the Granite Press because it was necessary, according to law, to notify one newspaper. He wanted to call them because they were the most likely not to attend. He didn't want any reporters at the meeting. We concluded the meeting and I returned to the office where I called Reece to tell the other board members about the meeting for Thursday.

I recalled the fifty-eight thousand dollars we had given for the land adjacent to the store on the north side. The town attorney's law firm had made out the deed and he had done the title search. I think he told me at the time it was a good deal. The street leading to the store is a dead end street. We had purchased the land beside the store because a cement company was next door. Our customers complained that they couldn't get to the store for the trucks blocking the road. Frequently the trucks spilled cement on the road. Our customers were complaining about getting cement on their tires and cars. When the plant was mixing cement the dust got on all of our bottles and on the floor ruining our carpet. It stopped up our heating and air condition system.

When the company stopped working we decided to buy it to protect the entrance to the store and to get away from the dust.

Thursday morning when I got a break in the office I went to talk to Blue, the other Republican town commissioner. When I told him about the land and the attorney's opinion he was pretty much disturbed, saying he was against buying the land but whenever he found out about it we had already bought it. He asked if I had kept Bert informed about it. I told him I had but I didn't have anything in writing about it. He wanted to know who had authorized the town attorney to investigate the store. I said I didn't know, he said he did it to check up on the ABC laws on his own. Blue said he would check up on it. He said he hadn't heard anything wrong with the store.

He wasn't sure he would come to the meeting.

"They damn well know I will tell them what I think and I don't feel like tangling with them over this now. But to help you I will come," he said.

I thanked him and said, "Bring Gene." He is the other Republican commissioner.

Later in the day Bert called again. He said Noble had called the state people to tell them about the meeting Thursday and they had requested the town attorney to do the legal work. I wondered what legal work there was to do.

At four-thirty I called for Reece and asked him to go with me to the meeting. We went upstairs into the same room we had been in before. This time for some reason I felt like it would not be proper for me to sit at the table on account of there were nameplates around for the commissioners. We sat somewhat back of the table on a bench.

When all the town commissioners were seated Bert convened the meeting and declared it in executive session. There was a little commotion near the door and two people left the room. Next, Noble stated it was his business to see that things in the town went according to law and he had asked the town attorney to clarify some points regarding the operation of the ABC store.

The attorney brought up the questions of law he had raised with Bert and me. When he brought up the land I asked him if he had told the state people about the cement plant. I don't believe he told them. He started on the CDs we had.

Jim interrupted him and defended the store's capital and the need for money in our operation. He said when the town needed money we cashed in the CDs and at any time they didn't have the money to meet the payroll we bailed them out. If we didn't have necessary money to run the store who would help us? The law says the town can't loan the ABC store money.

The attorney made no comment and started attacking our audit, declaring we had too much capital and too big an inventory in the store. Reece jumped him on this and they tangled verbally for about ten minutes.

The meeting went on for about two hours. Bert finally adjourned it because the attorney said he had to go to another meeting. At the conclusion most of the commissioners commended the ABC board for doing a good job. We agreed to answer their questions about the CDs and land at the next town board meeting.

At home, Dorothy wanted to know if I was going to jail. She worries every time I have a meeting with the commissioners for fear we have done something wrong in the store. While I was eating, Bert called to tell me the two people who left at the beginning of the meeting were reporters from Hickory and Lenoir. He said someone had called them. The reporter from the Granite Press didn't come.

Shortly after I opened the office Friday morning Reece came by to tell me the reporter from Lenoir had called him in regard to the meeting. He referred him to the town hall.

About thirty minutes later my phone rang. It was a reporter from Lenoir wanting to know about the litigation between the town and the ABC board. I referred him to the town hall. In a few minutes Reece called again. This time the manager of the ABC store in Lenoir had called to find out what took place at our meeting Monday. He specifically wanted to know about the illegalities we were charged with. Seems like everybody was sure we had done something awful wrong.

Around three o'clock Reece called again. He said he bet I couldn't guess who had called him just now. I said the people in Raleigh, he said no our banker. He called to get an honest opinion of what was going on. About four o'clock Bert called to tell me there was a write-up in the Lenoir paper. I sent Sarah out to get a copy. The write-up was more concerned with city hall not letting them know what was going on and charging the town hall with illegalities about the way they handled the meeting on Thursday. They said the meeting was about some possible mishandling of ABC funds.

Later in the day I called attorney Thomas to plan a reply to the questions Noble wanted the ABC board to answer but he was out of town.

At noon Dorothy handed me two letters that had come from Noble. Inside was a copy of a letter he had received from the town attorney answering questions about the CDs and the land our town attorney had called Raleigh about. His conclusions from his telephone conversation with the attorney general's office were that the funds we held in CDs were in direct conflict of the law and that the purchase of the land is not allowed under the statutes. The other letter from the Institute of Government was not as condemning. Their conclusion was that we could retain profits, invest money and purchase land as needed to run the store.

35

Thanksgiving Day

11-23-1978 ✓

This has been a cold and wet day with the intermittent rain. We are beginning to have early days of winter with low temperatures at night and rising temperature in the day. I think the rapid drop in temperature makes my joints ache. Most of the time at night I sleep with my socks on to keep my feet warm. All the bugs that make night noises have gone into hibernation; they are not singing any more. About the only birds around are doves, starlings, sparrows and an occasional red bird.

Most of today has been spent in just living, doing nothing I don't have to. I think I know now what is meant in hymns sung about rest and why old folks were content to sit on the porch in a rocker and just rock the day away. I guess I am one of them now. Today I believe I would be content to just sit in the sun and rock the day away. It is because I am getting old.

Remembering my first Thanksgiving days, they were spent at my grandmother's house. After dinner we children went out in the woods to play Indians. When I was older a Thanksgiving Day had to be spent hunting for rabbits and quail. Now it is nice to spend Thanksgiving just relaxing and enjoying the day with my children and Dorothy.

Today Susie is home. We are enjoying her company. All the other children called to wish Dorothy and me a happy Thanksgiving.

My day began with the phone ringing about six o'clock.

It was Jeff, a man I had seen several times. This morning he said he had something he needed to talk over with me and wanted to know what time I would be in the office. Jeff is about fifty years old. The last time I saw him he said he was having trouble having sex with his wife and wanted something for it.

When his wife was in last week she said he wasn't doing any better and wanted me to change the medicine. I wondered if Jeff was calling about this or was he calling for me to fill out papers to get his wife on social security because of her arthritis. I didn't much like him calling me so early in the morning anyway. When he called he said he hoped he hadn't woke me up, I started to tell him why did he call me so early if he didn't expect to wake me up.

I lay back in the bed after the call reminding myself that today was Thanksgiving Day and I didn't need to go to the office at the usual time. Around eight o'clock the phone rang again. This time it was a patient with a fever wanting to know what time I would be in the office. I told her I would be in at ten o'clock the same time I told Jeff. After this call I decided I might as well get up. There would be other patients calling.

Dorothy got up and prepared breakfast while I dressed for the office. We discussed what to do about Thanksgiving. She called home to her mother's to see if her sisters were coming. None of them were coming so we decided to stay home.

At the office around ten o'clock my first patient was Tate, a fellow that seems to have a very good life. During the fall he spends his time hunting quail and rabbits. During the spring he fishes when the hunting season ends. Sometime in the spring he puts out a tobacco bed and about the last of April he starts setting his tobacco plants out in fields. When it is too hot to fish he tends his tobacco. About the last of August he pulls the leaves off his tobacco plants and dries them in a tobacco barn. Late in September he sells them at the tobacco market in Winston-Salem. He comes home from the market and starts the cycle over again.

A few days ago while hunting he thinks he stuck a briar in his thumb while crossing a fence. I have been picking on it for the last three days without finding anything. Today he believes he stuck a wire in it while feeding his bird dog. With this new history I think I will stop picking on it and let it heal up.

When he left, two young men came in with a girl about twenty years old. She was holding her right hand wrapped in some brown paper towels. She had caught her thumb in the car door. She was in a great deal of pain saying she was going to faint. I kept her head down while I dressed her thumb. I have had some patients to faint and I dressed the injury while they were out. The last patient I had with an injury like this locked the door on her thumb. She had to call her husband to unlock the door.

My next patient was Jeff. He wanted to know if I would examine a girl about nineteen years old. He and his wife were planning to let her stay with them. She had no other place to go. Jeff wanted me to do a thorough examination to be sure she didn't have any venereal disease. As he told me what all he wanted me to check for I wondered if she wasn't the reason he had poor sex with his wife. He wanted so much done I referred him to the county health department.

Before closing the office at noon, I saw Dudley come to the theater so I went over to see him. He was making some more posters announcing his fiddlers' convention. We had left out one of the "d"s in six of our posters. Guess we can't spell worth a fiddle. I have a patient who frequently tells me my pills are not worth a shuck.

At lunch I told Dorothy we were making some progress in our disco program. She wanted to know if I would have it ready in time for our New Year's Eve Party. I told her I thought we would. Steve had agreed to come over and run the equipment. We can have a caterer to bring over the food.

Dudley said if I wasn't going to have a party he wants to have one in the theater for his gospel singers. I told him he could come to ours.

I will have to ask Reece if our guests can have alcoholic drinks. I need to talk to him anyway because the auditor is changing the way our auditing is done. I asked Reece to look up the receipt for the town attorney's firm when we bought the land beside the store. They had charged us $345 to do this work while his firm was on a retainer fee from the town. At the next meeting we are going to ask why if it was illegal for us to buy the land did his firm let us buy it.

To help ease things along a bit we are going to cash in half of our CDs the first of the month. It will give the town something to think about as to whether or not to give the money to the schools or keep it for the town.

Reece said Wednesday someone from Lenoir wanted to know if the property is for sale. Reece said it wasn't now. There may be more to the ABC outcome than just giving the town the money and selling the land. The town manager Sam Noble may lose his job. Blue, the commissioner who worked so hard for a city manager form of government will not support him any longer.

Johnson will vote with Blue. Noble got his job with a split decision with Bert breaking a tie vote. Now he has lost Bert. He is supporting the commissioners who want to move the police department in with the fire department four or five blocks from the center of town. The police department is opposing the move. They are a very powerful group in an election. With no more support than he has now he will have a rough time staying in this town.

Now the town attorney may come under fire too. He knew at the time or ought to have known whether or not it was legal for the ABC board to purchase the land. For him to come up with it being illegal now after four years seems to be a bit out of line. To use a newspaper reporter term, he could lose his job. People could think he is not a smart attorney.

Blue is anxious to know who is going to pay him for investigating the ABC board. He said the town commissioners had not authorized his investigation.

Time will tell who is right.

36

Power of the press

Sunday morning started with a call to come to one of the rest homes to see a new patient. I suggested coming at ten o'clock but Doris, the owner of the home, wanted me to come now. This was a new resident and she didn't know much about her. I agreed to come right away.

At the rest home I was greeted by one of the ladies who led me to the patient's room. While I was checking on her the other ladies gathered around to see what I was doing. They had the radio on and a minister was preaching. I made some comment about it being an early service. Seems like this led to some discussion on church and singing. I then remarked that I had gospel singing last night in the theater. I wondered if they would want to come. They all said yes, they were tired of looking at these four walls. As I was leaving I thought I would ask Dudley what he thought of letting these ladies in free to our next show.

I saw a few patients at the office and then went to church.

The afternoon was rather quiet. During the night I worried about the letter the ABC board needed to have ready for the town board on Monday night. Monday morning I went by to see Attorney Thomas. We drafted a rather simple straightforward letter.

Around four o'clock Reece called to tell me that he had heard from Mr. Hester with the state ABC board in Raleigh. He said our audits were all right. He said Noble had called him wanting to know when he could expect answers to the letter the town had written to the Granite Falls ABC board. I wonder why Noble hadn't asked us. Reece said Mr.

Hester told him he thought most of our trouble was coming from a reporter in Lenoir. I was real glad that the state people were satisfied and that our operation was within the law.

At seven o'clock all the members of the ABC board were assembled in the council room again. Attorney Thomas was with us. All the town commissioners were present. After convening the meeting Bert read our letter answering Noble's questions. There were no questions from the town commissioners. I think it was because we had an attorney with us. Bert appointed three commissioners to try and work out a satisfactory solution to the land acquisition on the west side of the ABC store.

There were three or four reporters and after the meeting I think they talked to every one. One asked Jim about the land. He told him it was a little like as if your wife was needing an operation and the price was two thousand dollars. Well, you might not think that it is worth that, but you damn well will get busy getting the money up. Well, we needed the property to protect our business and that is why we bought it. It would not be worth a nickel to us somewhere else.

I called Reece later in the evening to see what he thought of the meeting. He said he didn't think we accomplished a thing. There would be other things the commissioners would bring up. He said he heard Jim tell one of the reporters that it was nothing but some dirty politicians trying to get control of the store.

I am beginning to agree with Jim. Some people want to change the ABC board and will do what is necessary to get us out. I am beginning to worry about the personal cost of being involved. I can't keep my mind on my work for wondering what violation I will be charged with. The town commissioners can continually make charges that we are not operating the store right. Newspaper reporters will take their story.

We are the liquor people and guilty to begin with, according to some people, of wrecking society. It is all right to throw rocks at us but they like the money we give them. Now we have the newspapers all having a field day making prophesy that the store will close and the courts will have to settle the illegalities if there are any. COULD is a powerful word to use in the press. Anything could happen and to get people excited it is the word to use.

37

Cost of involvement

12-6-1978 ✓

This has been a very beautiful Wednesday. Several years ago on a day like this I would have been bound to go fishing. At present I am content in trying to make my time account for something constructive. A combination of events has brought me to this conclusion.

The last time Jim and I went fishing we caught a nice mess of crappies and gave them away. We were on the lake about five hours. The second thing is after raising minnows in my minnow tank I am convinced I can catch fish if they are plentiful and near my hook. With these conclusions I had to come up with some better use of my time than just catching fish. Now I am content at present to spend time working in the theater or with my patients.

You needn't believe this conclusion will hold past this spring when the sun is warm, leaves come out on the trees and flowers begin to bloom. I will spend time on the lake again, fishing will be my excuse just to get out and commune with nature.

At the last town board meeting Bert appointed a committee to decide about the land the ABC board had purchased. They are to make recommendations as to whether we should keep it or sell it.

Since the meeting I have been wondering about the cost to a person being involved in public positions. Is it worth the cost and why should anyone accept a position that is political?

Near election time people will tell you to run for this or that position, town council, county commissioner or on some board. Your answer is you are too busy. Politics is dirty business and you don't want to get mixed up with it. But government is a little like housekeeping. Some people must look after it. If capable people don't accept the position, less capable people will fill the position and we will have to live in the house—clean or dirty—until the next election.

When the house gets too dirty capable people will have to accept the positions to clean it up if they still have the opportunity to vote. How much are they willing to pay to keep the house clean? Remember in a democracy there is more than one opinion about who should have the job and you will be constantly criticized in order to get members of their party in positions. This gives them power and jobs, none of which are permanent. For like a high tide washing footprints off the beach, they may be washed out of office with the next election.

At the meeting with the town board, questions were asked by reporters that suggested the possibility of error. This is embarrassing to the person questioned. It is a threat to their character. Having posed the question with reporters it is put in the paper. Your name is in the paper associated with possible violation of some law. Your wife, your children and relatives begin to wonder if you are guilty. Your enemies are sure you are or else you wouldn't have been questioned and they are glad to say they bet you are guilty. Wherever you go, people may say, "Isn't he the one that was named in the paper in connection with this or that?"

The people involved can't erase their discomfort easily. The questioner can dismiss himself by saying he just wanted to know, a little like the saying, "Do you still beat your wife?" It is no wonder people hesitate to run for this or that office. We make the cost of involvement too high.

I don't believe one can escape being politically involved when people are involved, even if only three people are involved. We are all wanting to be accepted by other people. We are always judging people to know if they are smart or dumb, rich or poor, strong or weak, fat or thin, honest or liars. Someone must make decisions on how we will live together. This is done by voting on someone who volunteers to do the job. You can vote for him or her or volunteer yourself. Some of the dirt in politics is scheming to get people to vote for the volunteer. Someone will take the job.

My office practice is a bit political too. If I don't please my patients they get another doctor. Yesterday a mother came to see me. I felt very sorry for her. She was in the office about two weeks ago for some medicine for her nerves. She had been drinking fairly heavy. She had started drinking because her troubles are more than she can bare. Her husband is leaving her and her twenty-three-year-old daughter is having her second operation for breast cancer. She isn't expected to live. She wanted some nerve medicine until her daughter dies.

Yesterday I was out to see Jim's uncle. He is about ninety years old. He has heart failure and kidney failure. Jim says after he dies he will be the old man in the family.

I watched some of my elderly patients as they arrived in the parking lot. Generally there are three or four people in the car with them. Frequently the car is old and in bad shape, a lot like the patient. As soon as the driver of the car I watched today unloaded the patient he went to the front of the car to check on the engine while I checked on the patient.

Sometimes when the patient comes out to the car it won't start and I have to supply jumper cables to get it started.

At the theater, Dudley's fiddler convention was well attended though no fiddlers showed up. He had five bluegrass groups that carried the evening. Dudley was all smiles as he sold a ticket, then ran around to be at the door to take it up again. He would grin at me and say that there were more people coming. He was so anxious to keep people coming that he didn't get the show started until eight o'clock.

Our disco party for New Year's Eve is progressing. Saturday afternoon Steve and his girlfriend came over to the theater to operate the disco equipment. He thinks he is all set for our party. We locked the equipment in the office for fear of someone stealing it. Dorothy would have an awful time if we lost it. She is already worrying about something going wrong.

Steve said he could solicit private parties for Christmas and use our disco equipment, but I told him even for $200 each evening I wouldn't take a chance on something happening to our equipment.

We already have our invitations. Dorothy wants to get them in the mail soon. Steve and his girlfriend are looking forward to the party. It will be his first big party. He said if he gets sick he has trained his girlfriend to operate the equipment. We should have no trouble.

38

Beginning of Christmas 1978

12-19-1978

This Tuesday has been a cold and wet day. From the office window I noticed the clouds hanging low to the ground like they were a year ago when Dorothy was returning from a visit with Susie at the University of Maryland. It was twenty-four hours of anxious waiting before she got home. The plane couldn't land in Hickory because of fog. It had to land in Atlanta.

She spent the night there and arrived in Hickory the next day around five o'clock in the evening. Since Wednesday Dorothy and I have been concerned with traveling. Susie drove down from the University of Maryland Thursday and Mary flew home from Los Angeles. When I came home for lunch Friday they had gone out for a Christmas tree. They decorated it in the afternoon and at five o'clock we all went to Hickory for dinner.

I went in my practice car because they were going on to the airport in Charlotte for Gail flying home from Iowa. She was due to arrive in Charlotte at nine o'clock. I wanted to come back in case some of my patients called and too I wanted to see how Dudley was doing at the theater. At nine o'clock they called from Charlotte. The plane had been delayed in Chicago due to mechanical trouble. It was three-thirty Friday morning before they came home.

Because of this uncertainty of events I sometimes wonder what it would be like to be able to foretell their outcome.

What if you knew in advance what was going to happen? What if you could look at a cloud and tell whether it is going to rain or not?

159

Sometimes I have written out what I thought would be the outcome of an event. The event didn't turn out as I had predicted. What caused the different results? My lack of knowledge for one thing. The weatherman uses instruments to determine what will happen with the cloud. With my knowledge, experience and instruments I can predict pretty well what will happen with a certain illness, but something may happen like an accident or another illness to change the outcome. The more you know about an event the better your chances are of predicting the outcome of the event.

I would like to know how our disco party for New Year's Eve is going to turn out. When I go to the theater I imagine how it will look full of people. Will the music be right, the lights burn and flicker, the heaters work and the commodes work. We have sent out one hundred and fifty invitations. Lots of people have said they will come. At church yesterday a lady told Dorothy she was coming, though we had not invited her. Dorothy had sent her daughter an invitation since she was a friend of one of our daughter's.

With all of these irregularities it will take a lot of knowledge to predict the outcome. It is the uncertainty of events and working out a happy ending that give the joy of success.

Sunday at the breakfast table Dorothy and I discussed our position here in the community. With all our children away we are experiencing the empty nest syndrome, a feeling like an event is over and we are entering another event that will require some adjustment in our way of life. We have not been a flat and quiet couple in the community, not vanilla people as opposed to all the other flavors of people there might be.

Some people in the community may have looked to us for our opinion. We have been involved with various activities since our children started to school. It is probably through our children in school that we began to take an active part in politics. We found that a child couldn't just stand in line with a ticket and get equal treatment. When you don't know you have got to pay. Our children were as good as any of the other children. When there was a parade or a homecoming at school and pictures taken, our children were not included in the pictures. I asked the owner of the newspaper why he didn't put pictures of my children in his paper. He said it was because I didn't pay him to have my children's picture taken.

This is when I realized something more than a plain ticket to the opportunities in life was needed for my children's success in life. For recognition of the child in school and community the parent's reputation, the parent's occupation, rank in the occupation, political party and rank in the party, education of the parents, address of the parents, the church they attend and position in the church, friends of the parent and their education all have an influence on the seat the child gets.

After a lot of thought Dorothy and I concluded the only way we could gain some opportunities for our children was through political involvement in the community. A parent can be just a plain good person and his child a good child and get a good plain seat in life. To get a better seat for your child someone has got to pay to get the picture taken. Through political involvement one belongs to either the winning party or the losing party. Either way you are a member of a group of people that has influence in your community. Some of the members may be able to help you gain your objective. Members of the opposing party respect you because sometime you may be on the winning side.

Now sometimes when you get to talking and thinking out loud someone begins to look around at the present company to see if they could be the subject of the discussion. In this case Dorothy began to think we might begin at home with some improvement in our lives even though the great event of raising our children is over. Right off she said because we are older some of our habits become worse and more offensive to other people. She especially thought I should dress better. Old men in baggy clothes looks pretty bad. I had to agree with her. I have seen patients I thought who would have been more pleasant if they had been wearing cleaner clothes. Others with tobacco juice draining from the corners of their mouth were a bit repulsive. Some that had not taken a bath in weeks were not good company.

Even though you are old one can still try to improve on yourself. From my patients I know that physical defects get worse as you get older. I promised to continually try to make myself better even to watching my language.

A great part of life is spent in the company with other people and the more acceptable one is the better your chances are of being accepted by them in their activities. An old person can't afford to accept unnecessary handicaps like shabby appearance in body and mind. They need all the friends they can make.

During the last few days Dorothy has been Christmas shopping. Saturday she spent most of the day in Hickory. I worked in the theater adjusting the lights and popping corn for Saturday's event. Dudley has the Green Valley Boys coming to put on a country music show at eight o'clock. I didn't get to stay for it.

Dorothy and I were invited by the Northwestern Bank to a Christmas party in Hickory. About a hundred directors and their wives were there. We returned about nine-thirty. Dudley had already closed the theater. It was a little early and I wondered if something had happened.

Sunday morning I went to the theater to check on the lights. I thought Dudley might be there too. I used some Christmas lights along the side of the auditorium. They seemed to be just the right thing to give enough colored light. With them blinking and the mirror ball going around reflecting spheres of light the size of grapefruits on the walls and ceiling it was a tremendous effect, a lot like being in a planetarium. I wondered how it would be with the music playing. I was so enthused about it I called Steve to come over in the afternoon to see how he liked it. He was pleased about it and promised to come around two o'clock.

When he arrived he had his girlfriend with him. She didn't come past the lobby so I went back to speak to her. I think she had been crying. Her eyes were a little red and full of water. With all my urging she wouldn't come down to help with the stage lights. She left the theater in a few minutes and sat in the car. I wondered if they had other plans and I interrupted them by calling Steve to come by to see the lights.

Monday morning Dorothy went shopping again and I saw patients in the office. There were not many. I think they are shopping for Christmas. Around ten o'clock Dudley came in to give me the report on the show with the Green Valley Boys. He didn't have over fifteen people to come to the show. One got drunk and had to be carried out. After about thirty minutes there was some disturbance with the performers. They got to cutting up on the stage. Dudley said they were drinking and he had to end the show early. He wants to go back to gospel singing.

About two o'clock, Blue the Republican town commissioner came by wanting a copy of the reporter's write-up in the Hickory paper about the last meeting of the ABC board with the town commissioners. He said the report said the commissioners were going to keep an eye on the ABC board. I told him I had a copy of the write-up, but I didn't remember seeing anything about the commissioners saying they were going to keep their eye on us. He wanted the report for the next town board meeting.

He was going to tell the reporters about putting a name to whatever a commissioner had to say. He felt like when the reporter said commissioners it included him and all the commissioners. He wants the reporter to give the name of the commissioner doing the talking and let what he reports be for him only. I agreed and said I would get him a copy of the report.

I wondered if the town attorney would be at the meeting. Bert said he would not approve the past minutes because of a dispute about who was the town attorney when the ABC board bought the land beside the store. I called Blue late Monday night to find out about the meeting. He said the ABC business didn't come up. The meeting was about putting the police department in with the fire department, but he wanted to keep the article about keeping the eye on the ABC board in case it came up at the next meeting.

On the way to the office this morning I stopped in Jim's store. I wanted to know what the doctor in Winston-Salem found out about his wife. She has been having severe headaches and fainting spells ever since our last meeting with the town commissioners. Jim was wondering about the possibility of a brain tumor. He said all the studies were negative.

After closing the office Dorothy and I went to a Christmas party at the Rotary Club. We had nine young teenagers using bells to play the Christmas Carols. None by themselves would have sounded good, but all together they made beautiful music.

After the program Dorothy and I went to Laney's funeral home where the family of Lawyer Abernethy were receiving friends. He was a very good friend and a Rotarian. He died sometime Monday morning. He frequently came by the office just to talk about hunting, fishing and politics. He had high blood pressure and I checked on him for about twenty years. I did his medical work and he did my legal work, all professional courtesy. In the last few years he changed doctors. We still remained good friends and he continued to come in to visit. I think he changed doctors because I changed my political registration to Republican. He was a staunch Democrat.

We worked together in several town elections. He helped in a school vote and was a big help in winning the ABC vote. In other elections we supported the same town commissioner.

Two things I learned from him about politics stand out in my mind. The first was to be pretty careful about how much criticism you draw from the opposing party. If you can, select a candidate acceptable to both parties. It is better than accepting a person completely unacceptable to the opposing party.

The second thing is that your candidate's acceptance by the voters pretty much depends on the way you present the candidate to the voters. A candidate's dress, speech, physical appearance and character all have a lot to do with his or her acceptance by the voters.

To support this philosophy he had a little story that goes something like this. A young lawyer was working with an older lawyer. Each time he got a case ready to go to court he asked the elder attorney if he thought he would win the case. Each time he got the same reply.

"It depends on the way you present the case."

After some time the young attorney asked why he always got the same reply.

The elder lawyer replied, "One morning I had this case for a man in which his wife was suing him for a divorce on the grounds of impotence and in the afternoon a case for the same man in which his maid was suing him for bastardy. I lost both of them. I lost both cases by the way I presented them."

My stories are a lot like that. Whether or not you like them depends on the way they are presented.

39

New Year's Party

This has been one of the coldest days of the winter. I don't believe the temperature has been above ten degrees all day. Most of my minnows in the minnow tank have frozen. There is a sheet of ice on the bottom of the tank an inch thick. I raked some leaves into the tank hoping they might help thaw it out

Our Christmas was very pleasant. All of the children came home. Gail had some delay in Chicago and appears to be going to have the same trouble getting back. When she called this morning the airport in Chicago had changed her schedule so that she will be leaving tomorrow. We got up this morning around five o'clock planning to take her to Charlotte to catch her plane, but when we called we found out she couldn't get out of Chicago today. Marty left for Western Carolina this afternoon. Mary will leave Friday and Susie on Saturday.

Dorothy and I worry a great deal about the children getting jobs. We have spent a lot of money on their education and so far there isn't much to show for it. They are all trying their best. I talked to Mary today about painting houses. I told her she might fall and be unable to paint for a long time. I wanted her to come back home and work on her art here. Gail is in about the same shape. She thinks with more education she will be able to get a better job. At the rate she is going it will take her another two years to finish school. We told her to stop working at school and concentrate on getting through.

This business of working at school for two or three semesters in order to get one free is just keeping the children in school. They soon

166

become captive of the school system in that they are doing a little work and not finishing their education. I think it is a way of keeping the students out of the labor market.

We gave Marty the same advice. We hope he will finish his schooling and get a job rather than continue in job training.

We are being drained dry of our funds paying rent. Too there is the possibility of something happening to Dorothy and me so we can't help them on down the line so it seems best that they get through school as soon as possible.

Most of my patients now have the flu. Right now it is a rather mild flu compared to some we had a few years ago. I expect it will get worse as the winter progresses. This is usually the case. The patients that get it in March are usually much sicker than the ones that have it now. It seems that the longer the virus is around the stronger it gets.

On Friday I became anxious about our New Year's Eve party planned for Sunday night. Dorothy wanted me to have Dudley cancel his engagement with the Blue Grass Boys of '76. I told her Dudley would be upset. Too, the attendance had been so poor I didn't believe there would be enough people come to mess up the decorations we had up for our party. I told her I would tell Dudley to be very careful about our decorations.

I had worked out a backup set of lights to reflect off the mirror ball. Pinkney, an electrician had brought me a transformer so that I could burn flashlight bulbs. It worked very well except that for some reason on Friday morning when I turned it on to test it, two of the bulbs blew. Steve had his electrical control box so he could make the side lights reflect off of the mirror ball too. We had double coverage on the lights. We had six colored spotlights focused on the mirror ball so we had balls of light going around everywhere in the theater. Unless a fuse blew somewhere we had the lights under control.

Saturday morning I cleaned out Dudley's office, making it into a cloakroom. There was room for about a hundred coats. During the afternoon we strung tinsel along the stairways and across the back of the auditorium and the lobby. This tended to separate to some extent the lobby from the auditorium. Mary made two paintings for the restrooms. For the men's room a young man holding a cane pointing up stairs, for the ladies room a lady wearing a black glove pointing up stairs. We had to adjust the light so they were easily seen. Then we hung a big banner across the back of the lobby saying Happy New Year. Mary made the banner using paper and spray paint.

Mary did most of the decorating. She took down most of my pictures of old movie stars. The ones she left she arranged in a neat row across the back of the lobby. It gave a distinctive touch to the lobby I had not been able to achieve with all my clutter.

Saturday night when the Blue Grass Boys came they were pleased with the appearance of the theater. They said they had never played in a place nicer than this. The attendance was so poor Dudley and I agreed to cancel all future events. We were getting nowhere with gospel or country music shows.

Sunday morning the weather began to clear suggesting we would have a cold and clear day. After church we all went to Hickory for lunch. When we returned I went to the theater to meet Steve. He said he would be at the theater around one o'clock. While I was waiting I wondered again if we should be having such a big party, a hundred or so people. There were so many things that could go wrong. What if Steve had an accident? I had no one to run the disco equipment. Marty might be able to operate it, but Steve had the records. What about party crashers coming in off the street?. I had invited the chief of police. He might help me on this if I needed him. I reconciled myself saying if it was a success I would be glad that we did it, if it failed we would know not to do it again.

Steve didn't come so I closed the theater and came home to await developments.

I had hardly settled down when the dogs began barking in the back yard announcing the arrival of someone. Steve had just missed me and came to the house. He wanted to go back and set up the equipment.

We went back to the theater and soon had it set up, but he wasn't satisfied with one of the needles on one of the turntables. He left to go to Hickory to find a better stylus. It was now four-thirty. He said he would be back by six o'clock.

I waited in the lobby for the caterer. We were going to serve punch cookies and sandwiches. The catering people arrived at five o'clock as promised. They put up a long table along the back wall of the lobby between the auditorium and two small tables in the concession area. After draping them with green crape paper that seemed to accentuate the orange walls they filled the tables with punch bowels and food. There were two containers of meatballs kept warm with Sterno heat. Beside these, there were containers with cubes of yellow and white cheese. It almost looked like a banquet.

When Dorothy and her sister Mary came out at six o'clock we were ready for the party. I began to wonder about Steve. There wasn't any use worrying now. There wasn't anything I could do about it. Dorothy was getting anxious too and asked where Steve was. I said he had gone to Hickory to get a needle for the disco equipment. She was upset, but realized there was nothing we could do about it now. She went to the lobby and came back wanting me to dim the light in the coatroom. It was so bright it detracted from the decorations in the lobby. I found a stepladder and changed the bulb. It made the lighting much better.

Now Susie and the other children, Marty, Gail, Mary, and Phyllis arrived. Susie wanted an extension cord to use in the balcony to show old movies. I had the silver screen pulled down on the stage. I wasn't too excited about this. I didn't think they had much of a place in the party. The previous movies she had shown on Saturday night were so light they could barely be seen. I found her an extension cord and she headed up the stairs to the balcony. Gail wanted a flashlight so she could operate her camera. I finally found her a large flashlight.

The other children waited in the lobby for our guests to arrive.

It was now seven-thirty.

Steve returned with his girlfriend Dennese. They had been looking all over Hickory for a needle for the disco player. Now to get the needle on the machine he needed a small screwdriver. I left to go to the office to get one. All the time I was remembering that it is generally a bad policy to start working on equipment just before it is needed. There is a good chance that you will lose something or break something so that it will not work. I brought three small screwdrivers and soon Steve had the needle holder off and in three parts.

Dorothy and her sister were looking on. I am sure they were wondering if Steve could get it back together. Some of the guests were arriving so they left to go to the lobby. At eight o'clock the time for the party, Steve got it going.

Our first guests were Pete and his wife Marie, members of the ABC board. I left Steve to go to the lobby to welcome our guests. The next couple to come was John and Hellen, then Jean and Mable. Dot and Jim came along with my brother Melvin and his wife Mary.

Other people were coming so fast I don't remember their names. Some of the people we thought wouldn't come came and some we thought would come didn't. We had a group of about seventy people. They seemed surprised at the theater. Most remarked how good it looked. They enjoyed the roominess. They could eat in the lobby, move into the auditorium and watch people dance or go to the front and dance to the disco music.

You could sit in the auditorium and watch the colored balls float along on the ceiling and walls. In between times, Susie in the balcony had her movies going on the screen. Someway she had found how to darken them so that you could see them very well. I think the guests enjoyed the movies as much as anything. Somewhere she had found a movie we had made of the dam at Rhodhiss running over and of me fishing at the racks in front of the powerhouse. The white bass were running and I caught several. I guess it was the first time some people had seen a fisherman wearing a hat and suit fishing.

Everybody had a good time. None of my fears materialized.

At midnight Steve played a special record made by Guy Lombardo of New Year's Eve in Times Square. From the balcony, the children threw down balloons they had stored in plastic bags. We forgot to get any noisemakers, but everybody had a good time anyway.

We closed the theater around one o'clock on New Year's morning. We felt sure the theater was a good place now to have a big party. It gave people three areas of activity, the lobby, the auditorium and the front of the stage for dancing.

Monday morning, Pinkney came to the office. He had developed another way besides the mirror ball for having colored light flash around on the stage. By using a slide projector we could reflect light off the face of eight small mirrors he had glued on a piece of cloth over a speaker. When the light was passed through a color wheel onto the mirrors streaks of colored light, first red, then green and yellow were reflected onto the screen. The speaker caused the cloth to vibrate so the beams of light danced on the screen. They appeared a lot like a flame of fire beginning in the lower corner of the screen and extending up to the top on the right hand side. I had never seen anything like this. We will use it in our teen disco program.

40

Town meeting on ABC

1-18-1979 ✓

Today has been a nice winter day with the temperature around fifty degrees under a clear blue sky. The sun is low in the south so that in the afternoon it shines almost directly through the kitchen window, warming the chairs and table. Yesterday was such a nice day I had Johnnie trim out some of the maple trees in the back so I can make a bigger garden this spring. The trees shade the area so the sun doesn't shine on my plants to make them grow.

Dorothy said this morning at breakfast I should be helping Bert with the town hall rather than thinking of my garden. I agreed, but there doesn't seem to be any way to help. There are two commissioners supporting him against four that are against him. I told her I thought all we can do is what is right and be patient.

At last week's Rotary meeting, Bert asked how the ABC board got along with the committee the town had appointed to discuss the land purchase and distribution of our money. I told him they agreed for us to keep the land for now and we agreed to give money to the police department instead of to the ABC officer. I told him we would draft a letter to present to the town commissioners at the next town board meeting.

There was some encouragement from the town meeting last night.

The main subject at the meeting was the ABC Board. We were charged with not giving over our money properly and that we had purchased land we should not have purchased. They must have forgotten that we purchased land on the upper side of the store about six years ago for parking. We had also enlarged the store without any complaint. Now everything we do is illegal. We met with the committee Bert had appointed and they had gone along with our recommendation to hold the land, to give money we were giving to the ABC officer to the police department, and to give more money to the town. I have one of the articles that came out in the paper and a copy of the minutes of the town board. I hope the town commissioners will be content with this decision, though I have known them to reverse their decision the next day.

I am afraid the commissioners and the newspapers will keep the ABC store in the papers until some people decide to close the store. I don't believe many people will campaign to keep it open.

The liquor people don't care because people will buy their liquor anywhere. The beer people gave the money for the campaign when we won the vote to open the store. The opposition, the Christian Action League through church support can get plenty of money to run a campaign against the store. I think it would be very easy to win an election to close the store. I don't believe any of the commissioners would support keeping the store open. With all the criticism of the store now by the commissioners, I would not support a campaign to keep it open.

Most of my patients have the flu along with sore throats. It is peculiar that the flu occurs at this time of year. I don't know of a flu epidemic occurring in the summertime. In the summer it is mostly measles or chicken pox.

Until we had the vaccine, Polio Myelitis occurred in the spring. During one polio epidemic I had one family to have five children become paralyzed. In flu epidemics, the elderly frequently developed pneumonia and before we had antibiotics they frequently died with the pneumonia. Because of this, older doctors called pneumonia the friend of the elderly.

One of my patients wanted papers filled out to get his social security. He said he had paid for it and now he wants it back. This is an attitude now of a lot of people whether it is social security or insurance.

He said he would have been better off if he had been left alone to invest the money himself. I told him he couldn't have kept his money. It was taken out of his check where he works and sent in. We don't have control over a lot of our affairs. We must pay social security, pay taxes, and fill out forms. We must prove that we spent this or that so we can get some money off our taxes. The government is taxing so they can give the money back in the form of revenue sharing.

Every community is trying to get this money back in the form of grants. This pleases the government so they tax more because they are now out of money. This causes the cost of things to go up.

Around ten o'clock a patient came in to inquire about an injury I had treated her mother for several years ago. Her mother now has a swelling of the hand. She said her doctor wondered if it could be coming from the old injury. She wanted the plant her mother is working in now to pay for the swelling she is having now.

I looked on the record. Her injury was to the mid finger of the left hand six years ago. When I gave the daughter this information she said she thought it was a more recent injury and left the office.

In about thirty minutes a plant supervisor came in for me to check his blood pressure. He was the supervisor who had brought the woman in to the office with the mashed finger in 1972. I asked him did he remember the woman. He said she showed him her hand yesterday. She had not been complaining until yesterday. He thinks she hurt it outside the plant and wants the plant to pay for it.

Another interesting patient was a grandmother who wants to visit her grandson about three months old. She doesn't like her daughter-in-law or her people. Her son is living with his wife's people so she can't see her grandson. She will buy her son a trailer if he will move out so she can visit or even let them move in with her and live rent-free. She thinks the daughter-in-law is lazy and unfit to care for the baby. I advised her to leave her son and his wife alone. In time, they will move out into a house of their own and she can visit them then.

In the afternoon, Dudley came by to talk about the theater. I am closing out the gospel and country music shows. After paying all of the bills for sixteen weeks of operation we had about a hundred dollars for each of us. Steve is going to try a disco program for teen-agers. Our first attempt will be Saturday night.

After closing the office, I went by the theater to see how Steve is doing with a color wheel like Pinkney loaned us for the disco program. He is trying to make one. He had two speakers with cloth over them but no mirrors glued to the cloth. He had tried dental mirrors on them but they were too heavy. Pinkney agreed to sell us his because he would not be using them. He had made it just to see if it would work. He said he would like to come up on Saturday nights just to see it work.

Steve gave him a season ticket.

41

Our first teen disco

1-19-1979

Our weather today has been variable with clouds this morning suggesting rain. Around noon the cloud formation broke up, the sky cleared and now we have a cold northwest wind blowing. Dorothy and I didn't go to church today. It was almost one o'clock in the morning when we closed the theater after our first teen disco dance.

I began this morning with a call at six-thirty. A friend called me to come see his father, a man about eighty years old. He said his father had called him earlier and was feeling bad. He wanted him to come to see him and the son wanted me to meet him at his father's house. I had seen his father several times a few years ago and he had not been cooperative in taking my advice about his health so I was not too anxious to see him again especially at six o'clock on Sunday morning.

I asked the son to go see him first and if he needed me to come to call back and I would come. The son accepted this, though from his voice I thought he was somewhat disappointed.

I lay back in bed, but couldn't sleep. I thought it was more my business to check on the old man than the son's so I got up and went to see him. When I arrived I saw a light in the front room, the same room his wife had died in five years ago. As I opened the front door I saw her bed over against the living room wall just like it was when she died. The old man slept on a cot on the other side of the room. It was still there. The covers were thrown back like he might have gone to the bathroom. I called our rather loudly with no response.

I went farther back into a hallway where I could see a little light coming from around a door. I knocked on the door and turned the knob opening the door into a small kitchen.

The old man was sitting by an oil heater near the table eating a bowl of cereal. He continued his eating as though I wasn't there. I said hello again and this time he noticed me and paused in his eating. There was some trembling in his right hand as he lifted the spoon to his mouth again. I had not seen this before. When he noticed I was watching his hand he stopped using the spoon, lifted the bowl to his mouth and drank the cereal down like milk. I think he thought I saw something wrong with his hand and he wanted to hide it. He put the bowl down on the table and used his left hand.

People his age frequently have a light stroke before they have a big one that takes them away. If they don't want to go to the hospital they will try to hide it so I won't know the trouble.

I checked his pulse and blood pressure. This was all right. I inquired about his water. He had not been able to hold his urine and had to urinate right away with each urge or he would wet his clothes. I smelt urine in the living room and the kitchen. His pants were wet now. I told his son his father may have uremia from kidney blockage. He would need to bring him to the office Monday morning where I could do more testing and that we would probably send him to the hospital.

I closed my medical bag preparing to leave. The old man turned to me.

"Are you going to leave me without doing something for me?" he asked.

"Yes, I am going now," I replied. "I will see you the first thing Monday morning in the office. Tom will stay with you today and if you have any bad trouble he will call me. I will be in town all day."

"I might die before Monday," he said.

"If you do, and go up, put in a good word for me," I responded from the kitchen door. "If you go down, tell them you don't know me."

He laughed and I left him with Tom, his son. Driving home I was glad I had gone to see him. I could go home and rest knowing I didn't have to worry about him.

Dorothy had breakfast ready when I came home. I think both of us were pretty tired from our disco program. We had wondered all week how it would turn out. We advertised it one time in the paper. Steve had wanted to put some posters in schools but I was afraid the principals would not allow them since we were not giving any of our money to the schools.

To help with the concession stand and tickets, I offered Hadley twenty dollars. He accepted, but said it wasn't enough for a night's work. Sometime Wednesday he called me to tell me he was leaving me to take over an auction house near the post office but he would help me Saturday night since he had promised to. Steve said his father would like to help with the disco so on Thursday I called Hadley to tell him not to come Saturday.

Around three o'clock Saturday afternoon Steve started setting up the disco equipment for the evening. I popped the popcorn and opened up the concession stand. While popping the corn I noticed Steve was having trouble with one of the turntables. Something was wrong with the power going to the unit. He worked on it until six o'clock. It seemed that we would have to cancel the event or use a plain record player. Finally he thought he had a friend who would loan him one. He put the case over the unit preparing to store it when he noticed a flicker of light across the instrument panel. This quickly inspired a few sharp knocks on the case with the end of a screwdriver and there was a flicker of light again. He soon found a loose fuse to be the trouble and we were set for the disco program.

Our first customer arrived at eight o'clock, a mother with four children. She said she was real glad the town was finally having something for children. Steve's father and mother took up tickets. Before starting the dance we had about thirty children. It looked like disco dancing would be a success.

They enjoyed watching the balls of light going around on the ceiling from the mirror ball and the flashing light on the screen made by Pinkney's color wheel. Some danced and some were too bashful to dance.

About nine o'clock we notice we had a lot of girls leaving. When they returned they were accompanied by one or two boys with ticket stubs. We think before the girls left they collected ticket stubs from their friends to give to the boys outside.

We didn't care because we wanted people to see our disco dance. Next time we will use stamps for the arms or back of the hands. Steve said to make it more enjoyable he will have planned programs for all to participate in. If we can get all the children interested we will have less running up and down the stairs. I guess they haven't ever seen stairs before, at least stairs they seem free to run up and down on.

Another event due to take place tomorrow night is a meeting between the town board and the committee Bert appointed to work with the ABC board about the land and money. When the committee left the ABC store last week it was in agreement for us to keep the land, but to give the town more money.

42

Our house fire

1-29-1979 ✓

Last Thursday night about one o'clock there was a house fire on North Main Street. Some of the neighbors saw the smoke and called for the police to send the fire truck. All of the family got out safely. One of the firemen cut his thumb knocking out a window and called me to sew it up about three-thirty this morning.

Later at the office a lady brought a little girl to the office. She had got her thumb caught in a car door. She had been living in the house that burned. I could still smell the pine smoke in her clothes.

Some years ago our house caught fire. I had to call for the fire truck. I had been burning hickory logs in the fireplace in the playroom. It had been a cold day and I had a fire going all day and into the night. Around ten-thirty I was planning to retire, but I noticed the room seemed to be filling with smoke though the fire in the fireplace was dying out. Dorothy had put the children to bed and left the room to go to bed.

I couldn't understand why the room was filling with smoke when the fireplace had red coals. In a few minutes I began to smell something like pine smoke rather than smoke from hickory logs. I was about to decide it was due to the fireplace getting adjusted to having a fire in it. I got up from the couch and began to walk about the room deciding whether or not to go to bed. As I made a turn at the back of the room I happened to look at the top of the mantle above the fireplace. There in the corner I saw thick gray smoke drifting out into the room.

For a moment there was a numb feeling when I realized the house was on fire. I called the fire department and while I was waiting for the truck I got Dorothy and the children up and outside into the station wagon. I told them to be sure to stay in the wagon and all together while I went back into the house to check on the fire. I could hear the fire siren going off downtown and soon heard the one on the fire truck getting louder and louder as it rushed down the street to my house. When the truck arrived two of the firemen rushed into the house with fire extinguishers. They pried the mantle from the wall where the blaze had broken out. They had it out in a few minutes. I think if I had not noticed the difference in pine smoke and hickory smoke we all might have been burned to death.

Returning now to my practice, the fireman's thumb is getting along well, though he broke the wound open yesterday in a fight.

Sometime Friday afternoon a patient came in that I had not seen for a long time. She was just passing through on her way to a new town. She wanted to know if I could give her some capsules stronger than the ones I gave her five years ago. I couldn't remember right off what they were. She said they were pink and to help her relax. She had run out of them and since she was moving she wanted some to take with her. At present she felt nervous and couldn't eat. Most of the things she ate made gas on her stomach. The gas caused her not to rest at night. No sleep at night made her eyes weak. Due to this she had her glasses changed two weeks ago, but they are pinching her nose so her sinuses are bothering her. This causes drainage down her throat making it sore and she has to cough so that something gets under her dentures making her mouth so sore she can't eat. But the irritation under the dental plates is not as bad as the drainage from her sinuses stopping up her windpipes so she can't breath. On this account she must cough a lot and this is making her back hurt with pain down her left leg.

Frequent coughing has caused some incontinence so she must wear a pad all the time. There is also some pain in her ears if she coughs too hard.

I was about to say something when she said she forgot to mention she had pain in her neck. While she was relating her symptoms her husband was telling her to hurry up because he wanted me to take his blood pressure. With this interruption I seized the opportunity to tell her she had best see her doctor in the new town she was moving to. He would need to give her the capsules so he could check on the side effects that may give her some trouble. Her husband agreed and gave her a little pull out of the chair so he could sit down for me to take his blood pressure. It was a little high and I renewed his prescription.

All this time I had my regular patients waiting to see me. I had spent about forty-five minutes with these two people. When the husband asked me how much I charged I said fifteen dollars. His wife said that's awful. I said if you think you can get a doctor cheaper someplace else I wish you would stop there next time. I guess they must have thought I should have seen them for free for old time's sake.

Friday night the weather was bad with ice hanging from the trees and in some places cutting off the power. Reece had to use the hand-operated cash registers at the ABC store for several hours.

I was concerned with a tree hanging over the lines coming up to my house. I hesitated to call the electrical department because they had been up since four o'clock this morning cutting trees so people could get their power restored. I called the police department to tell them to tell the electricians if they got caught up there was a tree that looked like it was going to fall over the lines coming to my house. They never came, but around six o'clock the temperature warmed so the ice melted off of the tree.

When Dale came in this morning I was caught up with my patients so I thought I would ask him about life. He is a Sunday school teacher and somewhat of a philosopher. I asked him just what was the point of life. Tomorrow if I live I will be doing the same thing I am doing now. Yesterday when I saw him at his store he was becoming disgusted with all the work and regulations he was having to comply with. He said if I would tell him the purpose of life he would tell me the point of life.

I said perhaps we could determine the point without knowing the purpose. To this he disagreed saying we were all put here for a purpose, some are smarter than others and can do things that other's can't do. His purpose was to run his feed store and fill out forms.

I said I didn't believe we all had specific assignment in life. To this he said yes we do and my assignment was to get him something for his toothache as quick as possible so he could get back to his store.

43

A suicide

2-1-1979

We are having very cold days now. Today the high was in the upper thirties with the night temperature predicted to drop to ten above zero. Tuesday night we had a little snow.

I think some of my patients are just wanting drugs. Last week I had four patients come in complaining of having migraine headaches. Each one was about an hour apart and from out of town. When I suggested something for migraine each one said the only thing that would relieve their head was a slightly pink or orange tablet, Talwin, they thought was the name of it. The first two got by without any trouble. When the third one came in asking for the same drug I became suspicious. I didn't give him any Talwin. As he went out the door he tore up the prescription because it was not for Talwin.

About four o'clock the fourth one came in. He began to cry with his headache. He said if he didn't soon get something his head would be so bad it would knock him out and he would have to go to the emergency room for some shots for his head. I finally believed his story and wrote a prescription for twenty-four Talwin tablets. When he started to pay me he said he had left his billfold in his car and would run out and bring me the money.

I gave him his record and the prescription saying he could settle at the front desk. He seemed to be better already. I felt like I had been deceived. He left the record at the desk, but he didn't return to pay me. Dorothy said she saw him through the window when he drove off smiling in the car with another man. Since then I have had three other people wanting this drug, but I haven't given any a prescription for Talwin.

Last Friday night around two o'clock the police called me to know if I knew anything about an elderly lady who had been going to the health department here in town. I said no, I had no idea who it could be and suggested they contact her social worker. Saturday morning as I came to the office there were several police cars and the sheriff's car at an apartment where an elderly lady lived. Later in the day I learned she had been found dead in her apartment. The police first thought she had gone away to visit some friends. They thought this because she had told several of her friends she was going on a trip.

Her apartment was locked with a padlock on the outside door so they concluded she had locked up her apartment and left town.

After calling everywhere they decided to break into the apartment where they found her body lying on her bed. They found a suicide note on a bedside table telling what to do with her things and how she wanted her funeral arranged.

At the bridge club Saturday night Laney said he thought she had been dead about four days. She didn't smell so bad until they moved the body, then fluid began to run from under her arms and her inguinal region, giving the apartment an awful smell.

He could not embalm her because she had requested in her note no embalming. To keep her from smelling in his funeral home they planned to put her outside someplace where she could stay cold until time for the funeral. He doesn't have a refrigerated room for holding bodies.

Dorothy and I have missed going to church the last two Sundays so we planned to go this Sunday. On the way to church Dorothy said the preacher was going to tell us something to watch out for. She didn't know what it was. After we got seated I planned to listen so I would know what to watch out for. I became distracted before the sermon started. The congregation was standing singing the first hymn when a man and his son came in. They were visitors. They came down the right hand aisle along the wall and to the pew ahead of me. There were four people on the pew. An elderly couple at the end on the left hand side and a lady with her young daughter at the end on the right hand side. Her daughter was on her left side. The lady was standing so there was about room enough for one person between her and the end of the pew. There was plenty of room along the middle of the pew. The man stopped and moved into the pew beside the lady and expected her to move down so his son standing against the pew in the aisle could sit with him on this pew.

She didn't budge an inch.

At the end of the first verse I noticed him give the lady a little nudge to move down, but again she didn't move over. At the end of the third verse his son moved up to the pew ahead leaving his father sitting squashed in beside the lady. She never did give him any room. During the sermon I wondered why this lady didn't welcome this man and his son to the church or at least move over so they could sit together on the pew. Older church members have their pew loosely staked out according to family names on the stained glass windows and other members seldom take their pew, but they will always let visitors in their pew if need be. But this time for some reason the lady didn't move. I think now she might have been a visitor too. Since she was there first she had a right to hold her seat. I wondered if this was what the preacher said to watch out for.

There are situations in which it requires a great deal of thought about what is the best thing to do to be considerate and helpful. On one occasion I was in church on our family pew and three visiting women sat in the seat ahead of me. There were also two strange men who came in and sat beside Dorothy and me. When we were singing the first hymn the man on the end noticed the lady ahead of him had her skirt caught in her crotch and to be helpful he gently pulled it out. She turned around and scowled at him as if she were going to slap him.

His face turned red and I know he was embarrassed. When we stood to sing the next hymn after a long prayer her skirt was hanging loose so he thought to be helpful he would put it back like she had it for the first hymn. This time she did turn around and with a great scorn gave him a sharp slap across the face. He and his friend left without hearing the sermon.

Monday Reece and I met with Bert to discuss the audit for the ABC store our auditor had brought. He had added a few new lines showing what the store is withholding for operating expenses. He had discussed it with the ABC people in Raleigh and they had agreed our audit is as good as we can make it.

Bert said he would present it to the commissioners at the next meeting.

Wednesday night I worked on the disco lights in the theater. I fixed a spot light so that it will reflect a red light off the mirror ball. Now I have nice red balls flying about the ceiling and screen. Steve hasn't seen it yet but I think it is spectacular.

I have some worry about my method of practicing medicine. President Carter has announced a program for national health. He plans to afford it by having physicians and hospitals charge less for their services. I am wondering how he can set fees for us and not for other professions.

A few other things have happened today. One was a boy about twenty years old. He brought his wife in for some medicine for the flu. After examining her and prescribing some medicine, he pulled a small notebook out of his pocket and turned to a page where he had listed six drugs. He wanted to know what they were for. I am beginning to wonder if young people aren't trying to be pharmacists.

A little later in the day a mother brought a little girl in about seven years old. The little girl was smiling and showed no evidence of any trouble. Her mother said last night she fell from a cabinet and injured her straddle area over a cabinet door. She had been bleeding some from the vagina. When I examined her there was a small tear at the edge of the vagina.

Since the mother was with the child and the child seemed happy I let the case go as an injury, though I wondered a lot about sexual molestation.

44

Burglars

Last night it snowed about eight inches deep, the worst storm of the year. When I awoke and saw the snow through the window I thought I would not get up until around noon. At eight o'clock the phone rang.

Melvin was calling to see if I wanted him to come get me and take me to the office. He said the roads were very slippery and the snow was about ten inches deep. I told him I was not going to the office today and I would call him if I needed him. At nine o'clock I decided I might as well get up. Some patients would be calling me soon.

When I arrived at the office I was surprised to find my parking lot cleaned off. I wondered if the town had done it for me. Sometimes they have done it. In the middle of the lot was a Jeep but no one was in it. Perhaps they had walked up town.

When I went to unlock the office door it was already unlocked.

This was a bit frightening for I made sure I had locked it last night. When I opened the door going into the reception room the room was full of patients. Sarah, my assistant, had arrived early and let them in. I asked if all these people came in that little Jeep. She said only one came in the Jeep, some people had brought the others and gone on up town. She said the man from the filing station where I get my gas had cleaned off the lot. My love for the town dropped a bit. They were not as obliging as they were a few years ago.

When I had seen all the patients I looked over my copy of the ABC audit Bert is going to present to the town Thursday night. It seems that

189

one or two of the commissioners always complain about something. I think they are determined to get the ABC Board to resign.

Saturday night Dorothy and I were invited to a disco party in Hickory. There were about a hundred people there. As we entered the room a young man associated with Steve in the disco business came up and said he was stealing one of the ideas we used in our New Year's Eve Disco party. He was using movies like Susie did only he didn't have a large movie size screen. He had silent movies projected on the opposite wall. Most of the guests were sitting around laughing. It was a good idea.

Monday morning at five o'clock I had a call to come to see a lady living about two miles out of town. Her daughter said her mother was lying on the floor and couldn't move. She wanted me to come see her. She thought she might have had a heart attack or a stroke.

I dressed and without breakfast went over to a little store building where her mother lived. I think the building was once a small service station and grocery store. As kids, Jim and I sometimes rode our bicycles over there on Sunday afternoon.

As I entered the building I noticed it was cold and there was no heat in it. A man from across the street was trying to get a fire started in an old pot-bellied stove.

Inside the store along the right side were the same old wood counters I had seen years ago. A little farther back at the end of the counter was an old coin-operated drink machine and a table with bread and cookies. Along the back wall firewood was piled up to the window. Chairs and boxes were pushed along the left wall. Near the stove a woman lay curled up as much as she could. Clara was covered with a pink blanket. I had seen her many times and when I called her name she responded. This was good, now I knew she wasn't dead.

I started to lift the blanket off and her daughter cautioned me, saying Clara was all messed up. She was not able to move her. Without removing the blanket I checked her pulse, it was normal. Her blood pressure was low, but not enough to cause her to be unconscious. When I examined her feet and hands I thought she was frozen.

Her daughter said Clara had lain this way all night without any heat. After moving her feet and hands and talking to her I decided she was not in any immediate danger. Someone had called the ambulance and the crew was coming in through the door with a cot. The daughter told them that if I found it necessary to send her mother to the hospital she would call them.

With the help of the neighbor man and daughter we cleaned up the patient and got her to bed by placing her in a chair and carrying the chair to her room, which was a little addition on the left side of the store. We wrapped her in an electric blanket. In about thirty minutes Clara felt well enough to eat a little breakfast. The neighbor man had got a good fire going in the stove and the room was beginning to warm up. I told the daughter to call me if she didn't do well.

Back at the office the day went along very well. I didn't have any patients calling for Talwin.

Monday evening around seven o'clock I went to the theater to see if I could improve on the disco lights. I had been adjusting them for about an hour when there was a loud knocking on the back door and someone calling my name. I was up on a twenty-foot stepladder and it took a little while to get to the door. I didn't recognize the voice but I shouted out that I would be there in a minute. When I opened the door a policeman was there holding a flash light. He said my alarm system had gone off at the police station up town. He had checked my office and couldn't find anything wrong. The front and back doors were all locked and the windows were all closed. He thought I ought to go over to the office and reset my alarm.

The alarm he was talking about is a system that turns on a light on the switchboard in the police station. If something opens a window or a door the light comes on. I installed it after someone broke into the office three times within a six-month period two years ago. The police were not able to catch the burglar though they knew pretty well who was doing the breaking in. To arrest him they needed to catch him in the building or with my drugs on him. The burglar was finally caught in Boone when he had broken into someone's house. After the last time he broke into the office I decided if he stole some of my narcotics the state drug people and the police would be in the office so much I would not be able to do any work for a week. I decided to put in a system like we had in the ABC store.

"If it has just gone off there is somebody in there," I said.

He ran to his police car, which was parked halfway between the theater and the office. A second policeman jumped out of the car and ran toward the office. The first officer cranked the car and slammed it into reverse stopping just short of the office steps. I walked toward the office in the glare of the headlights. I wondered why he had backed the car so near the steps. The first policeman was waiting for me as I came around the car. He motioned for me to open the office door. I noticed I was leading the way and he was following behind me with his pistol drawn. I was about to open the door leading into the reception room when I decided since he had the gun he should be leading the way.

I motioned for him to get in front and open the door. He asked me for a light. I had my little pin light, the other office had the big flashlight. I didn't know what had become of him. He kicked open the door and shined the light about. We didn't see anyone, but we thought we heard a little noise coming from another room. I was a step or two behind him as he started down the hallway. I turned the reception lights on and heard him shout.

"Hands on your head and don't move."

I was not able to see what was taking place because he was in the emergency room area. I moved in a little closer and turned the lights on. The policeman holding his pistol in his right hand and with the pin light in his left was slowly approaching a large man with his hands on his head.

"Anybody else with you?" He said again in a loud voice.

"No," said the burglar.

The officer commanded him to put his hands on the sink while he searched him from head to toe for any weapons. He soon pulled out a large chrome table knife from one of his boots. When he was satisfied there were no other weapons on him he handcuffed him to my white examining chair near the sink. He turned around to see where he should look next. I turned on the lights from the outside to the first examining room.

Leaving the burglar bent over the chair, the officer tiptoed with gun in hand through the doorway into the examining room

"All right," he shouted, "Hands on your head and don't move."

He had found another burglar in the examining room.

I eased into the room to see what was happening. The officer had the burglar bent over my desk feeling for weapons. He found another large table knife like the first burglar had. He handcuffed him and brought him out to where the first burglar was. He asked him if there were any more people in the building.

"No," he said.

I was standing in the hallway where I could see into both rooms. The second burglar was a small person dressed in a black jacket and black pants wearing large leather gloves. When the officer sat him down in my office chair he appeared to be about five feet tall. The first burglar was about six feet tall, light complexion with light brown hair and blue eyes. He was wearing a light brown jacket and brown trousers.

I started to move closer to him for a better look. I thought I had seen him somewhere, but there were footsteps running up the stairs in the reception room. It was the first policeman who had jumped out of the car and run to the back of the office.

He said someone had started out the back door and when he called for them to halt, they slammed the back door shut and ran toward the front of the office. Looking around he was surprised to see the two burglars in handcuffs. The officer with me asked him to watch them while he and I searched the building for others. With him leading the way with my pin light in one hand and his pistol in the other we searched every corner of the building, but two were all we could find. At the back door the burglars had broken the glass, reached in and unlocked the door. They closed it after they were in the building so if someone didn't look close they would not know anything had happened.

When we returned to the front of the office again the officer went to the car and radioed for the police lieutenant to come to the office. Now I knew why he had placed the car near the steps, so he could radio for help if needed.

While we were waiting for the lieutenant the officer decided to search the large burglar again. He found a small vial with some pink tablets and handed it to me to see if I knew what kind of medicine it was. On the label it said "Talwin."

The patient's name, R.T., the same name he had given me about three weeks ago when he was crying with a migraine. He had gotten the Talwin on the same day of the break-in from another doctor. I was glad to see that I wasn't the only doctor he had fooled.

With the officer standing by, I asked him if he wasn't in my office three weeks ago.

"No," he said. "I have never seen you before."

The lieutenant had arrived and asked me if I would swear I had not given these two men permission to enter my building. I said I would swear and he directed the officers to take them up town and lock them up. When the office was clear of people I reset the alarm.

Tuesday evening it started snowing around five o'clock. Jim, Laney and I planned to go to Hickory for a meeting. At six o'clock I received a call to go see Jim's uncle. When I arrived he was dead. I called Laney to come get the body. We all went later to Hickory for dinner.

The speaker was a retired minister turned humorist. I remember one of his jokes. It was about a Texan visiting some boys in North Carolina. The Texan had been bragging about everything in Texas being bigger than anything in North Carolina. To get even, the North Carolina boys found a large snapping turtle and put it in the Texan's bed.

At night he saw the turtle and asked what it was. The boys from North Carolina told him it was a Carolina bed bug, to which the Texan replied, "It sure is a little fellow isn't it?"

45

La Maze

Today has been a nice pre-spring day with temperature in the sixties. It was so warm I raised all the windows in the office to let the wind blow through. For dinner tonight I took Dorothy out to the Page One, a new restaurant in Hickory for her Valentine present.

At the office most of my patients were enjoying the spring-like day. The flu seems to be subsiding. I still have quite a few patients with sore throats from the flu and my usual patients with nervousness and high blood pressure. During the morning there were not many patients so I could take a lot time with the ones I had.

One patient was a neighbor of Clara, the patient I went to see who was lying on the floor in the old store building. She said she was not doing so well in the hospital. I had referred her to the hospital the next day when she began to complain of pain in her left thigh. They found a fracture of the neck of the femur. She might have gone to sleep in the chair beside the stove and fell out. I saw one patient her age pulling on the bottom drawer of a dresser. Her hands slipped and she fell backwards fracturing her femur from a very little fall.

My next patient was a young man complaining of pain in his right thigh. He had been waiting three weeks for it to get better. Since it was still hurting he decided to come to see me. He had tried various analgesics and even some La Maze treatments. He said it was a matter of mind over matter. He had tried getting his mind off of his leg to make the pain go away, but he was never quite successful. When I asked him where he had heard of this treatment he replied he had been going to La Maze classes with his wife.

The classes teach his wife to relax so when she goes into labor she will not have much pain. His part in the delivery seems to be to coach his wife in all the things she has been taught.

It reminded me of a joke I heard at a meeting. A lady had bad migraine headaches and had tried all kinds of remedies. Finally the doctor suggested she try putting her index finger to each side of her head and saying over and over that she didn't have a headache. After a few days the system worked. She was so pleased with the doctor she brought her husband to see the doctor to see if he could help their love life. In a few weeks the doctor had the love life going as good as new. After a few months the wife noticed that before making love to her the husband spent fifteen to thirty minutes in the bathroom. One evening he left the door open and she eased over to where she could hear and see her husband. He was standing before the mirror with his fingers pressing on his temples repeating one phrase over and over.

"This is not my wife. This is not my wife."

A chauvinist joke—not very funny.

Yesterday I went to Ben's garage. One of the mechanics said that little alarm fooled them. He meant the little radio I have hooked to a switch on the front door. When the front door is opened the radio comes on in the back of the office so I know someone has come in. The alarm that caught the burglars was one that came on in the police station.

Until Wednesday I thought it was infallible unless I should fail to turn it on. I had made an appointment with my auditor to work on my income tax. I turned the alarm on and locked the front door so no one would bother us. We talked a few minutes and then it occurred to me that my car was parked outside and my patients would think I was in the building. They would beat on the front door until I opened it. I went outside and moved the car around back and came in the office through the back door. We worked for about two hours. As he was leaving I noticed the alarm system had been tripped, the red light was on. Then I remembered I had tripped it when I came out to move my car to the back. Now I wondered why the police had not come to investigate. I called the police station and Ted, our former ABC officer answered. He is working in the police department now. He said it had been on for about two hours. The police had driven by the office and everything looked all right.

On the way to the house I concluded that devices are still dependent upon human interpretation for proper action. The night of the burglary the officer had decided something was wrong and came by for me to go reset my alarm. Wednesday the officer rode by the office and saw nothing unusual, my car parked back of the office where I very seldom park, a strange car in the parking lot, the burglar system on in the police station, all of this looked usual, all right.

At the next town election the two commissioners favorable to Bert are up for re-election, only one of the opposition is. This means to gain anything, the two favorable ones plus another new one favorable to the mayor will have to win for Bert to have an even chance. This will be hard to do without some specific issues.

This week the general assembly in Raleigh passed the resolution allowing the money we spent on the ABC officer to be given to the town police department so the matter of our ABC officer will not be a big issue. At the last board meeting one of the commissioners brought up the salaries we are paying our employees. Our salaries are in line with those other ABC stores are paying. Perhaps the commissioners will be content now.

46

A sudden home death

3-1-1979

A lot of birds are showing up so spring is on the way. Most of the sports activities now are centered around the championship basketball games. There is also some concern about an energy crisis. President Carter has indicated that the price of gasoline will increase about 10 percent a year. With heating oil already high, I am wondering how I will get to the beach with the increase in gasoline. A round trip takes about fifty gallons.

Last night Dorothy and I went out to dinner with Emory, a friend seventy years old who moved here from the state of New York about four years ago. He is a rather knowledgeable person, a little like an encyclopedia. We began our discussion with a statement he made about something he had read sometime ago. Emory had read somewhere that in so many million years the earth explodes from the inside and all that is on top goes inside and the world starts over again. I have never heard of this.

Last Thursday afternoon at two o'clock I was called to a home to see a man who had died suddenly. Gaither had been my patient on some occasions. The family couldn't find his doctor so they asked me to come. A doctor or coroner must verify that the person is dead before the body can be moved. These types of calls are rather depressing. There isn't anything I can do and in some ways I think the family holds the medical profession responsible for the death. We should have known what to do to have prevented it.

When I arrived at the house located on a steep hill I had to drive around to the back yard, which was already filled with cars. I parked back of the last one and walked past the police car and the ambulance parked next to the back porch. Some people were on the porch and made way for me to go into the living room. Just inside the door to my left were three of the ambulance crew talking to two policemen. Along the back wall were four or five young girls and three elderly women sitting on a couch. One was sobbing a great deal and the other two were trying to comfort her. A large woman was standing in a doorway to my left talking on a phone. I was wondering where the body was when a door to my right suddenly opened and I was motioned into this room.

Gaither was lying across a bed on his back with his clothes on. His brother said he had recently returned from the hospital for a heart condition. After lunch he felt a little smothery and came in the room to rest. While sitting on the edge of the bed he gasped a few times and then fell backwards onto the bed. Hid brother called the ambulance and the police. The ambulance crew had tried to resuscitate him without success.

I listened to Gaither's chest for a while and then told his brother this man is dead. I closed my medical bag and went into the room where all the people were gathered. His brother closed the door behind me.

The large woman who was on the phone when I came in asked me to check on the woman who was sobbing so much on the couch.

I checked on her blood pressure and listened to her heart. I couldn't find anything wrong so I gave her a few nerve tablets from my medical bag. As I moved closer to the door preparing to leave, Gaither's brother asked me what should be done about his brother. I told him to find out from the family what undertaker they wanted and he would come pick him up. "When you call tell him I will sign the death certificate."

When I returned to the office a young woman was waiting to see me. I had seen her several days ago for what I thought was a pelvic inflammatory condition. She had separated from her husband a year ago and was going now with several boyfriends. I overheard her talking with Dorothy in the waiting room while I was washing my hands at the sink. I first thought she was talking about her condition but when I heard her say that one good piece was worth three bad ones I turned the water off to listen more carefully. I was relieved when she said something that let me know she was talking about hairpieces.

Before closing Friday, Bert came by to tell me that City Manager Noble was not satisfied with the ABC audit. He couldn't understand the amount of cash we were holding. Bert told him we had not made our distribution yet. To find out how we stand with two bosses, the town and the state, I asked Reece to call the state ABC people in Raleigh to find out what is our relation to the town. He said they said that about all the power the town board has over the local ABC Board is making the appointments each year.

At the theater our disco program seems to be holding. Saturday we had about thirty young people. Some were dressed neatly for a disco party, others were wearing slacks or jeans and some kind of jackets. We had our disco lights blinking and balls of light going around on the ceiling, but most of them spent their time running up and down the stairs and out to the front street. There was one little girl about fifteen years old who kept her finger in her mouth most of the time. She spent the evening running from the concession stand to the front and then outside to the street.

Another very pretty blond girl about the same age frequently ran upstairs on the girl's side and then back down on the boy's side screaming as loud as she could. I think the yell was to make people think some boys were chasing her.

A man wearing a bright pink shirt and blue jeans acted most peculiar. The first part of the evening he spent on the dance floor on his stomach and back rolling around to the music like he was having an epileptic fit. Several times he stood on his head on the stage, keeping time to the music with his feet kicking in the air. When he came to the concession area he was sweating and panting for breath. When he ordered a drink, he didn't care what kind it was, he just wanted to wash down a B.C. powder. With his drink in hand he moved to a large ashtray and lit up a cigarette. I was observing him pretty close because last Saturday evening he tried to unscrew all my light bulbs along the edge of the stage.

Outside the ticket office two unusual characters kept looking at the ticket window. I thought they had robbery on their mind. One was a large person built a lot like a female; the other was about a foot shorter and looked like a Mexican. In a few minutes a group of girls and boys came running out to the street again and they moved away.

Cars were beginning to circle the theater. Some of the cars were so souped up they shook the theater. It began to pour down rain so contact between people in the cars and girls on the street had to be broken off. While all of this was going on in front of the building and children were running up and down the stairs, some other children were having a good time dancing on the stage.

About eleven o'clock a young blond boy came in asking about his sister. At the last event someone had given him something that knocked him out. His father had found out about it and restricted him to the house for a month. I don't know what he could have taken. When he came in the front door with some other boys he seemed to be laughing though there wasn't anything that I saw to laugh at. He fell halfway down the aisle. I helped him outside and left him and another boy to go inside to call the police. When they came after fifteen minutes some of the boy's friends had taken him home.

We closed the theater around midnight. Because of all the running in and out I think the future of our disco program is not bright.

47

Self-analysis

3-12-1979 ✓

Our weather is very delightful; the temperature is in the sixties with a blue sky and warm sun. I noticed a jonquil blooming in my parking lot today and a yellow bell bush in the yard at the old library building. At noon I saw some of my tulips budding near the south side of the house. I haven't seen many birds today, only a sapsucker in one of the maple trees back of the house.

My water hyacinths in the minnow pond all froze. I have one barely alive in the aquarium in the office. I think I will give up on my minnow raising. I don't believe I will have much time to go fishing anyway.

The beautiful weather is in contrast with my mood. Things have been going very bad. I am reminded of a poem called Invictus written by William Ernest Henley:

Out of the night that covers me,
Black as the Pit from pole to pole,
I thank whatever god may be
for my unconquerable soul.

In the fell clutch of circumstance
I have not winced nor cried aloud.
Under bludgeonings of chance
My head is bloody, but unbowed.

Beyound this place of wrath and tears,
Looms but the Horror of the shade,
And yet the menace of the years
Finds and shall find me unafraid.

It matters not how straight the gate,
How charged with punishment the scroll,
I am master of my fate;
I am captain of my soul.

Some of my despondency is due to the conduct of the people in the theater. We are having a good attendance, about thirty or forty people each evening. I am glad of this, but they destroying everything in sight. Each night someone stops up the commode in the girl's restroom. Another problem is drinking. About half of the people are drinking, though I have posted signs around the theater saying no drinking. They go outside to the cars to drink or take drugs. Because of the drunks, we have to make rules to check on every body. This means the inconsiderate people are making the rules that affect everybody. From this you can see that it is wrong to say that if someone drinks it is his business. At the theater we have to be concerned with the person drinking or on drugs because they are creating a disturbance among the non-drinking people.

Another element in my despondency is my apprehension about Dorothy. She has been spotting some for the last six weeks. We have been worried that the condition might be cancerous. She has an appointment with a Gynecologist and I suspect she will need to have a hysterectomy.

I was late getting to the office. I think because it is my birthday I am being a little slow. Sarah had already opened and I think deliberately called all my worst patients. There were three of them sitting together.

The first one wanted to know when her head was going to stop hurting. It had been hurting for the last ten years and no one, not even the major clinics, had been able to help. After listening to her story again for thirty minutes she was content to try her usual medication again.

The other two patients were similar in that there was nothing I could do but listen and keep them on the same treatment. I wondered while I was listening to them if they ever thought how the doctor might be feeling.

During the time I was seeing them the phone was continually ringing with patients wanting to know when they could come to see me. To keep calm I continually told myself this was going to be a bad day and I was under a lot of emotional strain thinking of Dorothy. If I would just remember to keep doing the best I could with each patient the day would end without any great trouble.

At eleven o'clock Paul from one of the plants called to tell me the woman I had seen six weeks ago with an injury to her hand was having trouble again. I smiled a bit when I told him to bring her back to the office. This was just another irregularity of the day. I had told Dorothy and Sarah when I first saw her she would not be happy with our treatment.

In a few minutes she came in and wanted an appointment with an orthopedist. Since she was hurt in the plant and they are paying the bill she believes there is no use in not going to the best specialist she can find just to be sure nothing is wrong.

After lunch, things seemed to go a little better. A few of my patients were better. When there was a little break and no patients were waiting I recalled another person sixty-one years ago who on this day might have had a lot of trouble and apprehension. It was my mother. I was born in 1918 during the flu epidemic. After the discomfort of delivery there was a new child to care for, her sixth living child. She probably wondered what the child would become in life. Could she influence it to be a responsible and worthy person?

A child is a mother's creation. She feels joy for its successes, grief in its failures. It is a great joy for a mother to live to see their children succeed in life. My mother died shortly after I finished medical school.

It is also a great joy when the children call the parent wishing them a happy birthday. All my children called me during the day wishing me a happy birthday.

After dinner I began to review my life up to this point and consider how I arrived at the place I am in life now. What was my Zenith? Why am I like I am? I think during medical school I planned to do general practice. I was impressed by the local doctors I knew in my hometown. After finishing medical school I went for an internship in Gorgas Hospital in Panama C.Z. Some of my friends were there and it seemed like a good place to fish.

I stayed there a year and then went into the U.S. Army on active duty. My tour of duty for two years was rather uneventful in that I spent my time in the States in convalescent hospitals. I didn't like the army because I was too independent, though I made some very close friends. I think my trouble was that I didn't understand organization and rank.

When my time was up I returned home to set up practice with a local doctor. After a year I accepted a residency at Rex Hospital in Raleigh where I met Dorothy. I worked about two years in the hospital and one year in Coats, N.C. I didn't like the tobacco spray so I decided to come back home.

I married Dorothy in 1948 and we set up practice here in Granite Falls. I have retained my independence to a great extent and spent a great deal of my time with my family and friends. I don't believe I would have been able to do this if I had stayed in hospital work. A great many people like me here and ask me for medical help. I treat each one as though it is me asking for help.

When I first set up practice here I thought you received whatever you were entitled to by waiting your turn in line. I have found out different.

I have found out also it is very difficult to be an independent person. One must to a great extent be supportive of programs of the people and not make hasty decisions about policy dealing with people. Whenever we bought this lot for our house and developed the road I found out that things go a lot by who you are, your value to the community and your politics and whom you know that might speak favorably to the powers that be for you. We were denied paving and acceptance of the road by two of the town commissioners.

With this enlightenment about how things work with people I began to take an interest in politics. It is what controls almost whatever you do. It is the master science. No matter how good you are you are still under the influence of politics.

At this point in my life I can say I have achieved what I aimed for. I have a wonderful wife and family. I have been recognized as a medical doctor in my hometown. I have many patients. I think my mother and father would be pleased with my success.

I have enjoyed my life. I am what I have created. To achieve something one must decide on it and hold to it. There is a lot of joy in striving for your goal. Two important things in life are a good name and good health. Good health is a lot inherited, but we must make the best of whatever we are given. Everyone must try to protect his body through good habits and self-discipline.

A good name is earned as you go through life. Your name is you, all that you have been, all that you are. It represents your work, your character. It too must be protected by upholding goodness, honesty and dependability.

After sixty-one years I have learned a little about living with people. To succeed in life one must get along with people. This takes a lot of thought and consideration.

48

Spring again

4-5-1979

A few days ago we had our first thunderstorm for this year. The following day was rather cool. At present we are having delightful weather with temperatures in the seventies. At night it drops to around forty. Today we have had a very beautiful day with a little wind.

Due to the nice weather most lawns are turning green again. Cherry trees and plum trees are in full bloom. I have three Nectarine trees in bloom for the first time. Our camellia has pretty red blossoms and the azalea are showing evidence of blooming soon.

Even with all the flowers blooming and the early turning green with spring grass, I am still pretty low in spirit. Dorothy is planning to go to New York on a tour for this weekend. I worry about her flying.

I also received a summons from the court to appear against the two burglars who broke into my office last month. I worried about this for a week and finally called the police to see what had happened, as I was never called. They promised to call me about thirty minutes before I was needed in court. They said that the case had been postponed because the little burglar was being tried in Boone for several other crimes he had been arrested for. He had turned state's evidence (agreed to tell on all the people who helped in the crime) in exchange for a lighter sentence.

After the lawyers have gotten all they need to know from him, they are then going to turn him over for trial for breaking into my office. They figure that he will draw enough time for this, to keep him locked up for a long time.

This morning I had an early call to the office and when I opened the back door to get in the car there were a lot of birds singing. Some were doves cooing, some jaybirds flying about in my neighbor's garden building a nest in his June apple tree. A pair of cardinals was busy in a brush pile in the pasture back of the house. Later in the day when I went down to the minnow pond several small frogs jumped in.

With this pretty weather Jim wanted to go fishing, but due to the muddy water we decided not to go. Some years go we would have gone thirty or forty miles away to find clear water but now we are getting too old to go so far for one afternoon. When we went fishing then we went with the aim of catching a good mess of fish for supper, now we go mostly just for the relaxation.

At the office things are changing too. Most of the patients now want some kind of paper to support their visit. Most have some kind of insurance and need to have a blank filled out so they can recover their money and money for time away from work. One patient came in today with a paper to be filled out declaring she is totally disabled so she will not have to pay county taxes.

I am having some trouble adjusting to all the paperwork and receipts. I try to remember that the patients probably don't like it anymore than I do. I think that some of my depression is due to all the work I do and at the end of the year I give it to the government in taxes.

I become irritated at having to fill out all these forms that I had nothing to do with. Politicians make all these laws and then tell the patient to get the doctor to say they are thus and so, so they can get paid or exempt from something. If the doctor doesn't grant the request he will lose the patient, if we grant the request then the politicians scream that the doctor is wrecking the program by letting too many people make claims for more money.

Even murder has become a medical question.

Yesterday, a patient asked me if it was all right to get someone to kill somebody. This was my first inquiry about murder. It raised the question of whether or not the patient was mentally ill. He said some people were getting in his yard while he was at work and tearing up his shrubbery. He had called the police several times without getting any results. He would like now to pay someone to shoot the bastards whenever they climbed over his fence.

I told him I didn't know of any one he could get for this job.

Another patient wanted to get a deed reversed. She signed a paper along with her brother deeding some land to her neighbor. Someone told her she sold the property too low so now she wants it back or more money from the neighbor. My part in the scheme is to certify that her brother was incompetent when he signed the deed.

We had a very smelly patient come to the office a few days ago. She said that she had come just like she "wuz." She is a short lady about seventy and about as big around as she is tall. She has a little face with close set fiery eyes. She was wearing a dull red sweater over a faded brown dress. Her hose were rolled below her knees.

Dorothy accompanied her to the examining room and then went to the backroom to get some candles. I sensed something was going on when she asked me where the matcher were. She said that she wanted to light the candles to kill the terrible odor. Then I recalled that at the last visit, this lady told me she milked three nanny goats and looked after two Billy goats. This time she had come straight to the office after milking the goats. The odor was so bad that I opened the windows as soon as she left.

After she left, I had a male patient about the same age. He was about as dirty as the goat woman, except he didn't smell. He is about six feet tall, weighing about 170 pounds. He shuffles his feet along like someone walking in the dark. He wears a dirty brown had tilted down over his one good eye. His brown double-wasted coat is generally unbuttoned, showing his olive green shirt with faded blue stripes. He wears the same pair of black pants with the fly half open at the top. Generally he has on white socks and run over brown shoes.

When he sits in the examining chair, I can see that his face is twisted a little to the right, making the left eye with a gray cataract look frightening. Looking at the left corner of his mouth, there is a brown stain extending down the chin and neck into the shirt collar. Before we can start the interview, I must find him something to spit his tobacco in. He has diabetes, congestive heart failure and arthritis.

Another interesting thing happened a few days ago. A boy about fifteen years old came complaining about eye trouble. He was accompanied by another boy about the same age but about two inches taller. During the interview, I asked them about their schoolwork an other activities. the smaller boy was more energetic than the larger one. he admitted that he was the boss over the larger boy. I have noticed this with the boys who come to the disco. They are frequently in small groups of three or four with one always leading the activity.

In seeing patients waiting in the reception room, I sometimes form a first impression of what might be the complaint. Yesterday, a boy about seventeen was sitting in the wooden chair near the door. I thought he might have gonorrhea. He had long hair, a beard and was wearing shorts, a little early for shorts. When I examined him, his complaint was that he had had a wreck on a trail bike and had a large burn along the inside of his left thigh.

I am having a lot of children brought in with sore throats now. This frequently happens in the spring. Years ago, it was sore throats and measles. While I am examining the child with the illness, the other child that is brought along because there is no one left at home to look after it, frequently asks for some medicine too or for me to look at some scratch or bruised place. This is to get recognition. I wonder why attention is so important. I think it must be necessary to make the other child feel worthy or accepted as a person. They would feel like they were denied something if I didn't recognize them.

Yesterday, a father brought his son and his daughter to the office. The son was about five years old, the daughter about four. The son had a sore throat. he was a very bright little boy. While examining him, I thought of the responsibility a parent has to his child. It should be his duty to see that the child develops into the best person possible, able to survive and prosper in society. To do this, the parent would need to spend a lot of time working with the child. With society the way it is now, this is most impossible.

Both parents work, leaving the child in a day care center. There, the child is in a group and probably spends most of the time watching television. Later, when he starts to school, he is under the influence of teachers and other children. Then there is the group-planned activity after school so that the child is soon lost to the parent.

At the theater we are still having our disco dances with children running all over the building. I have been wondering if we will ever make any money at the theater. So far we are about making expenses. I called the insurance company the first of the week to see that the insurance was still in effect and was surprised to find that none of my policies were covering activities at the theater. After some pleading, I finally got the company to insure each weekend activity against liability for twenty-five dollars a weekend. That is about all we take in. The insurance company said that people are so suit-conscious now that they are afraid of almost everything.

I can agree with that. whenever a patient is involved in the slightest accident, he wants everything cleared by x-ray just to make sure. If socialized medicine ever comes, the cost will be tremendous because people will want everything since it doesn't cost any more to them.

Recently, I have been giving a lot of thought to what direction to take in my life at this point. I am sure I am on some important plateau of life. My strength is not near what it was some years ago. I can't tolerate tension and anxiety as well. I am searching for an aim for my activities rather than just the daily routine. I would like to be like a little girl who comes to the disco. She loves a little boy she dances with very much. He stood her up last Saturday. She spent most of the evening going to the front door looking for him. After about an hour, I asked her if she wasn't awfully mad with him. She said she wasn't. She loved him too much to get mad.

It would be so nice to be able to work and deal with people without becoming tense and anxious or upset. Perhaps some of the feeling of being on some plateau is due the fact that I have just completed executing my will. It seems a little like being at an airport getting a ticket for some tremendous place and knowing all the time that you are not going to be the one to the use the ticket.

For the time being, the best aim I can come up with for the day and for the rest of my time is to try to be a better person. After thinking of this, it seems possible that this could be the whole aim of a person, even beginning in childhood with the parents. their aim is to help the child develop into a worthy person. it would be well for this person to continue this development into a lifetime goal of being a better person. In doing so, he would continually have to be serving humanity and serving other people.

49

Drawing conclusions

6-17-1979 ✎

The weather has been warming until now with the temperature sometimes in the eighties. Last night, we had what people call a soaking
rain, a slow continuous drizzle that soaks into the ground. It was a
needed rain, in that the gardens and lawns were getting dry.

I have a bird feeder that a former patient had given to me years ago
for Christmas. I was surprised at all the birds that have come to it.
There are a lot of cardinals, jaybirds, brown thrashers, peewees and
chickadees. Some birds on the ground are walkers and some are hoppers. The doves and starlings are walkers. jays, sparrows, bobolinks and
some others are hoppers. The pecking order starts with the large blackbirds with long tails, then jaybirds, cardinals, bobolinks, and brown
thrashers on down to the sparrows. I suspect if the crows find the
feeder, they probably will be above the blackbirds.

Yesterday, I mentioned my bird feeder to one of my patients,
remarking about the crows. He asked me if I knew that crows had a
funeral for their dead. I said I didn't know that. He then said that they
would wait in a field for an injured crow to die. At sundown, all the
crows around, would leave that area and would never come back to
that field. I said I had never heard this about crows.

He then told me another thing about crows. He said that they
would have court for the guard crow if it had let something happen to
the gang of crows. He recalled one afternoon when he was a boy on his
farm. Crows were making a lot of noise in one of the hollows. To find
out what the trouble was, he slipped through the woods and down the

side of a hill into the hollow. There, in a small clearing surrounded by large pine trees, were crows in all the trees, and in the clearing there was one crow all by itself. Occasionally, it made some kind of noise. After about thirty minutes, the crows in the trees stopped cawing. The crow on the ground made a few sounds and then all the crows in the pine trees descended on the crow in the clearing and in a few minutes they had killed it and flew away in various directions. He said that the crow on the ground had probably been a guard crow and let something happen to the other crows, so they killed it.

So far, I haven't seen any crows at the feeder, though today I heard some down along the creek.

My practice seems to be holding about the same as last year. The big change is in the request of patients. They most all want some kind of record now, a receipt for taxes or to give their employer showing that they were at the office. Some need a statement to give their employer so that they can get pay for being out of work. I think most all of my patients now have some sort of insurance.

Some of my patients go to the county health department each week to get their blood pressure checked. The health department puts the findings down on a pocket card and when the patient is out of medicine they come to me expecting me to write a prescription for the medicine without checking on their pressure. Yesterday I had such a patient. He said that I had told him that he would need to take the medicine all his life and thought that he had a permanent prescription at the pharmacy. He was very upset when I told him I would have to check on his pressure before writing a new prescription. He couldn't understand, or didn't want to understand, that if he has medication with my name on the bottle, I am pretty much responsible for him whenever something happens.

I think he had got caught by an order I gave the pharmacist just a day or two ago. I called and cancelled all my orders allowing patients to get medication as they desired because of an alarming incident that happened last Friday.

When I returned to the office after lunch, there was a fairly old model pickup truck in the parking lot. I didn't recognize it and as I went into the office, a man about twenty-five years old inquired if I was the doctor. I answered that I was and asked the trouble. He said that he wanted me to write a prescription for an electric wheelchair for his father. I then asked if had been treating his father. He said yes I had been treating him and that cortisone had affected his hands so that he could not use a conventional wheelchair. He had called Medicare and had been told if he could get his doctor to write a prescription for a wheelchair they would pay for it.

I asked if he had his father with him and he said yes, he was in the truck. I didn't recognize the man. I took his name and after looking through my records found that I had seen him in 1971, eight years ago. I had written a prescription for cortisone, but had no record of examining him or rendering any other treatment. I went back to the pickup and inquired if he had any bottles of mine showing that I was still furnishing the cortisone. He said yes and handed me a vial with a 1971 date on it.

When I called the pharmacist he checked the prescription and said I had marked it to be filled whenever the patient desired and they had been filing it each month since. I then requested that he not fill any prescriptions beyond a year without checking with me. I wrote him a new prescription for a month's supply so that he will have to check with me whenever it runs out. We discussed the wheelchair further. He had rather severe arthritis and needed a wheelchair. I suggested they try a conventional chair first and if he was unable to use one then to check out the electric chair. It will cost about a thousand dollars, but this is not concern of theirs as they are expecting Medicare to pay for it. I expect they will call me tomorrow.

Some patients are very nice and appreciative of my services. Yesterday I received a thank you note from Mollie for the services I had given her husband. He died about a week ago. she called for me to come to see him just as Dorothy and I were closing the office Thursday evening. We had started out for dinner. I told Dorothy to wait until I made the call.

When I got to the house, he was sitting up on a stool with his elbows braced on a kitchen bar so that he could hold his head up. He was using nasal oxygen from a tank he had at home. His color was gray to light purple. I couldn't hear any heart sounds. I tried massaging his chest and he gasped a few times. I think I felt a slight pulse.

With Mollie helping me, we lifted him from the stool to a reclining chair and called the rescue squad. While waiting for the rescue people, Mollie called a friend of his who came with his wife right away. I continued artificial respiration and heart massage until the rescue squad arrived. They came in with their mechanical resuscitators and took over. I felt like he was dead and I think Mollie thought so too, but due to the fact that sometimes something else can still be done, I agreed for the ambulance people to take him to the hospital under what they called a code blue. I felt like Mollie would feel better knowing that all had been done that could be done.

It was a pretty sad feeling seeing the ambulance pull out screaming with a friend and patient I had cared for the last thirty years. Thinking of him now, I don't think I will give any more concern to the patients that grumble about their prescriptions being refilled. If they don't like me for their doctor, I will be a great deal better off without them.

Today I went to the office to see a young patient. His mother has called for me to see him because of chest pains. After seeing him, he and his mother expressed their appreciation in every way they know how.

I am not doing well at the theater again. I closed the disco last week. Our attendance had dropped off so that it was not profitable to continue. Too, I think Ron was getting tired, so we are closing for the summer. I am sorry for the children. For some of them, it was the only thing they had for Saturday night.

Last Friday, a week ago, when I went out to check the temperature, the thermometer was not on the minnow tank as I had left it. I looked in the water and couldn't see it. I felt sure someone had stolen it. Checking around a little ways from the tank I noticed the honeysuckle vines were turned, suggesting someone or something had come up from the creek to the tank.

I followed the turned vines to the creek and across a foot log and down the creek and toward a house. Along the way, I found a notebook belonging to a boy I know lives in the house. I felt sure he had visited my minnow tank and taken my thermometer. I wondered how best to tell him what I suspected. Finally, I decided to tell him that I had found his notebook while looking for my thermometer. When I dialed his number there was no answer. I decided to try again in a few days.

Meanwhile, I checked the trail again and found that the honeysuckle was turned leading across the lot from the tank and then down through the woods to the foot log and toward the house that belonged to the boy. I continued to check on the minnows and since none were hatching out, I decided to take out a cloth screen that I had put in the tank. It was on a slant in the tank so that it would seem like the bank of a lake. after laying it out under the oak tree to dry, I took another look in the tank to see if I could see any sign of small minnows. There in the bottom of the tank, I saw my thermometer.

When I pulled it out, it had considerable algae on it, so that I didn't believe the boy had returned it and thrown it in the tank. I think it had fallen into the tank and rolled under the cloth screen so that I couldn't' see it.

I am still trying to determine how I came to such a wrong conclusion.

50

ABC appointment

7-7-1979

We are having most unusual weather for this time of year. The last time it was this cold in July was in 1930. At present I am sitting in the playroom with my coat on, the windows shut and the heat on. The sun is hidden by a big light gray cloud that has given us a slow drizzly rain all day, though the weatherman predicted a fair and sunny day. Now at nine o'clock in the evening. It feels like the temperature is sixty degrees. Ordinarily this time of year it would be about eighty degrees. When I ate lunch with Melvin and Mary he said he had to turn his heat on to keep warm. At the office this morning Sarah closed all the windows to keep the heat in.

Dorothy and some friends left Tuesday to visit friends in Los Angeles. I thought since she had company to travel with her it would be a good time to go visit our daughter, Gail. Dorothy called today and said she was getting along all right.

It seems that there is no end to the worry today. In addition to gas problems, grasshoppers eating up the rangeland, and all kinds of bugs and blight attacking vegetables, we now have the Skylab to worry about. Now it has gotten out of control and is falling to earth. Today's paper sets next Wednesday for the day it is due to hit the earth. It sounds a little like doomsday is really coming though not so big as predicted. They think some of it will partially burn up whenever it hits the earth's atmosphere, but a lot of pieces are not going to burn, the largest weighing about five thousand pounds. They don't know where it is going to land.

Another worry already on the earth and closer at hand is the Kudzu vines growing across the creek around the ball field. Kudzu is a vine with a broad leaf that looks a lot like a fig leaf and grows a lot like honeysuckle. It was first brought here from Japan to control soil erosion. It does this by covering and climbing on everything. Jim said if I don't get it stopped now it will soon take over the creek and stop it up. My neighbor Alva, who lives at the west end of the ball field on the next ridge first brought its encroachment to our attention when she noticed mosquitoes, rats, snakes and some other vermin were coming into her yard from the Kudzu vines. The county owns the ball field so she sent a petition to the county school board asking the county to get rid of the nuisance plant. I signed it to keep the Kudzu out of the creek. She said it had started taking over her yard and was climbing the utility poles supporting the lights around the ball field. At night the lights shining through the Kudzu were so ghostly she couldn't sleep.

In her petition she states, "There has been snakes seen sliding from my yard into the vines and we are unable to kill them, large rats come into our yard and run back in the vines before our cat can catch them. At night mosquitoes come out so bad we can't sit in the yard no more. Not long ago some other kind of vermin came up in my yard just at dark and sat on his hind feet staring at me. I am afraid to live here."

There were a few other things listed in the petition that I don't remember. A few days ago she called her neighbor to come look at the vermin staring at her. They chased it into a garbage can, put the lid on it and called the police, but before they got there it had pushed the lid off and got away. Jim said if it had a short hairy tail it was a ground hog. We talked about groundhogs for a while and then he invited me down to his house for dinner since he knew that Dorothy was visiting in California. After a nice meal we discussed some of our fishing trips and the couple of times we went grouse hunting around Boone. Just before leaving I noticed a small statue of a bird dog on the fireplace. I asked him if it was old George, a brown pointer everybody knew because he roamed all over town when Jim didn't have him out hunting. Jim picked it up and rubbed it a bit,

"No, that's old Don," he said. "Don was a setter. Don was before George."

We had a very enjoyable evening.

My practice is dropping off some. I think it might be because some of my patients are on vacation. I was surprised to see the patient I had sent to another doctor sometime ago. He is the patient that used to have the big political dinners down east each summer and invited all the sheriffs, state patrolmen, judges and police. He did not get along well in the hospital and had come to see me again to see what he should do. I had referred him to a surgeon, but someway someone else saw him. I made him another appointment and he was very grateful.

When he left a couple that had been living together for two years came in to see me. The man had some friends in another state and had been out to visit them. While there he contracted gonorrhea. When he returned he gave it to his girlfriend and now I am treating both of them. I think they will get married after this. Each night he goes by his wife's trailer to pick up the little girl born to him and his wife to spend the night with him and his girlfriend while the little girl's mother works third shift in one of the plants.

I have another female patient about fifty years old with headaches. Mostly her headaches are on the weekend. I see heron Mondays. I think they are a result of anxiety. She is living with her boyfriend and her husband lives a few miles up the road with another woman. My patient is having trouble deciding whether her boyfriend is jealous of her first husband and what to do about family reunions and birthday affairs of her children by her husband. Her children are living with him. When she goes to church she doesn't know whether to sit with her children or her boyfriend. She always gets a headache on Sundays. She doesn't have any children yet by her boyfriend. I wonder how all these people living together and not married are going to know whose children are whose, especially when the children are old enough to marry. Will they be marrying their own distant kin?

There was a little flurry of activity at the last town board meeting. It was their last meeting of the year. Their budget year ends the last of June. Commissioner Tucker nominated a fellow schoolteacher, Commissioner Helton, to the ABC board to replace Pete Bumgarner. He said the ABC Board had not sold the land and we still had not turned over all the money to the town and now was the time for the town commissioners to make the change or just keep their mouths shut. Pete was appointed by a vote of four to two.

That meeting's minutes also reflect that the ABC board gave the town commissioners Seventy-five thousand dollars for the schools, which they voted to put in reserve for the town and not distribute to the schools. The opinion of the committee Bert appointed in December to work with us was that we should keep the land and turn over the money as we thought best to the town. I think it makes no difference what the ABC board does. Some people want us to resign or to be replaced.

51

A choking child

Our weatherman on the television called our weather a Bermuda High, a high-pressure area off the east coast extending to Bermuda. For the last three weeks it has been hot sticky weather with rain two or three times a day.

Last Tuesday Dorothy and I went to the beach with her sister Mary. She and Mary walked the beach while I fished. My fishing was very poor, four spots was my total catch for the trip. I can recall twenty years ago I could always catch fish in the surf, a few blues, flounder and Virginia mullet. Now I think they have been caught out.

However there is always something different about each beach trip. This time along the surf over the first breakers small gulls were flying about a hundred feet high. Whenever they spotted something in the wave below they would flutter in mid air as if injured, then dive straight down into the water. After the dive they flew along the top of the wave gaining speed to climb for another dive. We had a very pleasant trip and returned home Friday night.

At the office Monday morning I had a very interesting patient.

About ten o'clock a mother and grandmother brought a little girl one year old for me to see. The grandmother had recommended me to the mother because I had been her doctor. The mother said the child had been having coughing and smothering spells since Friday night. This morning it had got so bad her husband had to blow in the child's mouth and pump her chest to get her to breathe again. I watched the girl breathe while she sat on her grandmother's lap. I couldn't detect any breathing difficulty. There was no runny nose or sneezing. I checked the temperature and pulse, all were normal.

When I listened to her chest there seemed to be some wheezing on the right side. I asked if they had been giving her any medicine. They had been giving her cough medicine a doctor prescribed for her on Saturday. My first thought to this was to advise them to take the child back to the doctor they had seen Saturday, but then I recalled the grandmother had brought the child for me to see; she wanted me to do something for the child.

While I watched, the child coughed again very lightly, a little like a cough I hear when a child has the croup or whooping cough. It sounds a little like something is stopped up. My thoughts now were she might have bronchitis. I could give some antibiotics and see if they would help by tomorrow, but the practice of medicine is not so simple. Things are often not what they seem. Something more than just a simple cough was causing this child to lose her breath. I thought I had better look in the throat though there was no complaint of sore throat.

I used a tongue blade. The girl's throat was a pale pink, no evidence of infection. What could be the trouble?

When I removed the tongue blade the child gagged and started a series of coughs. After the fourth cough something happened and the girl turned blue. She couldn't breath. I thought she was going to die before she started to breath again. The child had some very serious condition. I asked the grandmother to take her to the emergency room of one of the hospitals and tell the doctor I recommended hospitalization.

About two hours later they were back in my office. After taking a chest x-ray of the child at the hospital the doctor told the grandmother the child had a mild case of croup and prescribed another cough syrup. The grandmother argued with the nurse, insisting that I said the child should be hospitalized. The nurse said she had seen lots of children like this and this one was not going to die. At the front desk the grandmother was still pleading for hospitalization and didn't leave the hospital until she was threatened to be expelled by the security guard. The grandmother said on the way home the child had a coughing spell and turned blue. They had to stop the car on the river bridge with all the traffic and blow in the child's mouth and throw her up in the air to get her breathing again.

I believed something was in the child's windpipe. Sometimes it blocked the airway and sometimes it didn't. If the child coughed something blocked the airway it was too serious for her to be sent home. I called the office of a group of pediatricians and asked them to see the child. They said to send her down.

To be sure they saw what I was seeing I told the grandmother to be sure they made the child gag the way she saw me do with the tongue depressor before the child left the hospital. She said she would see to it even if she had to stick her finger down the girl's throat in front of them.

During the afternoon I kept expecting a call from the grandmother or the pediatrician. Around four o'clock I called the pediatrician's office. A nurse answered. She said I couldn't talk to the doctor attending the child because he was just getting into the ambulance to take the child to Baptist Hospital in Winston-Salem. When the doctor examined the child's throat like the grandmother requested the child had a choking spell. They had been working with oxygen for the last hour to get the patient stabilized for the trip to the hospital. With special x-ray equipment they had found a piece of plastic in the trachea.

Around six o'clock the grandmother called me at home. The surgeons had just removed the piece of plastic from the trachea. The little girl was doing fine and could come home tomorrow.

Wednesday morning the pediatrician who went with the child to Baptist Hospital called me. He first thought the child had the croup and had started a treatment for the croup, but the grandmother wouldn't leave his office until he made the child gag. When he did the child turned cyanotic. He had to work for an hour in the office resuscitating her.

Sometimes I wonder why I am doing the kind of practice I am doing rather than being in a hospital. I think it is because I wanted to be with my family and close to people. I think the people appreciate me, judging from the vegetables they give me and the friendliness they show whenever they see me on the streets in town. This doesn't hold for the town commissioners, however.

52

Limbo

I am calling this writing "Limbo" meaning a time of uncertainty. Dorothy is due to have a hysterectomy but the time has not been decided. In town there is the appeal by Duke's father to get his land rezoned. From some of my patients I have heard some of the town commissioners are not satisfied with the ABC land and money. All of these uncertainties make this time a state of limbo.

Our weather is hot and depressing. Some people call it "Dog Days." I think it is because the constellation called the Dog Star is visible. We have not had any rain for a week or two. My garden is drying up.

My practice seems to be going along fairly well. My little girl that had the plastic in her throat is home and happy.

Mr. Allen, the man that gave the big political dinners is going to Baptist Hospital to have his spleen removed. He came by to bring me some beans and tomatoes. When he went outside a boy I had engaged to mow the grass was trying to get his lawn mower started. Mr. Allen stopped to help him. Both of them were bent over it and couldn't get it to run. I took a screwdriver and pair of pliers and went out to help.

The throttle had rusted shut. We could get it to run for about ten seconds. Due to frequent interruptions to see a patient I finally gave up and told the boy to come back tomorrow. We already had five other people giving advice.

In the office all my patients seemed to be in a hurry. At least it seemed this way to me. The problem was probably me. I had too many other things on my mind. I needed to get Dorothy to the hospital at one o'clock If some accident or real sick patient came in I might not be able to leave on time.

I left Sarah in charge at eleven o'clock and Dorothy and I went to lunch and on to the hospital. I left her at three o'clock to return to the office. At five o'clock. I came back to the hospital and stayed until visiting hours were over.

At home I spent a restless night worrying about Dorothy. In the morning when I returned to the hospital she said she had slept well. Her operation was scheduled for ten o'clock. Soon her three sisters arrived. They said they would stay with her until after the operation. When the nurse came with the stretcher to take her to the operating room I came back to the office.

Whenever the phone rang I expected it to be a call from the hospital calling about Dorothy. At eleven-thirty I went to lunch. When I returned Sarah said the hospital had been trying to call me and they had not operated. There was something wrong with her EKG and blood potassium. In some ways I was glad for I hoped she might get better without the operation.

When I arrived at the hospital Dorothy was very sleepy. They had prepared to operate and the anesthetist had prepared the intravenous anesthesia when he suddenly decided the blood potassium and EKG were not satisfactory. The doctor was going to discharge her tomorrow and give medication for three weeks and then do the operation.

Thursday morning on the way home I told her Granite Falls was in the papers again. There was a big headline in the Press "Granite Going To Court." Therman and Duke are appealing the judge's ruling on rezoning their property residential when the zoning board had approved zoning it commercial. Duke had a long letter to the editor expressing his feelings toward John for blocking progress in the town. In his editorial he said things are pretty bad in the country whenever they have come to the point where other folks can dictate what one can do with their own property. There were two open forum letters supporting Therman and a notice that there were some petitions circulating in town for people to sign requesting the town to rezone Therman's property commercial. The court date is set for sometime in September. I told Dorothy I was surprised at Duke for complaining so about other people wanting to control his property. He has been on the zoning board for ten years making decisions about what happened to other people's property, but now when his father's property is involved he wants an exception made. The rules are all right for other folks but not for Duke.

He will probably resign from the zoning board if the property is not rezoned.

53

Snake bit

I am calling this writing "Snake bit" in the sense Jim uses it when we are fishing. It means nothing is going right for you. You can have the same lure as your companion, cast it in the same place as he does, but for some reason your lure hangs a stump, a rock, a bush, or the hook fouls up with the sinker or float. While you are getting your line together for another cast your companion brings in a nice fish. You can call it a run of bad luck that lasts for several hours until for some unknown reason things start going right for you again.

The last few days have been going like this for me, Snake bit, as Jim calls it.

They began about ten days ago with a call early in the morning from a patient who said, "I have been stung by "waspies." Will you come to the office?"

I said I would meet him there in ten minutes. It was eight o'clock when the call came in. He was at the office when I arrived, holding his left hand up for me to see the swelling. I gave him an injection and some antihistamine tablets. Before I could get my coat on there was a commotion coming from the reception room and someone else calling for me.

As I approached the reception room from the emergency room a man was carrying a boy about twelve years old with a towel wrapped around his left ankle.

"This boy's been snake bit. We didn't see the snake," he said, putting the boy down in a chair.

The boy unwrapped the towel and pointed to the place on his ankle. There were two puncture wounds about an inch apart just above the ankle. There was a little swelling around each puncture site.

"He got bit about an hour ago. We didn't see the snake to tell what kind it was," the man said, wiping his hands with the towel.

It was now nine-thirty so the boy was bitten about an hour and a half ago. Judging from the swelling and redness around the area, I thought if it had been a poisonous snake he would have been much sicker and the area swollen a lot more than it was. I sent him to the hospital for further evaluation

Later in the day I called the doctor at the hospital to find out what had happened. He thought the bite was not from a poisonous snake. He observed him in the waiting room for two hours and then sent him home.

In the afternoon I became upset when one of my female patients came in to have her prescription refilled. She wanted it filled in the chemical name—the generic name. Her "enlightener" had told her if she got the doctor to write the prescription this way she could get the medicine much cheaper.

I was already prescribing the generic drug. I didn't mind refilling the prescription, but I didn't like the idea of an "enlightener" directing her treatment. Following this there were several patients wanting their insurance blanks filled out. I think the insurance companies are creating a disease among patients, suspiciousness about the doctor and getting their money back. I never know if the patient is really in pain or just trying to establish a claim to get money back from the insurance companies. If the patient were paying for his condition then there would be no question about his pain.

Things are changing so that people are expecting someone to look after them in most every way. Some time ago Dorothy and I went to Glennville to see our son Marty. When we were going through Hendersonville we were about out of gas. We passed several service stations with gas lines of four or five cars before we found one that we could drive in and fill up without waiting. When we pulled out onto the road again it was full of cars. As we turned a corner near the edge of town I noticed a sign on the same post with a road sign. The sign said "Mental Health Clinic." I told Dorothy this was the "sign of the times." Our society is now so unstable that each city must have a mental health clinic to treat the mentally disturbed people.

All the devious ways we are living, filling out forms to get something back, is driving us crazy. People are trying drugs to settle their anxiety. Most of our trouble is that people have no direction for their lives other than their immediate desires. They are busy going today without thinking of what will be needed tomorrow.

At two o'clock there was a call from the middle school. One of the students had been stung and was complaining that she couldn't breathe. Would I please come to see her? She had called for the ambulance but it had to come from Lenoir and might be too late. I told her I would come. As I drove up to the school and started to park near the walk leading to the building, I was waved away from the parking place by one of the teachers who said the space was reserved for the ambulance. I didn't like this greeting, thinking if the ambulance was going to take care of the patient why did they call for me. But then I knew if the patient was in trouble treatment was needed now.

I parked in another place and entered the hall of the building. It was a long hall with groups of children mingling about. As I passed they all seemed to look at me wondering what I was doing at school. As I hurried by I wondered what some of them would be when they were grown. Would one sometime be doing what I was doing?

At the end of the hall the secretary was waiting and directed me into the teacher's lounge. There on a couch was a young girl about fifteen years old. She was calm, conscious and didn't seem to be in any distress. She said bee stings made her sick. I sat my medical bag down and pulled out my stethoscope to listen to her heart.

She pulled away saying, "No, No, not him," meaning me.

I reacted rather strongly to this by putting my stethoscope back in my bag and saying, "I don't want to treat anyone that doesn't want me." And got up, preparing to leave. The secretary urged her to let me examine her. By now the principal had entered the room and was insisting that she be examined.

I was wondering what to do when an elderly lady entered the room. She said she was her mother. She talked to her daughter and asked me to examine her. There was a little swelling about the size of a fifty-cent piece on her left arm where she said she had been stung. I gave her a Benadryl capsule.

The ambulance crew was on hand now so I told them to take her to the hospital. I never like to treat a patient who doesn't want my services. Later in the day the mother called to say the hospital had not given her daughter any additional treatment and she was doing fine. So far neither daughter nor mother have paid or thanked me for coming to the school.

When I returned to the office from the school there were four patients waiting. One was an elderly man waiting with a lady about the same age, about seventy years old. I have had some disagreements with him about my fees. A year ago I told him if he could find a doctor to do his work cheaper I wished he would do it. Since then he has not said a word about fees. He has paid and said thank you.

Now he is bringing his neighbor, an elderly lady about his age. I think she has had some kind of stroke affecting her left leg. I have seen her three times in the last two months. I have been checking on her blood pressure. After examining her today he asked me if I said she should be in a nursing home.

"No," I said, "I have not discussed her condition with anyone. You have been present every time I have seen her, but it might be a good thing for her to go to a nursing home if she hasn't got any body to look after her."

He then said someone had said I had recommended this and that I had also said that she couldn't look after herself. To this I replied she should have someone to look after her.

He replied angrily, "If the son of a bitch that said these things says another word about it I am going to stick my knife in him."

I didn't reply, but I was thinking a lot.

I recalled the first time he had brought this patient to see me along with his wife. His wife waited in the reception room while he helped her back to the examining room. When I was through with her he helped me walk her out to his car. His wife was waiting in the front seat. He told her to get out and get in the back and helped this lady into the front seat. On subsequent visits his wife had not been along. I think he is developing an affair with this lady. Thinking of it now, I don't believe he has complained of a thing since he has been bringing her to see me. It might be that love has taken hold and he doesn't need any treatment. Even at his age it might be that a spark of love can relieve a lot of aches and pain in an old body.

My next patient was a lady carrying a little boy two years old with a towel wrapped around his left arm soaked in blood. She said he had cut it on a storm door. I unwrapped the towel to see what was wrong. He had a long gash near the elbow and one about two inches long at the wrist. He was quite excited so I told the mother we would need a lot of holding. She said she thought so too and had brought her mother along to help.

I placed the child on the examining table with the grandmother holding his head and the mother holding the pelvis and legs. After cleaning the cuts and injecting them with Novocain the child kept screaming. I had about finished suturing when the mother said she felt faint. She was pale and sweating so I told her to go to the reception room and sit down. I had the dressing about on when a lady from the reception room came back asking for a towel with cold water. She said the mother had fainted.

Sarah who was holding the arm turned it loose to prepare the towel. The grandmother holding the head said the lights were going out in the room. Before I could catch her she collapsed on the floor.

Sarah returned from the reception room and prepared another wet towel for the grandmother lying beside the sink. She revived the grandmother enough to sit in the white chair at the end of the sink. I finished with my dressing and she carried the boy out to the mother now revived and waiting in the reception room. When she returned I asked if there were any patients in the waiting room.

"Yes," she said. "They are all out there and some are standing up." I was surprised that there were any left with all the fainting and screaming for the last thirty minutes. I think that people are so concerned with their problem that whatever is happening to someone else is not their concern. This is not entirely true because a lady did come back to get a towel for the mother when she fainted.

After seeing all the patients I closed the office around six o'clock to go home to check on Dorothy. She returned from the hospital Sunday after her surgery. I worried a lot about her surgery since before the operation there was again the question of her potassium level and an irregular heart beat.

During the time of operation I considered all the things that could go wrong. It was a great relief when they brought her back to the room. Since her return home she has been having chest pains. I told her it was probably rheumatic pains, though I knew it could be a small pulmonary embolism or a slight coronary occlusion, both, if large enough, can be fatal.

In some ways I think it is worse to know all of the possibilities that can be taking place than to not know. Her operation has been a trying experience for both of us. A great help has been support from all our friends and the many get well cards. We didn't know we had so many friends.

I guess Duke and his father Therman are looking for friends to support their petition to get the town to zone their property commercial. They are going to court December 17th to settle the matter.

Jim and I are planning to go to the beach next Monday night. We have been busy preparing our tackle and getting our wives settled for the few days at the beach. We plan to return Thursday night. We have learned now what Raymond means by "Flower Day." Years ago when we planned to go fishing he said he would have to get some candy and flowers for his wife, he called it Flower Day, getting permission to go. When he got married the last time he said he put it in the marriage contract that he could go fishing whenever I called him. Now that Jim and I have no children at home with our wives we find that our wives don't like to be left alone either.

54

End of the theater

10-3-1979 ✓

September has gone by very fast. Generally it is a dry month with cool nights and warm days, but this September was wet with rain most every day. Tonight the air is a little cool, suggesting that fall is not far away. While mowing the grass I noticed the maple leaves are beginning to turn yellow. Soon all the leaves will have their fall colors of yellow, red and orange.

Dorothy is still a little sore from her hysterectomy. She had to rest a while this afternoon due to some pain in her right side. I think the pain is due to some adhesions. So far she has gotten along better than I expected. She is doing the book work at the office and filling out the insurance forms. Almost every patient now has some kind of form to be filled out in connection with his or her visit. A few days ago a lady was in the office wanting me to fill out a paper showing she couldn't wear shoes with steel toes. On her job she is required to wear them in the event of and accident. Because her second toe is longer than her big toe she said she couldn't wear shoes with steel toes. On examining her toes, for sure her second toe was longer than her big toe, but no more than I normally see on other people. I told her I couldn't excuse her from wearing the required shoes, but if she came back to the office with a blister on her toe from the shoes I could excuse her.

Another patient said she was tired and wanted a paper filled out requesting a rest leave for two weeks. I didn't believe this was a medical decision; she needed to work this out with his employer. If I were to request one rest leave I would have the whole plant wanting forms filled out for two weeks' rest.

Saturday afternoon and Sunday I spent a great deal of time worrying about getting a man's wife committed to an institution for alcoholism. They both have responsible positions in town. I wanted to help as much as possible. I was in the theater Saturday afternoon when the husband came to the front door and called for me.

He said we were going to have to do something about his wife. She was drinking too much and needed to be committed for treatment. He had already seen the magistrate and had commitment papers drawn up. He planned for the sheriff to seize his wife and bring her to the office for me to examine and then refer her to an institution for alcoholism.

I was unaware of his wife's drinking, but agreed to be available to examine her when he needed me. Sunday around two o'clock when the phone rang he said he had his wife in the car with the sheriff and would be at my office in ten minutes. He wanted his wife admitted to a hospital. This was different than what he said on Saturday.

I waited at the office until around three o'clock when he finally arrived with his wife and the sheriff. He came in and announced that he had her outside in the car. I asked him to bring her in to the office where I could talk to her. When she came in she was not wild or belligerent. She sat down and asked me to close the door so her husband couldn't hear us talk. She said her husband beat her up every weekend and was mean to her. I didn't believe this; I had never seen her beaten up. There was a strong odor of alcohol on her breath and her speech was slurred. She said she had been drinking, but not that much. I found a psychiatrist to admit her for a few days.

Monday morning her husband came by the office to thank me for helping him in a very difficult situation. In some ways these situations are a little like a triangle love affair in which no one ends up happy. At the moment the husband is pleased that his wife is sobering up, but when she comes home she may not be happy about the way she was seized and sent to the hospital. He will not be happy about this. Neither will she be happy with me for sending her, though she volunteered to go.

Because she is unhappy with me I will lose her as a patient.

There isn't any easy way out of a situation like this. I do what I think is right and best for the patient, though the patient may disagree with my decision.

Later in the morning a man asked me about renting the theater for a warehouse to keep cloth in. I agreed to talk to him about it in the afternoon. After two years of trying to make a go of the entertainment business I decided to give up. When he came to look it over he wanted the seats taken out. We took three or four rows out and put them beside the building. A lady came in and said her pastor wanted the seats for his church and asked would I let her have them? I said yes if you will move them. She agreed and was back in a few minutes with her pastor and some deacons. They had the seats out and gone in a few hours.

The man renting the building was happy, whistling all the time.

Tuesday morning I went to a Republican executive meeting in Lenoir. We were selecting candidates for the coming election in the county and state. Our town election is about six weeks away. We have three candidates running, Simmons and Johnson, both incumbents and one new man, Clay. The two incumbents will have a hard time getting elected. After so many decisions a lot of people are against a candidate. A new man has a good chance with a clean record. The opposition has two new candidates. For Bert to have any strength in city hall we will have to get all three of our candidates elected.

According to the paper, at one of the town meetings a few weeks ago one of the council members brought up the ABC audit again. They are wondering what about our money and want us to make another distribution, though it is not the end of the quarter. I called our auditor Monday and suggested he write a letter stating that we are not in position to make a distribution at this time.

Jim and I went fishing a few weeks ago at Topsail. A few years ago at the close of the fishing season I began to wonder about making a uniform for fishing. Seems like whenever we get ready to go I have to search around for all kinds of coats and pants. I wrote my thoughts down and will tell you how they go:

With the closing of the fishing season and the quietness of fall I begin to reflect on the past fishing events. The big ones that broke the line, the nice ones we caught and the places we went to and didn't go to. As I gather up all my old fishing shoes, pants, shirts and hats to pack in the closet until next season an idea struck me. Why not throw all these old dirty clothes away, design a uniform, a fisherman's uniform. With a standard uniform I wouldn't need all these old clothes. No longer would I need an assortment of shirts, pants and coats.

A ready-made suit with detachable sections and various colors would be fine. It could be designed to be comfortable in hot or cold weather, wet or dry. It could have pockets for sinkers, plugs and line. A hat to go with it could be designed for wet or dry weather. It would look nice and we would all look a lot alike, all in a fisherman's uniform.

This part started me thinking the other way. Fishermen are rather independent and vigorous people. They buffet the wind and rain, endure hot or cold weather going along with whatever natures gives. They come and go guided by their own will and fish pretty much the same way. They represent a genuine cross-section of the American spirit of freedom and individuality. When you look up and down the pier each fisherman has selected clothing to fit his aptness for the sport. For people like this I don't believe I could design a uniform for all their likes and dislikes.

A beginner would find the uniform had too many pockets; the skilled would not want but one or two pockets. Taking another look at each fisherman in action I see each one has selected his clothing according to his likes and knowledge of what is needed. Perhaps in life what we wear is a suit accepted by us according to our understanding of us and our life's work. A uniform created for me by someone else wouldn't feel near as comfortable as my old clothes. My old clothes are like old friends, I best keep them for another season.

55

Town election plan

10-27-1979 ✓

Now we are having delightful fall weather, a time of year called Indian Summer when the leaves are in full color, yellow, pink, red, orange and a few purple. It is fascinating to stand under the trees and watch the leaves come down. Some come twirling, some oscillating like the end of a pendulum and some sail down like little boats. Leaves have made my yard like a large quilt of fall colors.

Along the streets there are large piles of leaves waiting for the town to pick up. At night the temperature is around forty degrees making for good sleeping conditions. During the day the temperature rises to about seventy. The sun is very bright so it is nice to just sit some place where the rays shine on your back seeming to penetrate all the way through.

With the coming of fall weather, people are beginning to wonder about the cost of oil for heating their home for the winter. When I stopped at Monday's service station to get my tires changed he asked me about solar heat. He wondered about solar heat heating water on top of the house in tanks during the day and stored in a tank in the basement during the night. It could be circulated from the basement tank through the hot water pipes at night. I think he got the idea from some magazine.

Though we are having delightful weather, in some other areas we are not doing so good. There is a lot of pollution in our streams from industrial waste and from atomic energy plants.

The stock marked dropped rather drastically last week. It was probably due to the action taken by the Federal Reserve Board. They raised the interest rate for prime borrowers up to 15.75 percent. This is the highest it has ever been. It was reported that they raised it this high because the banks reported that they had a lot of money, however after a few days checking the news media reported that the Federal Reserve Board had made a big mistake. The banks did not have all the money they had figured they had.

I don't know what will happen next. Inflation is eating away everyone's savings. Prices continue to rise. With prices going up I am trying to raise my fees in the office. I have raised the price of some services, but mostly my fees are locked in by what is allowed by the compensation commission, Medicare, Medicaid and those set by the insurance companies.

Generally my practice is staying about the same. I am having a lot of insurance troubles from forms I fill out. Sometimes the day is filled with irregularities. It takes a lot of patience to get through the day.

Eggers, a game warden came by yesterday to find out if a dog could get hydrophobia from a squirrel bite. He was called out to check on a squirrel that had attacked two boys at school and they had set their dog on the squirrel. The dog killed the squirrel but in the process the squirrel bit the dog. I told him I thought the dog would get infected if the squirrel had rabies, and that if the children played with the dog later they also could get infected by a scratch from the dog's mouth. He had sent the squirrel to Raleigh to have it checked for rabies. I saw the report about the squirrel attacking the boys last night but so far Eggers hasn't heard from the laboratory whether the squirrel had rabies.

When Eggers left my next patient was a young man I have seen at the office several times. Today he was complaining of his foot. He had stepped on a tack in the furniture plant where works and came to me for treatment. When I asked him where he works he said he worked at a plant that does not send their patients to me for treatment so he had not brought a first aid slip from the plant authorizing me to treat him.

I started to call the plant to find out if they would pay me to treat him, when one of the supervisors from the plant came in. I have been giving him some medication for his headaches. I asked him to find out whether the plant would authorize me to treat the boy. He agreed to call and get authorization. After talking to several people he said they had agreed for me to treat the man and send the bill into their compensation carrier.

My next patient said that his insurance company had just called his plant and said I had not filled out his insurance papers properly. I couldn't find any error in my copies of the insurance forms. I asked him to ask the personal man to call the insurance company and find out what was wrong. He called me an hour later and said the insurance company had made a mistake and would send payment in the next mail. When I saw the next patient I noticed there was a ten dollar charge still due from his insurance company. When I asked him about it he said I had sent the forms to the wrong insurance company. After some specific questioning and review of the record I convinced him that I had sent the forms to the company he had requested. He asked me to send the forms in again. By this time I realized the day was going to be a very long one, not in the sense of hours but in getting people satisfied.

To make the events less disturbing I decided to think of time as continuous, all day and no night. Without the night, time becomes continuous. Now there is no end of time so there is no great necessity to hurry to the next situation, just take time to settle each one as they come. With this attitude the day went along without much anxiety and at five o'clock Dorothy and I closed the office to go to a fish fry Laney had arranged at the Granite Bizarre with the fish we caught last week at Topsail Island.

We left last Saturday night to go to Topsail Island after Jim closed his store. We planned to go in my red station wagon and I had it checked out for the trip on Friday, but Fin said Laney wanted to take one of his vans he uses to haul flowers to the graves for funerals. It was agreeable with me especially since I thought Finn planned to do the driving. When Laney took a van two years ago Finn insisted on doing the driving. This van was a new model and would be more comfortable and roomier than the station wagon.

To be sure we were comfortable Laney said he would put in his parlor seats for us to sit in. When I told Sarah we were going fishing in the funeral car she thought it was pretty funny. She said we would smell like flowers on the pier and at the next funeral all the flowers would smell like fish.

When I was ready to go things didn't go as I anticipated. Finn came by my house around seven o'clock and we drove to Laney's funeral home where we agreed to meet Laney and load up in his van. After we had loaded everything in the back Finn decided he didn't want to drive. Laney couldn't drive because of rheumatism and a cast on his right wrist so I was the only one left to do the driving. I climbed in on the driver's side and cranked the engine. Finn stretched out on one of the sofas back of me and Laney with his pipe going full blast climbed into the seat beside me.

He was real happy to be going fishing again. Due to poor health this was his first trip this fall. When I started off I crashed the gears. The transmission was a straight drive and it had been a long time since I had driven one. Finn yelled that I would have to do better or he would have to drive.

By the time we reached Jim's house I had it under control. As I pulled into the drive I saw Jim's wife, Dot at the kitchen window. She didn't look happy. When I stopped at the back door Jim's youngest daughter, Margaret came running out of the basement door to speak to me.

"Shame on you," she said. "Shame on you for taking daddy off fishing and making me stay at home with mother on my first vacation from school." She is a freshman in college.

"Discipline, discipline, look to discipline," I replied. I thought it was a good thing for her to spend some time with her mother. Her ill feeling made me feel pretty bad, but not bad enough to call off our fishing trip.

She turned to go into the house and called back, "I have got to be back in school Thursday so you be back Wednesday night."

I promised to be back on time.

Meanwhile Jim was loading his fishing gear in the back of the van. When he had it all in he slammed the door shut and said, "Let's go," and flopped in one of the sofa chairs back of Finn. He generally runs back into the house to tell Dot goodbye before leaving, but this time he didn't go back. I think I knew why and didn't say anything about it.

By Tuesday noon we had enough fish so we packed up and returned to Granite around nine o'clock.

Laney's fish fry turned out well. He enjoyed talking about the trip and believed he had caught the most fish. The Bizarre had cooked the fish so they were very good. Everyone seemed to enjoy the dinner. At events like this there is often some discussion about the coming town election. Someone tells who they are mad with in town, who the town manager has made mad and what some of the commissioners have done that made someone mad. It is a little like a song I have heard on the radio, "Play Another Somebody Done Somebody Wrong Song." When it comes time for an election all of these things are dug up and used as issues to get people to be concerned about voting.

My concern is over the way some of the town commissioners attacked the ABC Board. They charged us with withholding money they think we should have given to the town and that the land we bought beside the store to control the road was illegal.

I think they want to harass us into resigning so they can put in some of their party members in our place. Laney is concerned with the election because the city manager wants to take about fifty feet of his front lot to widen the street for trucks going to Rhodhiss. Dale is concerned because he is trying to get his land rezoned to commercial property so he can put up a shopping center.

The city manager probably isn't concerned because his job is pretty secure. He knows we have a poor chance of getting all three of our candidates elected. As long as he has four commissioners supporting him he is in control of the town. Mayor Bert is concerned because without getting at least two of our candidates elected he will have little to say about the affairs of the town. He has talked of resigning if we lose the election. At present there are four of the six commissioners who vote together against the mayor. In this election one of the four is up for re-election. The two that support the mayor are also up for re-election.

When Dale was in the office yesterday I asked him how he thinks the election is going. He said it was the quietest election he had ever heard of.

"Nobody is saying nothing; that's a bad sign. They have already made up their minds how they are going to vote," he said. Dale is mad with a member of the zoning board over his land deal. He believes he lied about the decision of the zoning board in order to keep his job with the college. Dale says the board voted to zone it commercial; the chairman says they did not vote to zone it commercial. Dale is so mad he refuses to be in a meeting with him for fear of "Swarping him one."

Dale has now fallen out with the city manager who put the notice of Dale's rezoning request in the Lenoir paper so John wouldn't see the notice in time to file an objection. Dale liked this, but when the city manager put an article in the paper criticizing the zoning board for zoning the property commercial Dale was ready to "swarp him one too." The article complemented the chairman of the zoning board for stating that the zoning board had not zoned the property commercial.

One of the most distressing things about the election for our candidates is that the police department is supporting the city manager and the candidates opposing the mayor. The police department has a lot of influence on an election. They are in contact with a lot of people at funerals, school crossings and visiting the stores in town.

Some weeks ago I talked to chief Barlow about the election to see if he would support our candidates. I knew from what he said about the last city manager he didn't like a city manager form of government, but this time he said he was getting along with Noble, the city manager, and as long Noble leaves him and the police department alone they will get along fine. The chief has about one and a half years to go before retirement. He said he had so much trouble with the last city manager he went down to his house one day with his shotgun intending to blow his head off. He was so mad he would have done it, but luckily for both of them the manager wasn't at home. I have not talked to him any more about the election.

There are about fifteen hundred registered voters in town. We would like for all of them to vote for our candidates Thursday. About half of this number will go to the polls and vote for various candidates. We have contacted all the voters we know who might give us support. We will find out Thursday what the voters think of the candidates.

56

Election night

11-6-1979 ✓

All the voters have been contacted that indicated they would vote one way or another for candidates in today's election. The ballots are being counted now in the city hall, our voting place for town elections. We are all anxiously waiting for reports from the polls as to what candidate is getting the most votes.

It is now nine o'clock and Bert called me to tell me that the ballots have all been counted. Only one of our candidates won, Glenn, the man from the industrial plant.

All of us did a lot of work trying to get our candidates elected. We met several times with our candidates and called all of our friends, asking for their support. We thought we had at least three hundred votes promised for our candidates, but according to the results we were pretty short. The count was 407 for Erby, 348 for Glenn, 316 for Helton 307 for Johnson, 287 for Finn and 248 for Chatman. Politics is a very sensitive business.

About thirty more votes for our candidates would have put them in office. In a town this small where everybody knows each other, I think the voters often carry a grudge against the incumbent candidate. Finn and Johnson were incumbents. Some voters may have been refused some request or feel ignored in some way or are even jealous. New people have not had to make any decisions yet so they may not have many enemies. Voters don't know them and they think a new man is better than one who has not paved a street, zoned land as requested or increased taxes.

In this election we were working for control of city hall. If my three candidates had been elected they could have supported Bert with a three to three vote. Bert could break the tie vote and have some control over city hall again.

Some of our defeat may have been due to our candidates not hiring "haulers," people who have a list of people they can pick up at certain times and take to the polls to vote for certain candidates. I didn't find out that the opposition was using haulers until a few days ago. Sarah said she wanted off from work for a few minutes to take her mother to the pole to vote but she was not going to vote at this time. When I questioned her as to why she wasn't going to vote when her mother voted she said she was to be hauled to the pole by someone. If she didn't let them haul her they would not get paid.

Just because a hauler takes a voter to the poles doesn't mean that the voter is going to vote for a particular candidate. But if the hauler is being paid a certain amount if a certain candidate wins, then the hauler will be strongly recommending his candidate to his voter. Each candidate may have his own haulers and pay them out of his campaign money.

We might have helped our candidates a little more if we had used "watchers" at the voting place. A watcher takes names of the people who have voted and every hour sends out the list to the candidates so they can see if their voters have voted. If they haven't they can call them to come vote or go after them.

When the total vote is not much over 300 for a candidate a block of thirty or forty votes for one candidate may be enough to elect the candidate. With enough money a candidate might win by using energetic haulers and the chain ballot. It works like this. The hauler goes to the pole as soon as it opens up and is given a ballot to vote in the election. He goes behind the curtain, marks the ballot for his candidate and puts it in his pocket. He pulls out a piece of paper folded to look like the ballot; he comes out of the booth and drops it in the ballot box. Now he has left the pole with an official ballot in his pocket given to him at the pole.

He gives it to the first person he hauls. They are to put it in their pocket, go into the voting place and get a ballot. They take the ballot and go behind the curtain, put the blank ballot in their pocket, pull out the marked ballot, come out and drop it in the ballot box. When they get back to the place where the hauler picked them up they hand the hauler the blank ballot and he gives them ten dollars.

Without special influence on the voter people may tell you anything about the way they are going to vote. When they go behind the curtain to vote they do as they please. One fellow I know ran for an office in an election in Rhodhiss. He said half of the people in town promised to vote for him. When the ballots were counted he got only one vote, his own. One can't tell for sure about an election.

57

Running a stop sign

11-13-1979 ✓

For several years I have been having some trouble with my right hip. It is not a very bad pain, but something of a sticking pain like it has a nail in it especially when I try to rest on it. Along with this discomfort I have developed a ringing in my ears that is very annoying especially whenever everything is still. I suspect it is the beginning of deafness. It runs on my mother's side of the family.

My hip seems to be getting worse so I have decided to have it checked on. I called an orthopedist to see me, but he said I should get it X-rayed first. In trying to decide what might be the trouble. I decided I might have a tumor of the hip with metastasis to the brain giving me the ringing in my ears. I decided to call the X-ray office Monday to see what I could find out.

Monday morning was a cloudy and wet day with a drizzling rain. It brought down the rest of my leaves. I haven't seen many birds. I think they have already gone south for the winter. They could still find plenty of seeds and things to eat but I guess they don't like cold weather. I suspect before the winter is over a lot of us will wish we could go south because of the cold and shortage of food. Iran, a country we get a lot of oil from is cutting off their supply of oil to us because we have not surrendered the Shah, their deposed leader to Iran. I think he is here to have an operation on his pancreas. The Iranians have seized about fifty Americans in the American Embassy and are holding them hostage for his return.

A news report this evening said we would soon be paying more for oil. This means most everything will cost more because it is produced in some way with oil, our principal source of energy.

To return now to my x-ray appointment, it was made for two-thirty this afternoon. During the morning I saw several patients before Dorothy came to work. One was a patient who had just returned from Taiwan and brought me a gift he thought was something very special. When I opened it, it was a little pink and blue ceramic figure about ten inches high. It was an oriental man sitting down cross-legged holding a large vase between his legs against his pelvis with one hand and in the other hand he held a small brush like he was painting something near the mouth of the vase. The vase was about five inches deep and two inches in diameter. He was holding it so the mouth was about three inches from his chest. When seen in an oblique angle it looked like he was holding one tremendous penis.

Because of this suggestion I wasn't too fond of it, but I showed as much appreciation as I could and fixed a place for it on a small shelf in the front office where I have some other gifts on display. Sarah watched me put it up but didn't say a word about it. I thought she just didn't appreciate Taiwan art and thought no more about it. When Dorothy came in around nine-thirty to take the deposit to the bank, instead of going out to the bank as usual, she came straight back to the drug room where I was getting up some medication. She inquired immediately as to where I got that thing I had put on the shelf out front. Before I could answer she demanded I get it down from there immediately.

"Get it out of this office now," she said. "It is some kind of a god and will bring us all bad luck. Go take it down now. Wrap it up and get rid of it."

When she would let me speak I told her where it came from.

"You remember David, my brother in law?" she asked. "Somebody gave him one like that and it brought him bad luck. He died a few months later with a heart attack. Don somebody had one somebody brought back for him and he was killed in an accident. Wrap it up and give it to one of the new town commissioners or the city manager, but get it out of here today," she said and left to go to the bank. She didn't come back after going to the bank, she was going on to a birthday party.

When I finished with my patient I took the little man with the vase off of the shelf and put him in the bottom drawer of my desk.

When I returned from the office after lunch there were a few patients. I had seen them all by two o'clock and told Sarah I was going to Hickory. I would be back in about an hour. As I went out the door to my car I remembered I hadn't found matching socks this morning, I had one blue one and one gray one. I would be a little embarrassed walking around with a white gown and different colored socks. I went by the house to change them. This made me a little late for a two-thirty appointment. To make up time I went out by the church to Miway Avenue and left to the intersection of Highway 321. As I approached the intersection the stoplight turned green so I proceeded across the intersection of Duke Street across the railroad crossing and turned right onto Highway 321. I was wondering what might be the trouble with my hip when I became aware of a blue light flashing in the rear view mirror and the roar of a siren. Looking in the mirror I was surprised to see a state patrol car right close to my rear bumper. When I stopped a patrolman came up to the car and asked me if I had seen a stop sign back there. I said no I hadn't seen one. He then asked if I had seen him coming down Duke Street. I said no I hadn't seen him either. He said for me to give him my driver's license and wait in the car while he wrote up a ticket. He left me to get in his car and I stood in the road beside my car.

While he was writing it up I felt quite depressed thinking that I am getting old and too careless to drive. I looked to see the sign he said I had failed to stop for and noticed a town police car approaching the intersection the same way I had come. To my amazement the police car didn't stop for the sign either.

I moved out in the street to stop him if he came down Duke Street, but he went across the intersection and past my office.

When the patrolman came back to my car I told him the police car just ran the same stop sign. To this he replied he didn't see it or he would have given him a ticket. He handed me the ticket and said I could go to court or pay one of the magistrates in town twenty-nine dollars.

I went on to Hickory to the x-ray office. They took several pictures and said my hip didn't show any trouble. This was a great relief. I was prepared for a bad report.

When I got in my car preparing to leave the battery was dead. It would turn the engine over once or twice, but not enough to get it started. After trying for about thirty minutes I went back in to the x-ray office and called for Sarah to come so I could kick the car off with jumper cables. I was embarrassed to ask some of the x-ray people to come out and help. When she came she had a sort of smirkish look on her face. I thought it was because my car was giving trouble. Now I think Dorothy had told her about the little man with the big penis. Using the cables I got my car cranked without any trouble.

Before going to the office I stopped at Melvin's office to report on running the stop sign. Chief Barlow was there.

When I told them about the patrolman stopping me Chief said he wished that SOB would stay out of this town. His men could patrol Granite without him. Melvin said he could have him indicted for some trouble he has had with him. I said I didn't want to have any trouble, I had run the sign, but it was in a bad place and needed to be changed. It was nailed to one of the utility poles too high to see when you were looking at the streetlight hanging over the highway. Chief said the state patrol was running a check on intersections and speeding all over town. They were parked on the hill overlooking the liquor store all day Saturday.

I didn't say anything to this. I knew how he felt about the liquor store, I think he wanted to replace me with a member of the Democratic Party.

I left and went by Monday's service station to check on my battery. There was corrosion on the terminals. While he was cleaning them he said Finn could have won in the election if he had worked. I didn't tell him but Finn worked nearly every day for three weeks trying to get support for our candidates.

I went on to the office where there were a few patients. As I walked through the reception room I noticed the shelf where the man with the vase had set. I recalled what Dorothy had said about him, a little god of bad luck. In just one day I had already had a lot of trouble. Before seeing any patients I pulled out the bottom drawer of my desk and took him way back in the office where he couldn't hear or see and put him in an old aquarium face down just in case he was doing some evil things.

58

Gold bugs

Today has been a rainy day. Soon the nights will be cold and the trees will be standing bare to the north wind. This has been a very difficult year. We have had lots of rain and a most unusual summer with one hot spell and the rest very mild. I didn't read much in the paper about the "Hot House" effect of polluting the ozone layer in the upper atmosphere.

Along with the change in climate there seems to be a change in people for the worse. A few days ago in Greensboro there was a meeting between some Communist workers and members of the Ku Klux Klan. It ended in a shooting in which five people died. Nationally we are still involved with Iran. They are still holding Americans hostage for the return of the Shah. He has been operated on for a gall bladder ailment and is in one of our hospitals. If we return him to Iran they say they will execute him.

I wonder why people can't learn to live together peaceably. Last night Dorothy and I attended a party with some friends in Hickory. Everyone seemed to have a nice time. It would be nice if people could get together like this throughout the world, but for some reasons this isn't to be. We are all too jealous, envious and egotistical to do this.

Perhaps things will be better in our town since the election. One of the winning candidates, Commissioner Erby had as his campaign promise to work for a better quality of life for our town. I think this will be better for us than more growth which all the other candidates have promised. More growth is just like the same thing we already have, something like a bigger garden with the same vegetables, nothing new. To improve on the quality of life means giving the people something that could add to their happiness and love for living here. It might mean people could live together because each one would be interested in accomplishing something or developing their talents. They might have something to occupy their minds rather than being available for every suggestion of criticism or attacking someone else.

At the party last night in Hickory there was some discussion about the death of a sixteen-year-old boy who lived in Hickory. He had robbed a store and was trying to get away from the police. They surrounded his car and the report is that the boy shot himself in the car. I wonder if this boy had any direction for his life? Was he recognized by society as being a worthy person? Possibly if younger people are around happy and well-directed older people they might try to mold their lives after them. Today not many young people stay married. They put their children in day care centers so they can work for material things, furniture, cars, a house and utilities. All of these things are necessary items for living today. With husband and wife working it causes a break up of their marriage. It seems we are creating a world in which material things are the most important things.

I believe all the material things haven't a lot to do with developing a good life. I think it would be best for society if the mother could stay home and look after the children. In addition to the counseling I do telling people how I think they should live, I am probably soon going to be confronted with giving patients a drug insert with each round of medicine telling them about all the side effects of the drug. I feel sure this will increase questions about the drug, thereby requiring more time to prescribe or give out the medication.

This is all part of government medicine. If the patient knows all the possible side effects they will be calling me to see if they are having any of them from the medicine. Some, knowing all the side effects, may elect not to take the medicine at all.

Dale might be one of these afraid to take the medicine. He is very skeptical of his medicine already. A few days ago when he was in the office I asked him if he helped count the ballots at the last town election. He said no, he just couldn't stand it now. He was too nervous. He said during an election there are always lots of rumors that may cause candidates to lose the election. They are deliberately started by the opposition. Often you don't find out what they are until a day or two after the election. On Wednesday after the town election someone said that the Hickory City Manager who was our city manager a few years ago called our city office to get his old job back. The report was that he had been fired in Hickory. Our candidates were supposed to know this and were going to give him his old job back in Granite if they were elected. Most voters despised this city manager and were glad when he left town. All our voters who heard this rumor would not have voted for our candidates.

Rumors like this are like putting a "bug" in someone's ear to influence their vote. I was reminded of this yesterday when Jim called me to come by his house to see some bugs on the trunk of the cherry trees in his front yard. They really weren't bugs, but the shells of jar flies that had molted leaving their shells stuck to the tree. They had turned into grub worms and were now in the ground at the base of the tree. I took some of these shells to the office and spray painted them with gold paint. Now they looked like gold bugs.

While looking at them I thought of the rumors spread in an election. The ones that are successful might be called "Gold Bugs" like these empty shells. They had good intentions for the candidates spreading them but the truth of the matter is they had no substance like these shells.

Later in the day I went by Jim's store to ask him and Dot to go out to dinner with Dorothy and me. He was sitting in one of the chairs he uses for people to try on shoes. There are about eight seats in a row like theater seats. He couldn't go because his daughter was home visiting and he needed to stay at home with her. He said Commissioner Erby had come by to talk to him and congratulated him for running such a good campaign. Jim said he filled him in on all of the ABC activities and went over the audit with him. He believes Commissioner Erby may work with us regarding the operation of the ABC Store and the town. I was glad to hear this.

59

Christmas '79

12-12-1979

We are now into the Christmas season. Christmas carols are being played on the television and radios. Christmas lights are in the store windows and houses. Dorothy and I went to Hickory today to get a Christmas tree. It is a Douglas fir, a little smaller than the one we got last year. Generally I have gotten one too big for our playroom and have to saw about a foot of it off before Dorothy is satisfied with it.

Though it is the Christmas season our weather is almost like summertime, temperature in the seventies. Years ago I would have gone fishing with my son Marty. We are expecting all of the children to come home for Christmas. You would think with all the activity building up for Christmas I would be getting into the Christmas spirit, but due to the international situation I am quite disturbed. The Iranians have not released the fifty American Hostages. President Carter and Senator Edward Kennedy are at odds about what to do about it. Senator Kennedy thinks as soon as the Shah can travel we should send him back to Iran as the Iranians are requesting. President Carter is holding out for the release of the hostages through international channels. Today the news seemed to indicate that the hostages might be released because Iran doesn't have any central government. There are some revolutionary groups in Iran fighting the Khomeini government. With all the international turmoil it seems like peace is a bit uncertain. We may use military force to try to free the hostages.

However I have other worries closer at home to occupy my time.

At the last town board meeting with the new commissioners Commissioner Tucker brought up the ABC store again. He is still concerned about the money we have in the store. Nothing we do satisfies him. If we would resign I think he would be happy. Yesterday Hub came in the office and said I should resign. I think he is working with one of the commissioners, but I can't get him to admit it. I told him I was not going to resign, but they could have my position when my times runs out in July.

My practice seems to be dropping off some. I think it is due to all the free services the government is giving. At the Rotary Club meeting last night the speaker said that about 53 percent of the people in this country are now receiving one or more government checks. I asked him how far he thought we were down the road to socialism. He thought we are about 70 percent there now. About 50 percent of my time is spent in giving out papers so people can get their money back from some agency.

Last night was an exception. A patient called at ten o'clock asking me to see one of his friends. He had burned his eyes helping him do some electric welding. I generally don't return to the office for something like sunburn or minor eye irritation, but having had personal experience with this type of injury I felt very much obligated to relieve any patient with this condition.

My first encounter with this injury was in a similar way. I was about seventeen years old and home from school. I was holding part of a plow for my father to weld with an electric welder. It was about two o'clock in the afternoon, and we used the plow in the garden until about six o'clock. That night I had a date and took her to the movies. Toward the end of the movie my eyes began to burn and soon there were uncontrollable tears streaming down my face. When the movie was over and I started to take her home I could hardly make out the road. Approaching cars seemed like some hazy blob of light. When I left her home I couldn't make out the road. My eyes felt like they were full of hot pepper. I drove about a mile and had to pull off of the road.

My eyes were worse. They felt like red-hot coals of fire. The only way I could get any relief was to tie my necktie around my head and over my eyes so tight they couldn't move.

It was about daylight before I could make out the road well enough to drive home. When I told my father what had happened he explained that I should have worn a mask like he did. After my eyes got better I resolved that if ever I could help someone with this condition I would do my best for them.

All that is needed is a few drops of Novocain solution dropped in the eye every two or three hours for a day or two. On this occasion the patient was so glad to be relieved of the fire in his eyes he didn't ask to have a form filled out though it is a compensable injury.

Along with pure medical problems I have a lot of psychological problems. One patient yesterday wanted to know what she should do about her mother who is about seventy years old. Some years ago she lost her husband and ever since then she has held a wake for him. On all holidays and special events, especially whenever it is his birthday she said her mother pulls down all the shades and makes everyone in the house whisper so as not to disturb her husband's spirit. My patient said she was getting damn tired of these wakes lasting all year.

Another patient was in crying about her marriage. Her husband was leaving her for another woman. She said she had known about it for some time, but had put up with it until last night when he stormed out at her for not having dinner ready in time for him to go on a date with his girlfriend. I asked how old his girlfriend was and was surprised when she said she was one year older than him. Generally the husband leaves for a younger woman. She said his girlfriend had called her sometime ago and asked her not to run her husband out of the house because she couldn't let him stay with her for fear of what the neighbors might think. She admitted to having intercourse with him but if he stayed all night the neighbors would think she had committed adultery.

Since I have told you about the woman pulling down the shades for a wake I will tell you about a couple celebrating their fiftieth wedding anniversary. The wife decided to try something different for this anniversary. She said to Frank, "Why don't we celebrate this anniversary by doing like we did when we first got married?"

"That is a great idea, Mable," Frank said.

Mable pulled down all the shades and they were both going around nude. Mable fixed breakfast and they both sat down to eat. "Frank," Mable said, "We should have been celebrating all our anniversaries this way."

"Why do you think so?" Frank asked

"Because both of my breasts feel nice and warm again just like when we were first married," Mable said.

"Well, Mable," Frank said, "it's no wonder 'cause you have got one in your grits and the other one in your coffee cup."

60

Last of '79

Today is a cold wet drizzly Sunday. Dorothy has gone to visit her mother. Due to having so many patients sick with the flu I have stayed here and kept the office open.

I went to church and after the sermon I went to lunch with Melvin and his wife Marry. When we returned I went back to the office to check on some ABC reports about the election years ago. The ABC Board is due to meet with the new commissioners January seventh to answer some of the same old questions. However before going into these reports I should tell you how Christmas went.

All of the children were home and had a great time. Dorothy wanted to have another party like we had last year in the theater, but due to her high blood pressure I felt like she could not stand the excitement. She enjoyed the children and took them shopping. After Marry and Susie decorated the tree she frequently came over to move some of the balls or bells to some new place on the tree where she thought a hole needed to be filled. A few days before Christmas I heard her say this was the prettiest Christmas tree we have ever had. It seemed so to me also when we had all the presents under it. We gave them out Christmas night with Melvin and Marry sharing their Christmas with us.

During Christmas day I was frequently called to the office to see patients with some minor complaint. One had cut his wrist opening a can, another had sprained his ankle and several had sore throats. I was glad to be of service and hoped to add to their Christmas joy.

I recalled one patient I saw Christmas Eve who was not having a good time. Her youngest son had run away from home and was arrested in Kentucky for public drunkenness. Her husband was on his way out to Kentucky to get him out of jail. While this was going on her oldest son had been stabbed with a butcher knife by his wife.

Another patient came in at closing time Christmas Eve. He said he appreciated me getting him fired. He was a young man about eighteen years old, five feet tall with blond hair hanging down on his shoulders. He was wearing a thin T-shirt and some kind of light blue pants. Without thinking I told him he didn't have to come to see me, he could have seen some other doctor.

He left without saying anything more. I soon recalled he had been in the office about three weeks ago. At that time he said he had a cold and had been out of work all week. Would I give him and excuse and let him pay me later? I said no, I had not seen him while he was sick. About an hour later his foreman had called to verify his story. I told the foreman the boy had come in and wanted an excuse for being out of work. He said he had a bad work record anyway. I suppose he fired him because he didn't bring in an excuse.

It seems that I am always involved in some kind of decision-making. My paper work is continually increasing. Even on Christmas Day as I was leaving for dinner one of my deaf patients brought her mother in to see me. Her mother has normal hearing. She wanted her blood pressure and heart checked. At the conclusion of the examination I wrote a prescription for her medication and when she paid me for the visit I gave her a receipt. We were in the reception room going out the door when she suddenly decided she would like to get some of the medicine from me. I agreed to get her enough for a few days until she could get the prescription filled in her hometown. I charged her five dollars for the medicine. She wanted this added onto her receipt, which she had stuffed into her pocketbook. It was a large multi-compartment handbag. She went through all the compartments, pulling out a multitude of papers before she found the receipt. With the receipt in hand the next thing to do was to find the five dollars. Again she scratched through the handbag and came up with three paper dollars.

For the other two dollars she now turned to her deaf daughter. To effect this communication it was necessary for me to find some paper for the mother to write on. When the proper communication had been conveyed the daughter started scratching through her pocketbook looking for two dollars. After some time searching around she called for the paper to write a message. She didn't have two dollars. At this point I called for the paper and wrote, "Merry Christmas, let's go to dinner." They both smiled and thanking me they went out the door.

During the next few days after Christmas I gave more consideration to the coming meeting with the town commissioners. I think the new commissioners expected us to resign whenever they won the election but we have not done so. They have asked us to come to the January seventh meeting to answer the same questions again. This time we have very little money and there are no irregularities that I know of. Mayor Bert thinks it will be a very important meeting. He has been going over the records, and plans to bring his personal attorney with him. He told me Friday his attorney would be available for the ABC Board if we wanted him. He didn't trust the city attorney to give him good advice from now on since they had not agreed on whether it was right or not for the town to keep the school funds the ABC Board gave the town.

When I asked Jim what he thought about having an attorney for the meeting he said we didn't need one. We should tell the commissioners we are running the store and for them to run the town. They did all they could do about the store when they appointed us to run it. They can bring charges if they like. According to our bill, we can employ an attorney if we need to and spend every dime we make to defend ourselves in attorney fees. They can just decide what they want to do.

I am in agreement and believe it is up to the town board to make whatever charges they can. We can then employ the best attorney in the state to defend us. I spoke to Pete, another ABC board member, today as we were leaving church and asked if he was in agreement with this. He thought we should have a meeting before the seventh to see if we can think of anything we haven't already covered. Tomorrow I will call Bert and ask him to meet with us.

I have decided that I will not be asked by the town board to serve another term after June and I don't mind being replaced. However, I don't think I will allow them to use the store for their political advantages. If they use the store to pay off their election workers or give out political favors in the county I would not be very much opposed to closing it. I worked for the store mostly to pay for a band for the school. Now that function has been taken over by the county schools so the store has lost its importance to the community except for the income to run the town. In that regard we never intended the town to be run off of the income from the store, the income was due to be used for things above the regular budget.

My office practice has dropped off some this year. I think it is due to all the free services the government is giving.

Gas prices have increased to $1.10 per gallon. Due to continual international trouble I think it would be good if man had a map to follow to keep him out of trouble. Whenever I told Dorothy this she said he has a map but won't follow it. She said the Lord gave him the Bible.

61

Fired

1-11-1980 ✓

Christmas and New Year's have gone. Now the weather has changed to very cold. We will be burning more coal and oil than last year. This will be very hard on lots of people in view of the price of oil and gas. Gas is now about $1.08 per gallon. The Iranians are still holding our hostages. They would not let the United Nations ambassador see them or talk with Khomeini when he was in Iran a few days ago.

Russia invaded Afghanistan on Thursday. President Carter is protesting and planning to cut out all grain supplies to Russia. The Vietnamese are still fighting and the Cambodians are asking us for food. The world seems to be in great turmoil.

Here at home we have a lot of turmoil in city hall. I think Mayor Bert is now having an open disturbance with Don the city attorney. From talking with Bert it seems that Don and Noble, the city manager, told Bert that they didn't have to keep him informed on what goes on in city. This has made Bert very mad and he plans to have his own personal lawyer with him at the next meeting. He said I should ask him to defend the ABC board at our meeting.

Today I called the lawyer for the state ABC Association in Raleigh to find out what I should do if we are asked to resign. His reply was that according to the state statute they could not fire us unless they had specific cause. So far I can't believe they have a specific cause. We are due to meet with the town board tonight at seven o'clock.

All this turmoil is having some disturbance with my practice. It is hard for me to keep my mind on my patients. Most to them just have the flu. However one is not getting on well. His jaundice is getting worse so I transferred him to the hospital in Chapel Hill.

At seven o'clock we all met upstairs over city hall, the same room I and three other men met in to start campaigning for the ABC bill years ago. They are all dead now. Bert had his lawyer, David Sentelle. When things seemed to be settled down Bert convened the meeting. He called on one of the ministers in the back to give the invocation. After this Bert made a few general remarks and introduced Attorney Sentelle.

Bert went over to speak with Sentelle and when he returned to the table there was some commotion near the front door. We all looked that way. A deputy sheriff in full uniform came in with a handful of official looking papers. He was the same deputy who had brought patients to my house for me to sew up. Now I felt sure he had come to serve some kind of papers on us.

Instead the deputy began handing them to four of the commissioners. Some of them began to sort of snicker as though this was some kind of joke. Sentelle noticed this and stood up and announced rather loudly that the deputy was serving indictment papers on the commissioners regarding the secret executive meeting they had had December 20, the time they decided we should meet with them. Don realized that some of the commissioners didn't recognize the seriousness of the matter and asked Bert for a few minutes to explain the situation to them. Don and the commissioners went down stairs. Sentelle went with them. For a few minutes there was some loud talking going on downstairs.

When things quieted down they all came back up stairs looking very sober. Don announced that to be free of the indictment they had agreed to let us hear the tape they had made of their secret December 20 meeting.

The tape was about Don's strategy to win the Starnes case in regard to rezoning the Starnes property to commercial use. Also Don didn't like Bert writing a column in the newspaper each week about what was going on in city hall. Noble didn't like the places in town where opinions were given about running city hall. One commissioner didn't think I was qualified to serve on the ABC Board. Towards the last of the tape Don told Nobles to put all his notices about the Starnes case in the Lenoir paper where they were least likely to be seen by the Starnes and their attorney. To this Noble said he guessed that a little hedging never hurt. After a few other comments about the legality of Bert's column the tape came to an end and a short recess was declared.

It was now about ten-thirty. Bert asked me if I wanted to continue or call for another meeting to answer questions about the ABC operation. I told them to let's continue. I thought the ABC board had nothing new to add and the state attorney had said we were not under the control of the commissioners. Bert called the meeting to order again. Noble then gave out a number of handouts he had stacked on the table to all the commissioners and some friend of his in the back of the room. I asked Noble why we didn't get any handouts and he replied that we were not supposed to get any. Bert said he didn't get any either.

Noble ignored him and began questioning the ABC Board about matters we had answered before. His questioning was followed rather systematically by all four of the opposing commissioners and Don. I sensed from the first few questions that none of our answers were acceptable. As soon as we gave an answer they asked something else without paying any attention to our answers. Finally around one o'clock they were interrupted by a loud voice in the back.

"I think it is a damn shame that us firemen in this damn town are risking our lives every day and a clerk in the liquor store is making more money than we are."

There was no comment made to the fireman's remark. I could have told him we were paying the same amount other stores were paying. It was up to the commissioners to keep the firemen happy.

After a few other remarks, which I don't remember, one of the commissioners asked us to resign. We declined to resign and a motion was made to fire us. This motion passed four to two. Immediately, a commissioner pulled a small scrap of paper out of his pocket and read off three names of people the commissioners had selected to replace us. Nothing more was said.

Bert stood up to adjourn the meeting. His face was flushed and he had fire in his eyes. In a low trembling voice he said to the commissioners, "You have made one of the greatest mistakes you will ever make."

62

Suing City Hall

1-19-80 ✓

I am in a very bad mental state. Most of my thoughts are centered around the outcome of the ABC Board and our dismissal a few weeks ago. There was first the feeling of despondency and resignation to give up and let the town commissioners have their way. However after talking with Bert who is still standing up to the commissioners, he encouraged me to file suit. After thinking of it a day or two I decided to take his advice.

I went to tell Jim and he agreed to support our suit requesting reassignment to the Board. I contacted the lawyer, David Sentelle, the same lawyer Bert had when we were fired. Jim and I and our families are waiting now for him to file our case with the clerk of court. It seems rather peculiar not having something to do in regard to checking records or doing something in our defense, but this is in the hands of the attorney now.

Dorothy is real glad about this. She has been very upset since we were fired. It was the night of our wedding anniversary. Our daughter Susie was with us so our embarrassment was much worse than if just Dorothy and I had been there alone. Our anxiety now seems to be worse with Dorothy than with me. Sunday when we visited her sister she told Dorothy that her mother was very upset to learn that Jim and I had misappropriated ABC funds. A few days later when we visited my sister in Lenoir she was distressed about newspaper accounts implying the same thing

When Bert called this morning he said the attorney would file the papers Monday for us to be reinstated. He will take up other questions later. I think Bert wants him at the town meeting Monday night. The town is having some trouble furnishing sewer lines for some houses the last city manager let someone build. In addition to this, Duke is going to be there with his attorney to talk about getting his land reassigned. He thinks it will look pretty bad for Don, the city attorney to have so many lawsuits going on at one time.

"With all these suits, people might think the town needed a new attorney," Bert said. He was of the opinion that the town would have to get another lawyer before Duke could get his land zoned for a shopping center.

Sunday morning when Dorothy and I went to church she was still quite apprehensive. She said she would not be going without me. Because of the ABC thing she thought all the people would be looking at her. I assured her everything would be all right. We had done nothing wrong and some people must take a stand if things are to be kept in some kind or order for right. We were a bit late, but a bit ahead of Dot and Jim. Dorothy and I went into the church and down the right side to a pew near one of the stained glass window given by members of my family. Dot and Jim went down the left side and sat on the pew near a window given by their family.

Rev. Alderman soon came into the sanctuary though a side door wearing his long purple robe. As soon as he seemed settled with his notes before him, the choir members filed in and took their places behind him. When they were all in place he made a few remarks about the communion they had last Sunday.

I began to wonder about the value of communion. It is used to signify unity in our faith and to renew our faith. It is also to let us know others of the same faith so that we do not feel alone. I can well understand its significance now. Going to church this morning Dorothy and I felt alone. We wondered what other people were thinking about us. Were they thinking the same thing of us as her mother and my sister were thinking? I wondered if we were doing right in opposing the desire of the commissioners. A lot of what they accused us of was just their opinion. Some time ago just fifteen more votes supporting our opinion made it legal for us to sell liquor in Granite Falls. We were the only town in the county allowed by law to have a store for the sale of liquor. Now by opinion of the town attorney we are guilty of doing things that we thought were good for the community.

Some ways, like with communion, a great deal of anxiety is relieved whenever we are among friends who support our faith by expressing that they are glad we are there and standing up for what we believe.

Some people are saying Bert should resign his position as mayor because of his association with the ABC Board. It is difficult to stand against the opposition alone. Only two of the commissioners support him. Dorothy and I have decided we will stand by him. Now I know communion is a necessary part of life. It means you belong to a group that may give you support in your hour of need.

Alderman, having finished his announcements called out the first hymn, one he said we didn't frequently sing. It was called, "GO TELL IT ON THE MOUNTAIN." Somehow I thought from this selection that his sermon might have some parables for me. I couldn't help punching Dorothy. The choir really got into the singing.

With the conclusion of the singing, Alderman announced the his text the subject of his sermon, "WHAT KIND OF A PERSON ARE YOU?" In it he called for individual morality and honesty. He seemed to wander a bit and I began thinking of my own troubles. Something he had said reminded me of the famous lines of Shakespeare's Hamlet, "To be or not to be." Should I oppose the commissioners or drop the suit? When my mind came back to his sermon he was talking about all the turmoil in the town. Seems like he concluded by saying you should get your morality up to the Joneses and the Johnsons.

When the choir started singing the closing hymn, I looked at Dorothy. Her face was all red and her eyes wet. She started talking about Alderman.

"He was talking about us in his sermon," she said. I told her to stop talking so loud. Alderman was talking for us and not against us. She said, "Are you sure?"

Again I told her yes and I took her arm and led her out of the church as fast as possible.

63

Devil influence

2-9-80 ✓

This is a snowy day. Outside the snow is coming down at intervals in large fluffy flakes like down feathers covering the ground with soft white blanket. On a day like this, I have very few patients and tend to become melancholy.

Most of my patients stay home by the fire or in their beds. "Snow Days" I call them. To me there is always something eerie about snow, especially at night. Perhaps it is the stillness and the difference in sounds. Dogs must notice it too. On nights following a snow they bark to each other from hill to hill all night long.

The snow today reminded me of Elsie's funeral two years ago. She was buried while it was snowing. Today at two o'clock I attended Joe's funeral. He too was buried in the snow. He wanted everyone's soul to be white as snow. In addition to being a preacher and a patient, he was a very good friend and a firm opponent to the devil. I will miss Joe

The television has just announced that we are having one of the worst snowstorms of the year extending from the Rockies to the eastern seaboard. It is expected to reach a depth of six inches here tonight. It seems that our weather is keeping up with our international situation. The Russians are still in Afghanistan and are looking toward the Iranian border probably with the intention of extending their border to the Persian Gulf, putting them in position to cut our oil supply line. To counteract this advance, President Carter has announced that he will use military force if necessary to keep the oil lines open. To support his threat, he has activated the draft calling for men and women between the ages of nineteen and twenty-one to register first.

To block the registration, eligible draftees have begun organizing anti-draft demonstrations. Senator Kennedy is attacking President Carter, contending that Carter is doing too little about our international affairs. He is calling for Carter to resign from the presidential race leaving him the Democratic Nominee for President. Among the Republican candidates for president it seems like Bush and Regan may be the two major contenders. For the independents it is John Anderson for president.

On the local level things are very tense.

It was snowing Wednesday night when I went to the county medical meeting. I and another doctor had planned to talk against expansion of the county health department into private practice. My friend didn't make it to the meeting. I brought the matter up but I got no support.

When I called my friend to find out why he didn't come to the meeting, his reply was that the snow was too deep for him to venture out at night. He suggested we continue our efforts and recruit more members for our support. This is rather typical of the way things turn out. People will talk in support of something, but when it is time for action they have some excuse. If I agree to support someone I don't like to let him down.

It is for this reason that I encouraged Jim to join me in the ABC suit against the town commissioners. I felt we couldn't leave Bert alone to the commissioners. I believed we had been discharged illegally by the commissioners. The State Attorney General had implied this in his letter two weeks after we were fired. With these factors in mind I signed the suit papers and then took them to Jim to get his signature on them. Our attorney was due to file them in the county court house on Monday morning and then the sheriff would serve indictment papers on four of the commissioners who voted to fire us.

We were expecting a great reaction to our suit papers from the people here in town. Monday morning Bert called the court house around ten o'clock to get the report, but our papers had not arrived. He said he was told some people had already called indicating that we were going to get some reaction to our suit. When we called again this afternoon around four o'clock there were no legal papers from our attorney. Throughout the day on Tuesday we had the same result; no suit papers had been filed. We were told that the snow had probably caused the delay.

Wednesday around noon Bert called me while Dorothy and I were having lunch. He suggested that I take my copy of the suit to the Granite Press so we could get it in their paper. The paper comes out once a week and this would be the last chance to get it in their paper. I left my lunch and rushed down to the press office. When I arrived, Cleonard asked if he might keep the report until morning because he was already two hours behind in getting his paper to the printer. I agreed and returned home to finish my lunch.

Bert and I expected the Hickory paper to come out with big headlines on Wednesday evening announcing the suit against the commissioners. Instead, though the report was on the front page, it was in a space about five or six inches down in the left corner. Though very disappointed with this report, there was still the possibility of a good report in the Lenoir paper. Surely they would give us a good report.

On Thursday morning Bert called around ten o'clock to report that the suit papers had come to the courthouse and to expect some action. Thereafter, each time the phone rang I expected it to be someone calling to congratulate me for filing suit against the commissioners, but nothing happened. Around four o'clock a reporter called to ask me about the suit. Jim and I had been advised by our attorney not to talk about our suit. I told the reporter this and hung up.

The report in the paper was a brief announcement on the second page similar to the one in the Hickory paper. On Friday, the Hickory paper carried a report stating that Jim and I were asking in a suit against the town commissioners to be reinstated to our positions on the ABC board. It was about the same as in the Lenoir paper except it listed the reasons the commissioners had fired us; the land purchase, the certificates on deposit, and an illegal bank account. We were fired without an opportunity to audit our books.

It might be that when Reece and Miller return from Raleigh they will have some instructions for the town from the state ABC Board disallowing the commissioners' action so Jim and I will not have to continue with the suit. This would be a nice result. I would like to have the suit over with. It is a drain on my mental and physical system and I am sure it is affecting Dot and Jim. While we were visiting with them last night they were both very agitated and frequently snapped at each other.

It is having its effect on me too. I am becoming very depressed about the possible outcome of the suit. Today while attending Joe's funeral I began to wonder if the devil didn't work through the town commissioners to fire Jim and me. Joe knew the power of the devil. Because Joe and I were good friends, his wife requested me to be an honorary pallbearer at Joe's funeral. After following the oak casket down the middle aisle of the church the funeral director sat us down on the second pew from the front on the left side leaving just a few feet between us and the coffin. Then he propped open the lid so we could see Joe lying in his casket on his back, his bald head resting on a small white laced pillow. He was still wearing his big thick-lensed glasses in their black frames. From my seat on the end of the pew, they reflected the minister's reading light, creating something of a halo around Joe's head. Joe was worthy of a halo.

While the minister was reading his verses over Joe, I remembered all the things Joe had told me about the devil while I was running the campaign to get the ABC store in Granite. He had insisted that I was violating the teachings of the Bible by advocating strong drink for our brothers here in Granite. The Bible commanded that I was my brother's keeper and I was not allowed to bring in things that were not good for my brother.

"Be sure your sins will find you out," he would say. Joe was sure I was sinning and for my part the devil would surely be after me. I was asking the people to vote for liquor and because of this Joe held me responsible for all the divorces it would cause, for all the little children left cold and hungry at night because their father and mother had spent their paycheck on liquor and for all the people killed in auto accidents caused from drinking liquor. Too, this liquor would be a bad influence on the youth of the town, driving them all to sin and hell.

He wished I would not support it and resign. When I told him I had filed suit against the commissioners, he said, "Okay, okey dokes. Show them you are right. Win the case and then resign."

In his early life he had run with the boys, doing the things young men do—wine, women and song. In his last twenty-five years he had become very religious. He said he had gotten saved years ago by the Lord who had cleansed his soul till it was white as snow. Now he was a self-taught preacher and knew a lot about the Bible, where to find certain verses of Scripture and to interpret it for the occasion. I always enjoyed his visits either at the office or at his home. Sometimes our visits were late at night when he called me to his home because of his smothering spells. We would talk about religion for hours. The room was pretty cold and to keep his bald head warm he had a pair of Mom's pink panties tied around his head.

He was a great believer in the devil. He believed the devil could work within people or work outside alone and invisible to cause a person a lot of trouble. Most often to give men trouble the devil would work through a beautiful woman. He would then name the great characters of the Bible that had been deposed by the devil.

After Joe's funeral I began to wonder more about the devil. Was the devil now after me? I reviewed the record of our committee that had worked to get the ABC store in Granite.

Five men and myself formed the central committee called the steering committee. We were all business and family men close to fifty years old without any known health problems. Shortly after the store was voted in, about two years, one of the members dropped dead at work. It appeared he died of a sudden heart attack. This didn't seem too unusual to me at the time for it is not uncommon for a man his age to have a sudden heart attack. About two years later the youngest member began to complain of right frontal headaches and some disturbance of vision in his right eye. He had a young wife and two small daughters. He was doing well in his business. I saw him several times for his headache, but nothing helped. His condition gradually became worse and was diagnosed as a brain tumor. It pushed his right eye out of the socket so that it had to be removed. He died an agonizing death about three months later.

I didn't associate his death with the devil because men his age sometimes have a brain tumor. I began to wonder about Joe and the devil when the third member had trouble.

He came in the office one evening just before Christmas after deer hunting in the mountains. He said he had coughed up a little blood while climbing a mountain. He wanted to know what I thought about it. I told him we should get his chest x-rayed, but he said he felt fine and was going deer hunting again in the morning. It was three weeks later when he came to see me again. This time I insisted on an x-ray of the chest. It showed an opacity in the right lung. He had the cancer resected. It was malignant and he died just before Thanksgiving day.

Not long after this the fourth member died of heart attack.

Now I began to be concerned about myself.

Joe might be right. The devil may be involved in my troubles with the commissioners. Perhaps since I am chairman of the ABC board I am due some unusual punishment. I wonder what is his plan. Will he cause Jim and me to distrust each other and lose our friendship? Will the devil cause us to lose our suit. Due to the anxiety the suit is causing I may lose Dorothy.

She is complaining of chest discomfort and irregular heartbeats. I have listened to her heart on several occasions and it is irregular. If it doesn't clear up soon I am going to have a specialist check on her. While we were visiting with Dot and Jim last night, Jim said Dot was complaining of headaches again. He thinks they are just tension headaches. While he was telling it I was thinking of my committee member that died of a brain tumor.

The devil's plan might be for us to lose the suit. If this is his plan then I think I know my end. It will be for me to wind up friendless, ruined financially and professionally. If I lose the first round he will tempt me to appeal, thus gambling more funds on a worthless cause. My patients will leave me, thinking I am some kind of mad man. Due to having my mind on the suit I may make a mistake in my practice.

I need my friend Joe now. I would like to talk to him again about the devil. He would know if my troubles are the workings of the devil. He would tell me what to do to defend myself. With Joe's help I could overcome the devil and, like Joe, cleanse my soul white as snow. I had better get my mind back on my practice or some of these things might happen.

An interesting thing happened yesterday. An old man about seventy-five years old was in the office. His elder sister was helping him along to the examining room. I was standing in the doorway of the examining room watching them make their way down the hall. While they were approaching me I became aware of the song being played on the intercom. It was "I'm just going home." The song and the old man captured my attention.

"Just going home" is about all that is left for Clyde. The exertion of walking was making him pant for breath. On his face was an anxious expression. His eyes were staring straight ahead, his mouth wide open, his left jaw sagging a bit letting saliva drool down his chin and onto his shirt. He was leading the way with his left shoulder and leaning on a crooked walking stick. His hand gripping the stick was knotty and brown. His gait was a shuffling one made by leading with his left foot and then dragging his right up to the left. His sister held to his left arm. from the swinging of his pants legs I could see his legs were thin as broom handles. A little slip and he could break his hip.

Watching him walk reminded me of some of the discussions I had with Joe. There were some verses in the Bible that had to do with aging. They are in Ecclesiastes. I was amazed when Joe first told me about them, that someone had written down the aging process of man so long ago. Clyde now fulfilled all of the predictions. As the Bible said, Clyde was a white-haired old man, dragging himself along. Clyde has been my patient for about ten years. Each year he becomes a little weaker.

Some cold night his sister will call. She will say she thinks Clyde is dead and will I come. I will say, "Yes, I will be there in a few minutes."

I will hurriedly dress and go out into the dark night alone down the road past dark houses where people are sleeping to a house with all the lights on and a few cars in the yard.

Without knocking I will open the front door and enter a large room used for a kitchen and dining room. The room is cold and there are a few people huddled and standing around a small stove in the center of the room. Clyde's sister will lead me to the door to Clyde's room. Clyde will be in the bed lying on his back. He will be covered with some old quilt and still have his clothes on. I will open my medical bag for my stethoscope and listen to Clyde's chest for a heartbeat. Hearing nothing, I will put my stethoscope back in the bag. If his mouth is open I will push up the lower jaw to close it. I will push the eyelids down, closing his eyes for the last time. As a parting goodbye I will pull the quilt over his head.

When I leave the room to go out to the people around the stove I will say to his sister, "He has gone home." Some low sobbing will begin and some slow movement as people retreat into the shadows of the room. I will ask Bonnie, Clyde's sister, if she wants me to call Laney, the undertaker, for her. She will say yes and I will make the call. He will know where to come because he has buried other members of the family.

After making the call and saying I am sorry to Bonnie I will pick up my medical bag and go out alone again into the dark night. As I walk to my car I will look up at the starry sky. I have read somewhere that when a good person dies a new star appears in the heavens. I will wonder which star is Clyde's.

64

A spring lull

3-14 1980 ✓

I am a year older now. When I was forty I thought sixty-two was old and now I know it is. I am pretty tired at the end of the office day. When I was forty I could go fishing for four hours after closing the office and even get up two or three times during the night to make house calls without feeling exhausted.

During the summer I frequently went fishing with a group of people on Saturday night around eight o'clock, journey about 300 miles to South Port or Morehead City to fish on Sunday until around five o'clock when we returned to the dock. We arrived home around three o'clock in the morning. I was able to do my office work without being too exhausted. Now a trip like that would take a week to recover from.

I should be enjoying this nice spring weather. Today we had a clear day with a little cold wind. From the sunshine the grass is beginning to turn green and the trees are putting out their spring buds. Already most of the birds are back from their trip south. Robins are on the lawns and trees. red birds, chickadees and doves are gathering around my bird feeder.

On the international scene we have not improved any. Last week there was some promise from the Iranians that they were going to let the international group from the United Nations visit the hostages, but after they arrived in Iran there was some argument between the ruling groups in Iran and the visiting delegation was not allowed to visit the hostages. It was a big disappointment to President Carter. Tonight Carter has requested Congress to grant him authority to increase the price of gasoline ten cents a gallon to help balance the budget and to cut down on the import of Iranian oil.

Some of the candidates running for president have dropped out of the race because they have not gotten support from the people. Baker, Connley and Dole have dropped out. Anderson, Regan and Bush are still contending with Ford who is thinking of joining in the race for another bid for the presidency. On the Democratic side Carter and Kennedy are the two major contenders. I am of the opinion Kennedy will soon drop out because the Chapaquitic matter is being brought up again by the Republicans.

To change my day from brightness to gloom, I have just received from the deputy sheriff a copy of the counter suits prepared by Don, the town attorney, against Jim and me. The suit did not include Pete, the other board member. He had open heart surgery two years ago and didn't believe he could stand the anxiety of going to court.

I am charged with illegal purchase of the land where the cement mixer plant was located, separately from the other charges. Jim and I are charged with taking our wives to the National Convention and with taking Reece, our store operator and Mavis, his wife. We are also charged with operating a fictitious bank account, and with not making proper distributions of cash to the town.

This seems to be a poor reward for years of community service. Dorothy is very discouraged and wishes we had never set up practice here. She wants us to move someplace else as soon as this mess is over. I was surprised when an elderly lady I visited with the flu a few weeks ago declared the same thing. She felt like the town was coming apart and would like to move some place else. I told her I thought we were in some great social change and the town is changing with it. One whole block of downtown is empty except for the Western Auto store.

Except for flu cases my practice is falling off. I have lost all the town employees. Yesterday when Dorothy called them about a fireman with a splinter in his hand she was told the town didn't send their injured to me any more.

Politically, I have not done much better. At a meeting last night I was asked to help raise funds for Beverly Lake, the Republican candidate for state governor. I am due to raise $750. I have not had much success so far. I have asked two of my doctor friends. One said he had never given to a political candidate. The other said he had children in college and couldn't afford to give this year. From a few other friends I have raised $125.

Sometimes even on a bumpy bad day there are some good bumps come along that make it all worthwhile. Yesterday Dorothy had a call for me to make. It was right at closing time. I had not seen the patient very much and he just wanted me to see the children because of their runny noses. One was crying with an earache. At first I didn't want to see the children, but then I remembered that I had recently concluded that my best asset is my practice. I told him to bring the children to the office and I would wait for them. With all the worry about the ABC suit and the concern of people that might support me I have decided that the only thing I have for sure is my service to give to people. To them I am important. I decided this today.

Around noon the water pressure in the office dropped. I thought the town had turned my water off. I called a plumber at one of the hardware stores and they sent a man within five minutes. He found a busted pipe. He was a man that had brought his little girl with a cut hand a few days ago. He said if I had mentioned it to him he would have fixed my pipe then.

After closing the office Dorothy and I went out for dinner. When we returned home there was a pan of large strawberries on the front stoop. From the size of them I wondered if they weren't from my competitor, Dr. Bill Corpening. We started practicing here at about the same time. I had heard from someone that he had strawberries so big you had to eat them like apples. I didn't see any that big so I concluded Dot and Jim had brought them. The phone rang about eight o'clock. It was Avis the doctor's wife telling me that she and the doctor had been over to see Dorothy and me. She said they were sorry we were having so much trouble. It is nice to have someone say they understand and would help if they could. I don't think our preacher ever said as much. Things change a lot when you have trouble. To some it seems like you have leprosy.

65

Conspiracy

I am thinking the ABC matter is now taking on the aspects of a political conspiracy. It is something similar to that of Shakespeare's play "Julius Caesar." Act II where Brutus early in the morning is receiving his friends to plan the death of Caesar:

> "They are the faction. O conspiracy,
> Sham'st thou to show they dangerous brow by night,
> When evils are most free: O then, by day
> Where wilt thou find a cavern dark enough
> To mask they monstrous visage? Seek non, conspiracy,
> Hide in smiles and affability:
> For if thou put they native semblance on,
> No Frebus itself were dim enough to hide thee from prevention."

I did not think so much about a conspiracy on the part of the town commissioners until after Reece returned from the state meeting. His report was not what I had expected. He hadn't talked with Hester as I thought he would. In fact, he had very little to report. The only satisfactory things he had to report was that Miller had reported to the state people that he was the temporary chairman of the Granite Falls ABC Board, indicating he is not wholly convinced he is the chairman in my place.

I would like for this whole affair to be as simple as the operations of a bootlegger I talked with recently

He was about seventy and suffering from emphysema. I had inquired of him what kind of business he was in. He had done some fertilizer business in his youth along with some bootlegging. I was interested in how he made the liquor still and inquired in detail into the operation and manufacture of illegal liquor. He had been caught several times so I inquired why he wasn't sent to jail. He said that they don't send a man to jail if he can pay out. He always saved up the fine to pay out before he ever started making or selling any liquor. Even though I think my insurance is equal to the fine of the bootlegger, I can't seem to relieve myself of the apprehension.

My practice seems to be steadily falling off. In some respect I am not too concerned. I am getting tired of working and giving most all I get to the government. There isn't any way of changing things except to stop paying taxes. I don't believe anyone can get elected to a responsible position who campaigns on cutting out programs, Medicare, Medicaid, or food stamps. Their only possibility is to campaign on cutting out some of the taxes.

Last night I had a call to the office. A man had a sore throat and wanted me to come out to the office to see him. He had large swollen tonsils and a temperature of one hundred degrees. I gave him some penicillin and asked him to return this morning. I charged him twenty-five dollars, which seems very high, but I think I should have ten dollars for going out and opening up the office and treating him. What happens to the other fifteen dollars? Ten will go for taxes and the other five for expenses for the office. It is right discouraging to receive the criticism for the high fees from the patients and the government when the government is getting half of the fees in taxes.

To help keep my sanity I try to think that possibly I don't need so much money and to consider myself as in a sort of retirement, for indeed I think that is the position I am in. I think that with all the third-party influence now, I should have settled where there is a hospital and continued with hospital medicine, but it is too late to make a change now. I think with my age and to try to move and set up a new practice, I just couldn't build it up in time to do me any good. I will stay with what I have and play it out to the end, regardless of how our ABC suit turns out.

Generally my practice drops off in the summer, but not as much as it has this summer. I think it is due to a lot of the boycotting that is going on. I still have some loyal patients. One is Gerald.

Last week, his wife went into the bathroom and locked the door. after a short while, Gerald heard her seem to fall. When he called for her she didn't answer. He finally had to take the hinges off of the door and found her in a coma on the floor. He called me to come to see her. I suspected that it was an insulin reaction when he called so I took some dextrose and a syringe to give her glucose intravenously. We had to pull her out of the bathroom onto the kitchen floor. I tried both veins at the elbows, but they both blew out.

She was still unconscious and I was about ready to tell him we should call for an ambulance, but I tried the vein in her left hand. It was a rather large one and I was able to get enough glucose into her to bring her around to consciousness, enough to drink some sweetened orange juice. In a few minutes she was talking again and both Gerald and I were very happy.

I was surprised when a fellow stopped me on the street a few days later and said what a remarkable thing I had done for Gerald's wife. With people saying things like that for me, I wonder how much strength the town commissioners can have. They don't render any service to anyone here in the community.

After lunch, I had a call to go back to the office to see a patient with dermatitis of the hands and legs. Floyd had been seen by several other doctors. They have not been able to help his condition. I thought from his history there was some chance his trouble may be due to lack of stomach. He has had two operations requiring gastric resection so that he now has about one-third of the normal stomach. With this much stomach loss there is frequently a lack of absorption of necessary vitamins, especially vitamin B12. I had given him an injection of B12 on Thursday and he was due to come in today before noon for another. Floyd claimed he forgot and would I come to the office and see him.

I agreed and met him there at two. He was much better and said that he thought I was going to mess around and cure him yet. At this I couldn't help laughing. It reminded me of a patient the x-ray doctor told me of a few years ago. That patient was an elderly farmer who was in the hospital for the first time for some trouble with his colon. He was in the x-ray room lying on the table with a gown and the technician, a young lady, was planning to give him a barium enema. She was holding the nozzle of the enema tube in one hand and feeling around in the inguinal region with the other for his anus. Suddenly the old man exclaimed, "Lady, if you are not careful you are going to stick that thing up my ass!"

Floyd laughed when I told him the story and then to better my joke he said that it was a little like the farmer he knew who went to the clinic and the nurse asked for a urine specimen. The farmer didn't understand the nurse so she repeated the order. He didn't comprehend so she tried again, this time making it plainer.

"I want you to pee in that glass over there," she said.

Comprehending this time, he replied, "From way over here?"

I was about to top this with my school teacher joke, but there was quite a commotion in the reception room and a cherry call, "Hello, doctor." I didn't' quite recognize the voice and stepped out of the room into the hallway to see who it was.

Looking hard, I couldn't quite make it out. There was first the image of a man, a dark man not black, dressed in a brown rawhide matching leather coat with leather pants, all with tassels along the seams. A step closer revealed a man wearing a black toboggan and frontier type leather coat and britches. In one hand he was carrying a bow about six feet long. It was a brown bow nicely made with extra snakeskin wrappings on the stress points. Where the arrow fits against the bow there was a leather grip with rabbit fur at each end. In the other hand was an Indian war club. On the distal end was a large black ball about the size of a soft ball and in the center of this was a shiny steel knife pint about three inches long. This club was a brown color with a lot of brass inserts. He waved it around his head a time or two and said what did I think of his bow?

I could see now who the man was. I was my friend Rick, the man who thinks he is an Indian, Chief Crazy Horse reincarnated. Rick Young is a white man, but from the clothes he was wearing, the bear claw necklace around his neck and his mustache and long hair flowing about his unshaven face, I couldn't tell until I was closer to him.

He handed me the bow. It was a work of art, carved from young white oak and fashioned expertly into an authentic Indian bow.

"Just pull on it," he said.

I tried it and could pull only a few inches. He then showed me the pictures of the bow and of the war club in the manual on Indian lore he had brought with him. They were exact replicas in all degrees. He then insisted on going outside and trying the bow. he was so excited there was no way of denying his request. Floyd and I followed him out to the parking lot. Rick selected an old oak stump about 100 feet away and midway between us and the street where traffic was flowing.

Without hesitating, he fitted an arrow with a glistening steel point that he said Indians later got from white men and pulled back on the bow. I was trembling for fear he would miss the stump and hit a car on the street. He let the arrow fly. It centered the stump.

"That wasn't but about half as far as I can pull it back," he exclaimed as he went to retrieve the arrow. Rick is about twenty-five years old. He is as delighted in his study of the Indians as anyone can be. It was a delight to see his excitement and enthusiasm.

This is as youth should be, a sense of freedom to follow your own inclinations. He apologized about the ends of the bow not being completed.

"They should be tipped with horse hair from the mane of a stallion instead of rabbit fur. I should have fur from a ring tail cat."

He was on his way to see someone at Drowning Creek who had promised him the needed hair.

Tonight at the Rotary meeting some members were discussing the world's economic troubles by arguing about inflation and the results of a good depression. Gerald, sitting to my right, said that a great deal of the trouble was with society. No one understands where it is going. He is somewhat of a philosopher, plus a source of a lot of information. He said everything is in circles, the earth and the universe.

Whenever I could, I injected that I thought society was like a great big amoeba. Being in it, it is difficult to tell where it is going. I am sure it is moving and changing every day, but I can't tell what direction it is going in. That is probably what causes all the anxiety. We don't know if where we are is the right place, neither do we know where we are being taken by this giant mother amoeba. We are just a little molecule inside and can contribute nothing to its direction.

I suggested that the course it is taking is due to the scientific discoveries that man has made and possibly the ideas that have been accepted as a way to live. It is not the same from day-to-day, or the same each year. We concluded that the smart man will be the one who can analyze its movement and determine the course it is taking.

66

One day at a time

7-27-80 ✓

I label this writing "One day at a time" because of my depression about our ABC suit. There isn't any way I can plan for coming events. It is in the hands of the attorneys. All Jim and I can do is to wait one day at a time until they ask for something. In some ways the country is in about the same shape. The auto industry is cutting back on their production due to foreign imports. Whether or not this is having its effect on the furniture industry I don't know, but it is cutting back. Textiles are having difficulty. Our plants are running two and three days a week. On the national front, the Shaw of Iran died today. The president's brother Billy is accused of being a foreign agent for Libya. The newspapers are saying he had the approval of President Carter to negotiate with Libya and has received $200,000 to influence legislation favorable to Libya. There is also the hostage problem. Iran has not released our hostages. What course of action they will take against us now that the Shaw has died remains for time to tell.

In my own case I must continually strive to please my patients. With the health department giving away what I must charge for, I must try very hard to keep my patients. For some reason the nurse at one of the plants doesn't like me. She would like to send all the injury cases to her doctor friend in Hickory. Sometime last week a girl about twenty years old was hit on the head above her right eye when a handle on a machine broke. The foreman put a bandage on the laceration and told her she could see me in the morning. It was around ten o'clock in the morning when she came to the office. If I had seen her earlier I would have put a suture in it, but since it was now a little old I pulled the edges of the wound together with a small butterfly bandage. In addition to the laceration she complained of a headache for which I gave her some analgesics and requested her to come to the office again the next day.

She returned as requested and was getting along well, but then the mill nurse called. The patient had come by her office to make out an accident report and she thought we should send her to her friend for a skull x-ray. When I asked about the necessity of the x-ray she said perhaps we could wait a few days. My conclusion from the conversation was that she wanted all cases referred to her friend. My best approach to this problem is to be available and do the best I can for all my patients.

This approach seems to be working. Even over the nurse's objection the foremen still call for me. A few nights ago, about one-thirty, a foreman called for me to see one of his men who had cut his leg. It was a deep cut about three inches long exposing the fascia of the right leg. After suturing it both the patient and foreman seemed happy. The man returned the next day for a dressing, but he missed his next appointment. I felt sure the nurse had referred him. I called the foreman to ask why he had not returned. I was pleasantly surprised when he said the man was on the job now. He would send him to the office in a few minutes. This supported my belief that it is hard to beat being available and considerate of the patient's feelings.

I am fairing a little better with the nurse in another plant. We are concerned with a patient we think might have a brain tumor. The hospital report was negative for a brain tumor, but showed trouble with the carotid arteries. We are both pleased with this outcome. We believe this condition can be corrected with surgery.

I am having to help get a member of a family committed to a mental hospital. To gain a little time in this case, I encouraged the family today to try the patient first in a rest home where the patient can be observed and kept under strict control. It is possible the patient may like the rest home and agree to stay there. Some patients have made these facilities their home and like the company and comfort they afford. However, it is a very difficult time for elderly people when they have to give up their home to go where other people can look after them.

I have another patient I have been looking after for years that I would like to have in a rest home. Maxine has been depending on her daughter for help. They have gotten along very well at times, but then for some reason some kind of family difficulty develops. At present the daughter is going through some type of severe mental disturbance, making life very difficult for both of them.

I was called to come to the home by some of the relatives a few days ago to find out what we could do about the situation. The daughter threw all of Maxine's medication out into the yard. When I came to the house and examined Maxine, she stayed in the room declaring that her mother didn't need any medication and that her blood pressure was normal. After taking the blood pressure I assured her the pressure was high and the medication was needed to control it. To this the daughter declared that medication was not necessary and that she didn't want any more whiskey brought into the house either. For the last several years I had brought Maxine a pint of corn whiskey as a tonic. She would take about a tablespoon before each meal. It had been a pretty good tonic and I didn't believe it was too much for her. However, now it seemed too much, realizing that the angry daughter might inform all the neighbors by stating that I had been bringing her mother liquor and that it was causing her illness.

I concluded my visit stating that I would bring her some more blood pressure tablets that afternoon. When I returned in the afternoon with the medication Maxine slipped me a note folded in her check asking me to bring her on my next visit another bottle of whiskey hidden in my shirt. My usual way of bringing the liquor was leaving it in the brown bag against the front screen door. So far I haven't brought it. I am trying to get Maxine and her daughter reconciled to the fact that if they are going to live together they must try to get along together or else they are going to have to be separated, Maxine sent to a rest home and her daughter probably committed to a mental hospital, a place where she has been before.

Of the two, I am most sorry for Maxine. She frequently says that she is in something like a jail, though she is in her own home. Maxine believes that her daughter's troubles were set off by teenagers hanging around at night in the parking lot next to their home. The young people congregate in the parking lot to talk an drink. Sometimes they call obscene remarks to the daughter. She then calls the police to run them off, but because they are on private property the police can't do anything about it.

In addition to calling the police the daughter has called all of the town commissioners. They have refused to help by saying it is a matter for the police. They probably don't want to get involved. I don't believe they have much individual courage. The ABC store, the recreation complex, the Northwester Bank and some other things were not accomplished by the town commissioners. I doubt they can accomplish anything now because they do not have the support of the people.

When we stood up for the ABC vote in 1967 we were condemned to hell by the ministers and lost a lot of friends. Sometimes things for the good of the community require a lot of courage on the part of some of the citizens in the community. In the ABC vote I accepted the chairmanship of the drive and responsibility for the campaign. There wasn't anything for me to gain, but for the town I felt the proceeds from the store would help a great deal. For the same reason I worked to get permission from the Banking Commission for the Northwestern bank to come to Granite Falls. It was a personal sacrifice made by me and others for the good of our community. I don't believe the commissioners are willing to make this kind of sacrifice for our town.

Today while watering my watermelons I witnessed an example of courage.

I was standing near a watermelon hill where I noticed some black ants running frantically across a little clearing about a foot square in the grass at my feet. At first I thought they were running from the water I had been using, but then I noticed just inside the clearing a white worm about an inch long and about a fourth of an inch in diameter wiggling like it was in some kind of difficulty. I turned off the spray and bent down to see what was taking place. Two black ants were attacking the head of the worm. One had a grip on the worm just back of the head. The other ant was busy jumping about in front of the worm. Suddenly it darted in and bit some part of the head, but with the worm wiggling about it was easily dislodged.

The ant attached to the worm's neck stubbornly held on though the worm thrashed about rubbing it in the dirt. Other ants now rushed out of the grass to bite the mid section and tail, then scurried back into the grass. A few braver ants ran up to the head to view the struggle, but retreated without assisting the two attacking the head.

After about five minutes the worm suddenly stopped thrashing and lay straight out on its back. There was not an ant attacking it or even close by. Looking close at the worm I noticed the head was gone. The two attacking ants had bitten its head off. Two ants darted out of the grass and attacked the corps again, one at the tail and one at the head end.

At first it looked like they were fighting over it, but by watching the movement of the grains of sand under their feet I could see that one was pushing and one was pulling like two bulldozers. Other ants darted about but didn't offer to help.

I was about to leave the battleground when I noticed an ant dart across the clearing to a blade of grass where the battle had ended. In a second it emerged carrying something about the size of a match head with a little string attached. It was carrying the head of the worm. It carried it past the two ants moving the worm. One ant running from the opposite direction stopped it in the clearing long enough to touch the head of the worm with its antennae, then ran to a blade of grass where the attack on the worm had ended. In a second it emerged running across the clearing carrying upright the body of a black ant.

I suspected it was the body of the ant that had so stubbornly held to the neck of the thrashing worm. I would have liked to have seen the beginning of the attack. I wonder how this ant decided to seize the worm ahead of all the other ants. Did it find the worm first and hold it until other ants came to help. Perhaps another ant found the worm first and ran for help. The dead ant may have led the charge.

I don't believe any of the commissioners would have had the courage of the ant to lead a vote for beer and wine.

67

The dog days

8-4-80 ✓

This is the beginning of dog days, temperature in the nineties, hot and humid. I find myself getting tired pretty easy.

I am sure it is related to may age, but I can't seem to find any way to overcome it. I still have the ringing in my head. I think it is due to my ears. I probably have inherited some kind of deafness. Almost all of my mother's people had a hearing difficulty. Now, in addition to the hearing difficulty, which is manifested by a noise similar to that made by all the night bugs—the cicada, katydids and crickets—I am having some trouble with my eyes.

It seems that the best description of the feeling is that of smoke in the eyes. It is a burning feeling and then a feeling like the fluid over the eyes gets thick so that it disturbs the vision requiring frequent massage of the eyelids. I have some antibiotic ointment in the medicine closet, but so far I have hesitated to use it, thinking that I might be sensitive to it. If there isn't some improvement soon I am going to try some of it.

I am sure relief of my eyes will not relieve the heaviness that I feel associated with movement. It seems that to just move at times is a great effort. It is like I had just returned from a long walk and need to rest, but rest doesn't seem to relieve the condition. Neither does sleep bring renewed strength. I awake feeling about the same as I did when I retired.

I am sure this all adds up to aging. I suppose this is why some people will hesitate to vote for Reagan. They think he is too old to be president, but I am also sure some people have more energy and age slower than other people. Perhaps he is one that has a high energy level.

The ABC lawsuit is also a constant source of discomfort. I certainly don't understand the workings of the law. I keep thinking what if we lose? There will probably then be some counter suits. If my insurance doesn't pick up the cost, I probably will lose all I have. Partly for this reason I plan to sell out the beach property. One of the other reason is the expense of having them.

If I lose I will be a member of that group of people that doesn't have anything. I wonder how it feels to be a person without anything. There should not be a lot of responsibility associated with having nothing. One shouldn't have a lot of jealous people around envying what you have. There will be nothing to envy. Certainly there would be no trouble in having a goal. The only goal being to accumulate something again. No matter how I analyze it, I feel depressed. I can't see wherein I have broken any laws. I will try to put it out of my mind.

Today with all the feeling of litigation it is necessary to be pleasing to the patient. No matter how good the doctor is he is eventually going to lose the patient. This too is bad for the doctor and in some instances he has been charged with the death because he was due to be preventing the death. Even now death is being debated. Is it brain death or death from circulation? If brain death, circulatory death does not necessarily immediately follow. Sometimes I wonder what is a life. It seems to be a chemical reaction sustained by food and a constant temperature. Eventually though, even with these factors, it finally ceases to react and death follows. We can add various drugs to stimulate the reaction and make recommendations for adjusting this or that but eventually we fail. During it all we must be patient and hope for the best.

Sometime ago, after a rather hectic day, I concluded that my only purpose should be working with my patients. It is the most rewarding service I have to offer and is the position I am expected to fulfill. Seems like this reconciliation has acted to give me a lot of inner strength that is sorely needed on these hot days.

I had a few interesting patients today. One was a patient I first saw about ten days ago. His complaint was that there were fleas or some other kind of biting insects in his house. I looked at his legs where he complained most and it seemed that there were a few places that he had been bitten by possibly a flea or a mite. The places were painted with Mercurochrome so that it was difficult to see the lesions clearly. He thought the fleas were on his wife's dog or else the dog was going out into the grass and getting some kind of mites on it and bringing them into the house. They had the house sprayed for fleas twice and the dog bathed three times in some special solution. They were still having trouble and the patient had declared he or the dog was gong to have to move.

When I returned to the office from dinner the patient was in the waiting room. He started telling me about his trouble before he even sat down in the examining room chair. He said the damn fleas were eating him up and he didn't know what to do. The exterminators were coming to his house again this afternoon. I asked him to let me see the bites again. This time there were some punched out places in small clusters on the medial side of the left thigh and one on the right thigh. He said that they itched and hurt at times almost unbearable. He wasn't bothered anywhere else. There was a purplish area surrounding the lesions. I told him that I thought they were the result of shingles. I suspect that he had been developing shingles all along and not fleabites or mite bites from the dog.

Another man came in with a fishhook in his thumb. He had been fishing and caught two large stripers about twenty-five pounds each. When he called to see if I was in, I asked him to bring the fish along too. I thought if he didn't want them he would give them to me, which he as glad to do. The hook was in his thumb pretty deep, requiring some cutting to get it out.

After he left I began to think of ways to remove a fishhook without so much trouble. I first thought of a tube to slide down the shank of the hook, but then the pipe wouldn't bend. But if I was to split the pipe it would slide down the sides of the hook. If I sharpened the two edges of the pipe they should cut any tissue holding the hook at the barb. Using a pipe in a ballpoint pen, I split it and tapered the end. Then I slid it down the shaft of a hook. The tapered end and the sharp sides look like they would work well to dislodge a hood. My next thought was to find a small piece of sheet metal very think like a shim and fold it over. I have tapered the end of this folded metal and am planning to take it to the beach with me. If I find someone with a hook in his finger perhaps I can give this new idea a try.

Around four o'clock I had just returned to the office from making a house call to an elderly patient with episodes of diarrhea. I had given her an injection of Benadryl and morphine, which frequently controls the abdominal spasms in about an hour. As I entered the office the phone was ringing and it was her son asking that I arrange for his mother to be entered in the hospital because she was not a bit better. Though I suggested that the injection had not had time to work, he still wanted his mother in the hospital. I asked him if it would be all right for me to call the hospital and make arrangements before he called for the ambulance to take her over. He agreed and I told him I would call him back.

Before I could make the call Dorothy was motioning for me to come to the first treatment room. To support her motioning, there were a lot groans coming from the room so I went in to see what the trouble was. An elderly lady whom I had seen some years ago was in the chair next to the desk. She said if I didn't hurry up she was going to die. From her moans and from the expression on her face I didn't think she was in any distress so I asked Dorothy to take her temperature while I made the call to the hospital for my patient with the diarrhea. They agreed to see her and, if necessary, to arrange for admission. I relayed the message to the patient's son and felt that this patient was now taken care of and I began to give my attention to the elderly patient before me.

She related her complaints in a rapid manner. First there was smothering in her chest and high blood pressure. Her stomach was in a spasm and there was burning when she urinated. This had been ever since the last doctor's nurse nearly killed her when she drew her water to get a specimen for analysis. Ever since this, she had burning and pain radiating down her right thigh. It was so bad it gave her a terrific headache and made her blind. She was not able to stay by herself and was not going to go into a rest home. When I suggest that some nervousness might be the cause of her stomach cramps she then countered that what was causing her headache. A suggestive cause of the headache was countered with what was the cause of her smothering and so on.

I finally got her attention enough to suggest that we try something for the burning when she urinated and few tablets for the headache until the next visit. She agreed, saying that she needed to be in the hospital so they could find out what was wrong with her. I agreed, saying that if there was no improvement I would arrange hospitalization.

While Dorothy and Sarah were helping her out I went into the next room to see a patient I had not seen before. She was about forty years old, about five foot five tall and a little thin. There was some hesitancy when I asked her what her trouble was. She said she wondered if I could do anything about a sore breast. I said I would have to see it to know what I could do. She was wearing a blouse and skirt. She lifted the blouse up on the left side and then lifted up her bra. This exposed the left side of her chest to the shoulder.

The lateral half of the breast was eaten away almost exposing the pectoral muscle. The erosion extended up to the axillae and down along the lateral margin where the breast had been. The base of the ulceration was a dirty yellow and the sides had a dirty gray margin. I suspected she had cancer of the breast and it had destroyed the lateral half of her breast and had now metastasized into the lymph glands of the axillae.

I immediately told her there was nothing I could do and to cover her breast up. I had a very pungent odor. She said some doctor had given her penicillin for it and some ointment. I told her I didn't believe anything I could do would help and the only thing I knew to do was to refer her to a surgeon.

She admitted she had been told this before, but wouldn't go. On the way out I went out with her to the parking lot and talked to her husband. He too had been trying to get her to go to a surgeon. He said she kept thinking some kind of faith would heal her breast. I agreed that faith was necessary, but it might also be necessary to seek help too.

68

Mr. Republican

11-7-1980

Life for some people is a continual struggle for self preservation. After satisfying the basic needs of food and comfort there is an innate desire to be recognized by other people. This desire may be satisfied by being in a position to direct and control other people. It might be done if the person is physically stronger or mentally brighter.

If the person is just a general person he or she may achieve a dominant position through politics. In our society for some people life is a continual struggle between Republicans and Democrats for control of the lives of other people. Each party wants control of all government offices.

Perhaps politics is a lot like belonging to a church. One might limit his involvement. Perhaps this is where I have made a mistake. I have taken sides openly and am therefore fair game to the opposite side. At present, about all I am doing is waiting for the ABC matter to resolve.

I feel certain that I must make some changes in the way I am doing things from a political point of view. Even when I had helped friends win positions on the town board, there were no favors granted to me. In fact, I think they were especially careful not to do anything for me so that it would not look like they were being partial to me. I might have been better to have been a constant complainer and not had anything to do with anyone running for office. This line of reasoning doesn't seem to be very good because without having encouraged people that I thought were capable of running the town other less able people would have won the office. If one gives his opinion and it differs from other opinions then right away some people are opposing each other.

I am having difficulty understanding how a man can criticize one publicly and then call for his help privately.

The phone rang about five minutes after I had gone to bed. When I answered I was surprised by the source of the call.

"This is Jerry Chapman," announced the town commissioner. "I have a daughter that has a throat swollen almost shut."

He asked could I give her some penicillin? I inquired who her doctor had been, to which he replied that she didn't have a doctor. I wasn't to enthused about seeing his daughter.

"Are you asking me to help you?" I asked.

"Yes, sir, if you would," he replied.

I told him to bring her to the office and I would see her. I arrived at the office first and waited for him to arrive. As he came in the office I didn't say anything, just motioned for them to come on back to the examining room. After looking at her throat I could see she had a bad case of tonsillitis with her tonsils swollen so that they almost occluded her throat. Turning to Jerry, I asked him rather directly, "Do you want me to treat your daughter?"

"Yes," he said. "If I didn't I wouldn't have brought her down here."

Still looking straight at him I replied, "You didn't trust me in city hall."

"That's different," he said.

I didn't make any further reply, seeing that we would soon be in some kind of emotional discussion. I turned to the daughter again and inquired if she could take penicillin. She had never taken any so I started her on liquid penicillin, intending to give her an injection in the morning if she didn't have any trouble with the liquid. I treated her for the next three days and she cleared up her infection. I think if it had been my daughter and I had treated him like he had treated me I would have found another doctor. So far, the only understanding I can give is that they did this ABC thing all for political reasons like a game and I am not supposed to have any hurt feelings.

Our summer has gone now and we are coming up to election time when we elect people to make laws for us to live by until the next election.

Monday morning I awoke early. I was restless all night wondering if there was something else that could be done about the election Tuesday. We had canvassed all our precincts and had active precinct chairmen in each one. Also in each precinct we had telephone committees. There were haulers available for anyone needing a ride to the polls.

The polls showed the race between President Carter and Governor Reagan were about equal; we had a good chance to win if we worked hard tomorrow. The candidates had done all they could do. It was up to us now to get the voters to the polls and vote for our candidates. We were also to get to the poling places after the polls closed and count the ballots for the county commissioners and state representatives.

During the night I was very restless. I found myself continually recalling all the rallies I had attended. I knew all the candidates and could see their faces whenever I closed my eyes and thought of them. They were all good men. Frequently when I was about to doze off I found myself reviewing the drive up to the schoolhouse with the pictures of the candidates. What if in spirit they came alive and could talk to each other out there in the dark? Each would proclaim what he would do, what he was doing and had done. Soon in a fit of proclaiming and name-calling they would tear themselves loose from their stakes and destroy each other.

Thinking of them posted out there in the dark made me think of a passage from Shakespeare's play, Henry the V, Act Four, where the English and French army are waiting until morning to start a great battle.

> "From camp to camp, through the foul womb of night,
> The hum of either army stilly sounds
> That the fix'd sentinels almost receive

The secret whispers of each other's watch.
Fire answers fire, and through the night their pale flames
Each battler sees the other's umber'd face
Steed threatens steed, in high and beastful neighs.
The armourers, accomplishing the knights,
With busy hammers closing rivets up,
Give dreadful note of preparation."

When I awoke Tuesday morning it was raining. The radio and morning television reported a heavy voter turnout was expected for the election today. I heard an announcement stating the polls last night showed Reagan and President Carter to be equal in votes. Due to the heavy voter turnout it was predicted to be a bad day for Republicans. This was because Democrats outnumber Republicans two to one in registration.

At the office things were very slow. It usually is on election days. It was about one-thirty when I went to the schoolhouse to vote. Along the street I noticed some of the placards, both Democrat and Republican strewn along the street and walkway.

After closing the office I drove back to the middle school to help count votes. It was almost dark, but I could make out a few of the placards. Most of them were down and in the street. Two hanging from the cross arm of the water tank were slowly turning in the wind.

About twenty of us gathered inside around a long table. One of the judges asked us to swear on the Bible that we would do our duty. Holding up our right hand we all agreed. One of the judges then opened one of the large ten boxes. All of the ballots were poured out onto the table. I was given a tally sheet and one for the Democrat representative. We counted until about ten o'clock and then took a break. We finished counting about eleven-thirty. On the way out a Republican friend said, "I believe we whooped the shit out of them." He was going to Lenoir to the headquarters building to celebrate. I went home to bed.

It was about seven-thirty when I awoke. I turned the radio on to get the election returns. We were surprised to hear that the Republicans had won every office in the county. Our state candidates had won too. At the office it was impossible to hide my delight. Whenever my patients came in they were smiling too, even if they were Democrats. Being a Republican now was a pleasant feeling but it was soon to change. A man came in the office a little before noon for an insurance exam. I recognized him to be one of our candidates for the school board.

He too was happy. After discussing the election a bit I asked him what were the chances of removing the two schoolteachers that were town commissioners. I told him about their involvement in the ABC suit. He said he expected they would be backing off now. The Republicans were in charge and I was now Mr. Republican to them. They were the ones now that were going to have to do our bidding. When he left, the next person to come was Jerry. He had worked hard in the election and hauled voters to the polls. He came in to tell me now that now that we had won the election we needed to get rid of all important Democrats in the county. He then proceeded to name some very special Democrat "bastards" that ought to go first. Shortly after he left the office one of the special "bastards" he had named came into the office for treatment of his arthritis. An hour later a member of the press came in for treatment of his ulcer. He had not been in the office for ten years. I began to wonder how to handle the responsibility of being in charge of things.

How can I fire all of these people and keep a good feeling in the community? I can see already it is not going to be easy being Mr. Republican.

69

Christmas 1980

12-27-80 ✓

Tuesday it rained all day. On the way to the office I stopped to visit with Melvin. He was growing some tomatoes in five-gallon buckets in his office window. I said they seemed to be growing well, and asked how many tomatoes did he expect to get off of them. He replied he didn't know but Laney had five. To this I think I replied, "Big as this?" meaning Melvin's five-gallon buckets.

He said, "No, five bodies." He meant that five people had died Monday and Monday night. Laney had five bodies in the funeral home for burial in all this rain. I think elderly people keep a close watch on people listed in the obituary section of the paper. It is a way of keeping up with their friends.

The thing about Melvin's conversation that bothered me was that I had difficulty following the jump from the number of tomatoes I thought he expected to the number of bodies Laney had for burial. Seems like I am having difficulty following other things too. At the office I didn't understand things any better.

I had been treating a patient for a very bad dog bite on her right arm. It is healing up without difficulty, but will probably leave some scarring which I told her about before I sutured the wound. She understood this as a natural thing. When she came to the office on Tuesday I noticed my dressing had been changed. When I inquired about my dressing she said her lawyer had taken it off a few days ago when she was in his office with her son to get his driving license reinstated. She said he said she could get a lot of money because of scarring. I wondered why she couldn't have waited until the wound healed before seeing her attorney. It is not only doctors like me the lawyers are after, they are bringing suit against the hospitals too. It is on account of the tendency of lawyers to sue that the health department took out liability insurance last night. Two attorneys from the state health department were there to explain the laws to the health department. From their discussion I found out that there is too much emphasis given to the attorney general's rulings. From my involvement with the ABC Suit I have concluded he is just another attorney and may be as wrong as anybody.

I was very disappointed to hear this. I had counted on his ruling to help Jim and me in our ABC suit. When I inquired from his office to find out if the town had authority over us his opinion was that once the town had appointed us we were an autonomous body not subject to discipline from the town commissioners.

My practice is off about 50 percent. I have had an unusual case today. It involved a little boy about six years old. He had got his penis caught in the zipper of his pants close to the bottom of the fly. His grandfather was carrying him in and the boy was crying loud as he could, "My goober, my goober. Don't let him cut it off."

I used some wire cutting pliers and cut the part of the zipper that closes the opening. With this removed I was able to separate the zipper without much pain. He left smiling, his goober intact.

If you had been there while I was operating on the zipper to free his goober I would have asked you if you know why most women voted for Jimmie Carter?" They say it is because he had the biggest goober.

Just before closing the office, Jim came by. He wanted to pay me twenty-eight dollars, which was half of the cost of the dinner we had Wednesday night. Dorothy and I invited them to celebrate our wedding anniversary. It was also the end of the first year after being fired by the town commissioners. While in the office, Dorothy asked him to help her with some year-end reports. He said that was one reason he was retiring He was tired of filing out all kind of reports and being responsible for them. In addition, he was giving half of what he made to the government.

He helped with the report and visited with a few patients that came in. When he left Dorothy and I wondered if anyone would give Jim some kind of community recognition. While in business operating his clothing store he opened it anytime Laney called for a suit or dress for a deceased. If someone was burned out he gave them clothes. For a long time he was a scoutmaster and helped one of the commissioner's sons attain eagle rank.

With the community divided as it is now I doubt that anything will be done.

70

Jobs

"DOG CATCHER FIRED FOR POLITICAL REASONS" was the headline of an article on the front page of the Lenoir News-Topic today along with international news. Russia is still poised on the Polish Border is just about to agree to release our hostages and President Carter is preparing his farewell speech. Ronald Reagan is flying to Washington to be the new president. Now how do you equate firing the county dogcatcher with all this?

It is because all of this is politics the same as a drop of blood is part of a person.

It is true the county commissioners let the dogcatcher go and probably for political reasons. He was let go when the Republicans were in office about ten years ago and hired again when the Democrats beat the Republicans in the next election.

In his letter to the paper he stated he had been hired by the Democrats for political reasons and probably for the same reasons he was fired by the Republicans. The chairman had more to say about the dogcatcher last night. He said that since the dogcatcher was within a few weeks of mandatory retirement at age seventy-five the commissioners asked him to give up his job to a younger man. There were some remarks like he was the best dogcatcher in the county had ever had and a long time Democrat worker.

On this account he had to go. The chairman then repeated that the commissioners should fire all Democrats they can and give the jobs to Republicans, but he cautioned them that they cannot fire them for political reasons. There is a law against this. If they do fire them they may appeal to the labor board and have an investigation of unfair labor practices the people they fire have a right to sue the county commissioners. To move them out they can ask them to leave because they are uncooperative or as the case with Williams, head of veterans affairs and town commissioner, they can change the name of the job so it is no longer available.

While the chairman was talking I thought I heard some commotion behind a partition in the room. I punched Connley to tell him someone should investigate. We would be rather embarrassed if tomorrow's paper headlined our meeting. He tiptoed out to look behind the petition. Some members laughed when he returned. When the chairman brought up tax re-evaluation there was a great disturbance. Sherman sitting across the table from me was getting redder in the face by the minute as if straining with a bowel movement. Finally he could wait no longer.

He shouted out to the chairman that this was all a crock of manure as far as he was concerned. They had raised the value of his farm 300 percent. The meeting finally ended with the understanding anyone dissatisfied could have a hearing with the tax people. I called Jim this morning to let him know his store was being re-evaluated. He wasn't concerned.

He said, "We'd just as well spend our time studying about fishing and leave politics alone." Then he asked how I liked his Christmas poem? I said it was all right, but not as good as the one I sent him.

For Christmas I gave him a little bell to attach to the end of his fishing rod. The idea was when the fish bites it would ring the bell. I enclosed a note with it that went like this:

If when standing by the sea, your bent rod you fail to see, surely the peal of this little bell will tell when I am not around to yell, for sometime you might be by the sea without me.

His reply was:

Should I be standing by the sea and should the little bell toll with glee, I will think of thee and wish thee were there with me.

And when the fish is well in hand I'll think of thee in the red hilly land, caring for the ills of man.

While I was reading the paper last night there was an open forum letter criticizing doctors for charging too much and praising the health department. I think it was written in response to a report about the county commissioners going to cut down on some services.

Although the health department is seeing a lot of my patients, I still have a few loyal ones. A few days ago the mother of the boy that got his goober caught in his zipper brought her daughter in with the flu. I inquired about my little patient and was informed that his goober healed without any trouble.

Laney has been very sick again with the flu. Following each relapse he has an attack of arthritis. A few days ago I had a patient with the flu. After giving him some medicine he paused on his way out to say how much he appreciated me and my services. He said some of his friends at work had recommended him not to come because I never got anybody well, but he had always gotten along fine. I told him I appreciated this and that I always did the best I knew how. He said he knew this and that I was very religious man like himself.

He then related how he had been saved and spent a great deal of time reading the Bible. He often discussed the Bible with his fellow workers and anyone else he thought was interested. He believed there were a lot of hypocrites in the world and he was doing his best to change them.

This caused me to recall his last visit. He was complaining that he could not reach a climax whenever he had intercourse. I assured him there was nothing wrong and perhaps he would be able to function normally when he was married. At the time he was living with a seventeen-year-old girl in a trailer. Now with him professing so much self-righteousness and the world full of hypocrites I couldn't help getting his opinion about his own conduct. I followed him to the outside door and said, "Jake, I wonder what the Bible says about living with a girl and not marrying her?" I saw him blush some and grin a little. His reply was since she was not married or since he was not married it was not called adultery.

I pushed a little harder, asking for where it says this in the Bible. Jake has not been back to see me.

Wednesday afternoon the weather was bad so instead of going fishing I tried making a mold to make crappy jigs. I made a few jigs but they were all very rough. Jim came by to inspect them and said they were too big, but they might work later in the year. He showed me some he had made and tied with gold string he had found around the store. He said what we needed was some silver string.

Around five o'clock as I was returning up the hill from inspecting the minnows at the creek I saw a deputy sheriff's car coming up the road and pull to a stop at the front of the house. Sometimes a deputy sheriff or a policeman come to tell me a patient is at the police station and ask me to come to the office to see them, so I am not too surprised when they come.

This time it was different. The officer was unfolding a rather large sheet of paper. It was a summons from Don for me to appear in his office March 5 to answer questions about going to the national ABC convention from1972 through 1978. I was quite disturbed because he had taken all of the ABC records from the ABC store. I called Jim to tell him what was happening. The sheriff was at his door then. I called Bert and he had received one too about the land. He had called the clerk of court and they said Don had sent out six subpoenas only by now we were calling them Don's valentines. He had sent one to Hamby, the man we bought the land from. Monday night at the health department meeting one of the directors told me Don had a new Democrat appointment. The strategy committee. The duties are to make all Republicans look bad politically or wreck all Republican activities. I began to wonder how he is going to handle all of these activities. There is the suit against the town for cutting the power unannounced at one of our plants at six o'clock in the morning, the trouble Laney and Tommie are having with their land and the suit Jim and I have going. I have never known the town to be in such a turmoil.

There is a love song that goes something like this, "If I had a silver thread and golden needle I could fix this heart of mine," It is going to take more than a silver thread and golden needle to bring harmony again to this town. Only movement and funerals may smooth things again.

71

Depositions

3-8-81 ✓

At last things seem to be going well for Jim and me regarding our ABC suit. Thursday the old ABC Board met with the town attorney to give depositions about running the ABC store. It has been a time of great apprehension but at last I am feeling confident we are going to win. It seems now like a surgeon with a silver thread and golden needle will mend our hearts.

What does he look like?

A man about fifty years old wearing khaki work clothes instead of a white gown, a blue denim jacket and brown scuffed shoes. He is slightly stooped in the shoulders, about five-foot ten inches tall, gaunt and agile as a cat. When he walked into Robbins' office he moved along the wall by the chairs without touching any of them or the wall. When he eased into the chair at the table he looked like a man that had been on a six-week drunk. His hair was not combed and he was wearing a beard about two weeks old. He held his head down a little and was twisted in the chair toward the court recorder. When she asked him if he was going to tell the truth, he lifted his head up straight and in a very clear voice said, "I do, so help me God."

I got a frontal view of his face. It was tan; his nose was sharp and narrow. His lips were thin, forming a straight mouth. His eyes seemed to be dancing and full of fire. If he held to the opinion of the town attorney he gave me on Monday I thought my worries were over. All week I had been worrying about his deposition. Would he be helpful to the town or us?

I worried so much I frequently felt numbness in my left hand and arm. There was something of a lump in my throat giving a choking feeling. Even under stressful times with my patients I had some tightness in my chest. At night there had been very little sleep. Dorothy was having similar feelings. Frequently she wanted me to take her blood pressure and her pulse. She complained of her heart skipping. I tried to assure her it was all coming from our anxiety over the suit. I suspected that the other members were having similar feelings.

Though I tried to reason with myself that I could not come up with all the things Robbins might ask and I should stop worrying about it, it was not that easy to do. What about going to national conventions and taking our wives, what about buying the land to keep the cement off of the liquor bottles, what about taking liquor from the store? We had not taken any. We poured all damaged liquor down the sink. What about our ABC officer? We gave him money to buy setups to catch people for selling illegal liquor. There was no end to all the things that kept coming to mind.

When I rose Wednesday morning Dorothy said I should wear a suit. I agreed on my gray suit. When I came downstairs for breakfast Dorothy was crying with a bad headache. She said it was from her sinuses, but I knew it was from tension.

At the office I saw one or two patients. I was pretty tense and had to be very careful to keep my mind on my business. Once I loaded a syringe with penicillin and moved toward a patient with it. When she saw the syringe she said that doesn't look like B12.

Sometimes I was tempted to pray for our success, but I could never bring myself to ask God to help me with trouble I had got myself into with liquor. When we were running the campaign for the ABC store I was surprised at the man giving the invocation at our last dinner asking for God's help for our success.

Around nine o'clock I could not stand waiting any longer. The countdown was now in minutes. I gathered my material and drove to Jim's house. I pulled into his back yard and turned around. I saw Dot watching me through the bedroom window. I pulled up to Jim's top gate. Jim came out of his kitchen dressed in a blue suit. He didn't have any material. When he got into the car he asked me why I was taking all this material? I said Robbins might ask me something I didn't know. He replied if I didn't know to just say no. We drove down to Bert's plant Bert was waiting for us in his office. He said we were looking good.

Sentelle, our attorney, arrived from Charlotte, a little late due to all the fog. He looked over some material Bert had and said it was good, but to remember to just answer the questions and no more. After a few other precautions about our conduct we left for Robbins' office.

It was on the third floor of the Building and Loan Building. The door to his office opened from the left of a long hallway. Inside there was a large table about four feet by ten with three black leather chairs on each side and one at each end. The court recorder was seated at the far end of the table on a small typing chair with her back to us. Robbins took the chair across the table from her and Sentelle took the chair in back of her and across from Robbins. Pete took the end chair near the recorder and Jim took the one beside Sentelle. I took the other end chair. City Manager Nobles took the chair to Robbins' left. He had a big pack of papers. I guessed they were questions and answers he would feed to Robbins. Robbins was a little reluctant to start because Hamby had not arrived. One of his office girls came back and reported she had called about Hamby, the man who had sold us the land beside the store, and he was on his way. He should be here shortly. Robbins seemed pleased with the news and after wiggling about in his chair he had the recorder to swear Pete in and began his deposition.

Robbins asked about the land purchase and a few other general questions. Robbins then jogged out to the front office to see if Hamby had arrived. He had not so he swore Jim in and started his deposition. He asked him the same questions he had asked Pete and then some about conventions and school funds. Jim was calm and never got flustered one time. Robbins soon dismissed him and jogged to the front office again to find Hamby. He hadn't arrived. I was getting worried. Had Hamby promised Robbins some special information against us. Robbins decided to take Bert's deposition next. Robbins already had our written answers to most of the questions he was asking. I think the pile of papers Noble had were the written depositions we had already given Robbins. Nobles was munching on a sucker and grinning like a possum. I thought from his body language he was thinking, "We gotcha now."

The phone near Robbins made a funny sound. He grabbed it and said Hamby had arrived. He sort of wiggled out of his chair and went in a fast jog out of the room. When he returned in a minute or two and got seated he said Hamby was here and he would take his deposition now before lunch. He dismissed Bert and buzzed for Hamby. Hamby was led into the room by one of the office girls. She gave him Bert's seat. Robbins seemed quite happy. He must have thought now he had a special witness.

Robbins' shirt was dripping wet with perspiration. I think this was due to the strain he was under. None of us was sweating like Robbins. The recorder swore Hamby in and after the usual questions Robbins began his deposition.

I thought to myself, one of us is going to get it now. This man is smart and tough.

Robbins' first question was, "Did you own the land you sold to the ABC Board?"

"You ought to know, you did the title search," Hamby replied.

This set Robbins back a bit. His face seemed to cloud, but undaunted he asked his next question. "Did you bring your 1974 income tax record like I told you?"

"No," said Hamby, "I didn't. "My tax report is none of your damn business."

Robbins' face turned red. He shifted to questions about the sale of the land to the ABC Board. Hamby said Reece had contacted him about selling the land and that Robbins himself had called him encouraging him to sell the land and that fifty-nine thousand dollars was a good price. There were other questions but nothing that seemed to help Robbins. Hamby said his cement trucks blocked the road and dust blew on the store, but he couldn't help it. On this account he had decided to sell the property.

When Robbins finished with Hamby we took a break for lunch. We started again at two o'clock. I gave my deposition and then Reece gave his. I think Robbins never found out anything new. I feel a lot better now that this part is over.

72

Don's proposition

I long for the time when I will not be involved in continual conflict, but the more I think of it the more I am convinced that this life is concerned with people after people in some manner. We can't live without being involved with each other. We must pick the best choice for our time and hope for the best.

All around the yard there were beautiful azaleas blooming. Most all of the birds are back from the south. I have just been enjoying the beauty of nature. How all of this was planned out, the trees to put out leaves, the flowers to bloom, birds and bees to all follow seasons and over all of this man has been given dominion is an awesome thought. One that man doesn't give much thought to.

I became aware of it when I bought some seeds. After making the selection I noticed that the catalogue stated how long it took for the seeds to mature into fruit, about ninety days. It took some good planning to make seeds that grow and mature along with the length of the season. People live about seventy years, but when do they come to maturity as a seed to fruit? I wonder about the maturity of the town commissioners.

Wouldn't it be wonderful if man could regulate his affairs as well as nature? As man matures he spends a lot of time seeking to satisfy his ego. For this President Reagan was shot by a young man wanting to impress his girlfriend. A few days ago someone shot the Pope. Now we are considering whether or not we should restrict handguns. Should everyone carry one in his or her pocket? Congress is trying to decide.

Friday, Dorothy and I went to the City Barbecue for lunch. She went first because I was busy with a patient. Two ladies and two of the town commissioners were in the adjoining booth. Dorothy was sitting facing the two commissioners. When I came in I didn't see them and sat with my back to them. Dorothy said they had been playing some kind of a game children play to humiliate someone. They all agree at a signal to turn around making fun of someone.

Sometimes you get help from a good friend. A few weeks ago a man committed suicide and Laney had the body. For some reason a reporter was not satisfied with the cause of death and called Laney to verify the death certificate. When Laney answered the phone he told him this was the first time anyone had ever called to verify anything. He then asked him why he hadn't tried to find out about the certificates of deposit the ABC store held and who did the title search on the land we bought for the ABC store. Laney said the reporter agreed to look into it but he didn't believe he would because Noble would not give the paper any more news from city hall.

The lady with the dog bite has turned her case over to an attorney to collect damages for the dog bite and scaring. I have not been subpoenaed yet. Almost all auto accidents are turned over to an attorney. With things like this I am not surprised at anything. I Just try not to faint. Take the elderly lady I saw some time ago. She is about fifty, a widow, wears a tan hat, keeps her hair pushed back, her collar buttoned and wears a light black coat all the time. She is always very polite.

After I had completed my examination and the visit concluded she said, "Do you want to see something pretty?" What would you have said with her sitting there with a little smile looking you straight in the eye? My mind was blank; my mouth just said, "Yes" where upon her right hand slid into her large black hand bag and pulled out a rather large pearl handle pistol in a shiny brown holster and gently laid it on the desk pointing it at me.

I was quick to agree that it was a pretty thing with a cold blue steel barrel. She said it still had the original cartridges that her husband had put in years ago. Again stating how pretty it was I gently turned it so it wasn't pointing at me and kindly slid it toward her, suggesting she put it back in the bag. When she had been gone a little while I wondered if she had not wanted me to buy it.

Some people might have been carrying a pistol a few Saturday nights ago. The recreation department sponsored a boxing match at the Shuford Recreation center. They had about the same luck as I did with my boxing match. After a few rounds the fight became a free for all. Fans began throwing chairs at each other and into the ring. Some people say it was because the contestants were white and black and it turned into a race riot. Others say it was a grudge fight between the referees. At any rate five or six people were hurt and the fight canceled. At the town board meeting the commissioners discussed banning all boxing and wrestling in the city. A lot of people blamed the police for not keeping order.

None of the policemen were at the board meeting. I think they are too worried about their jobs. The city manager has moved the police department up to the fire station to conserve money. The police don't like it and have threatened to quit unless they are moved back to city hall. Some of them say the firemen keep all the bathrooms locked.

Bert and I were hoping the town board would not renew Don's contract, but because of all the suits the town attorney has going they thought best to rehire him.

Tuesday morning after the meeting Bert told me our attorney had called. Don had called him and made a proposition to settle with Jim and me. He said the town would settle if we would agree to purchase the land and give a token amount of money for the cost of attending conventions. Don's excuse for making the proposition was that he had heard we wanted to settle. As far as I know, neither Jim nor I have discussed settlement. I think with all the trouble the town is having with the police and suits, some of the commissioners are falling out among themselves.

73

Summer of discontent

6-5-81 ✓

Most everything now is as hot as the weather.

To let you know just how hot things are I had a patient yesterday who needed an ambulance to take her to the hospital. Our ambulances are dispatched by the police department. I called the police station and they said they would have one dispatched out of Lenoir right away. When I returned from lunch, Sarah said I should call the police station again, the ambulance had not come for the patient. When I called, the policeman said, "If you don't believe I called the Goddamn people come up here and I'll show you the Goddamn record."

I suppose some of the relatives had called him several times. It is peculiar how things are sometimes related, the ambulance and the police department.

In the last issue of the Hickory paper in the editorial section there was this comment: "Granite Falls officials, elected and appointed have lost credibility in the public fuss that erupted from a well-intended plan the town had to save money. This is unfortunate, especially because the flap probably could have been avoided or minimized. A little more deliberate thought, planning and execution could have made such a difference."

I think it is in reference to the move of the police to the firehouse. The police didn't want to move. Chief Barlow told Noble, "Just figure up my retirement pay and I will retire right now." Barlow retired then. Noble went ahead and moved the police in with the firemen. Now the firemen won't let the police use their social room or bathroom. This has caused the police to threaten to resign. They had a meeting about it without letting Noble know. He found out about the meeting and fired two policemen, one was chief Barlow's nephew. Two more officers resigned.

The newspaper headlined the event saying, "Two Police officers fired, Two resign." This got the people to talking about their protection. The police agreed with this saying they couldn't get along with Noble so they would demand his resignation.

At a meeting last night it was reported that Noble cursed the policemen and then fired them and took discharge papers over to the lieutenant to sign them so it would appear the lieutenant fired them. I remember telling Noble when he first came here that his days would be through whenever he tangled with the police department.

Now the commissioners are falling out with each other. Erby supported the police move at first, but at the last meeting he made a motion to bring them back. It failed to be seconded. Now with Erby split from the other commissioners and with Chief Barlow mad for Noble's firing his nephew things are getting hotter. Bert plans to hold the next meeting in the recreation center where there will be room for everybody.

My practice is about the same. Yesterday I saw a patient who was not so pleasant. He was a young man about eighteen years old, average size, had brown fluffy hair and a narrow face that reminded me of a possum. Two or three of his front teeth were missing. He had very bright blue eyes. He had gonorrhea. When he returned the next day for treatment he was grinning and said his father who had been in the army had told him how to tell the next time if a girl had gonorrhea. His father told him to stick his finger in his ear and then rub the earwax on the girl's thighs near her vagina. If she hollered with pain she had the gonorrhea.

74

Police pendulum

The regular town meeting is to be held in the Shuford Recreation Center. The big question is whether or not the commissioners can be persuaded to move the police back to city hall, their old office. I will give you more details later.

I am a little blue today because of the death of one of my patients yesterday morning. Sandy was about seventy years old. During the last year she developed a heart condition along with her diabetes and hypertension. These conditions were under control until yesterday morning around ten o'clock Her niece called for me to come to the house. She said Sandy had been sick all night.

When I arrived, Sandy was lying on the couch in the living room with a wastebasket near her head. I gave her an injection for the nausea and waited to see if she improved. After there was no response I called for an ambulance to take her to the hospital. They came right away.

I felt like she was having a severe heart attack. When we put her on the cot her breathing stopped. Using chest massage we got her breathing started. When they got to the hospital Sandy was dead. This evening Dorothy and I went to the funeral home where the family was receiving friends.

I am worried about another patient going into the hospital. About a month ago I had studies made of her bowel. She has a mass in the large bowel. She was operated on Tuesday. Her chances for a good recovery are not very good. She had a heart attack five years ago and developed a blood clot in the left leg. She recovered from the heart attack, but had to have her leg amputated because of the blood clot.

This afternoon I went to the Western Auto store to buy some paint. Jack came out to wait on me. He started talking about the condition of the town. He blamed Noble for all the trouble, but said it was the fault of the people for letting him run the town.

"People can get off the bus here and we will ask them to run the town for us," he said.

While we were talking, his long-time friend Wakefield came in and joined us. Wakefield was mayor before Bert. He too was of the opinion that we must do something to get our town back together again. Jack said rather angrily, "Everywhere I go, people are asking what we are doing here. We are acting like a bunch of children. We must work together again or let the outsiders have it."

Wakefield greed. "This damn shit isn't going to work. We had better get together and work to pull the town out of the trouble we are in."

Jack said we are going to spend about a hundred thousand dollars to remodel the fire station. "The only way to do the town any good," he said, "is to have four good men to run in the election. I don't care how many letters Tucker and Williams put in the paper, the people are mad now. It doesn't make any difference either how many letters Noble puts in, the people are mad. Boy, I tell you this is something else."

I had been there about an hour. I could have stayed all day the way they were talking but I needed to get back to my patients.

I didn't go to the big meeting at the Recreation Center. My patients told me about it all day long. All the commissioners voted to keep the police in the firehouse except Erby. It was a pretty hot meeting. Nobody agreed with anyone else. Some petitions were circulated calling for Noble to resign. I think the most outstanding character at the meeting was Wade. He is a big redheaded man, about six feet, three or four inches tall, about forty-five years old, reddish complexion from the sun and has fiery blue eyes. You don't want to meet him in the dark if he is mad. He is in the excavating and grave digging business. He had come by the office earlier in the day. I encouraged him to attend the meeting. He said he didn't have property in town but his mama did so he felt entitled to speak for her. He is mad anyway because the town is fixing to annex some of his property.

He finally got the floor at the meeting. I couldn't find out all he had to say. Bert called him down a time or two but Wade didn't stop until he had complained to all the commissioners and called for Noble to resign. For this he got a standing ovation.

Wade was so excited that he came by the office Tuesday morning to tell me about it. He said he had done some grade work for Don and had not been paid. If he found him out some place he might just kill him and take him home and put him in his freezer until he was digging a grave for a vault. To hide Don, all he would have to do is dig about four feet deeper, dump Don in and put the vault on top of him and fill the grave with dirt. No one would ever know what happened.

I said even with Don out of the way we would still have the two schoolteachers. There was no way to touch them. He just laughed about this saying, "You want to bet?" Then bending down and whispering in my ear he said, "Why I can plant some cocaine or marijuana in their cars any time and have the sheriff search the car."

Whenever he left I began to wonder how I was going to keep Wade from doing something.

In the afternoon paper there was a picture of Noble captioned, "Not going to resign." This may be the end of our form of city manager type of government. Finn and I worked for this type of government. I am sorry it didn't pan out.

One thing I have learned about dealing with the public is that if at all possible one should settle all complaints as quickly as possible. "Give everyone thine ear," even the dogcatcher. Talk with both sides trying to come to an understanding. Don't trust secrets in public office. Other people will find out and you will be caught on one or the other side of the problem. Talk with all people that may have an interest in the problem.

I should have had more people involved with the ABC matter. Every time there was a question I should have had other people giving their opinion. Anyone left dissatisfied or ignored is going to be working to get that man out of office at the next election. Perhaps the campaign for 1981 has now started.

75

Humpty Dumpty

Somewhere there is a nursery rhyme that goes, "Humpty Dumpty sat on a wall. Humpty Dumpty had a great fall. All the king's horses and all the king's men couldn't put Humpty together again."

City Hall has now had a great fall. It will take a long time to put it together again, probably another generation.

The Hickory Daily News and the Lenoir News-Topic carried headlines announcing "Granite City Manager Resigns" in their Friday issues. You recall the meeting at the recreation center to discuss the firemen and policemen merging in the firehouse. At the conclusion of the meeting there was a request by some people for the city manager to resign. Following this meeting, the papers had Noble's picture in the paper captioned, "City Manager Not Resigning." Well, now he is resigning. Some of the commissioners want him to stay, so there is a big split in their team. The town council accepted his resignation and voted not to advertise for another town manager until after the November election. I thought the next election would be against hiring a city manager and suggested this to Bert.

Noble's resignation has great significance to our ABC suit. With Noble out of city hall Bert can get information without Noble watching. Too, Don will now be cut off from information in city hall. With the breakup of the commissioners, their teamwork is lost.

The city attorney, Don, is in about the same position as Noble. For Don to hold his job he will need to get three commissioners and a mayor to support him.

Most of my patients Friday and Saturday were happy about Noble's resignation. Even at church they were happy. After the service, there were people outside in little groups talking about it. At first I thought they were talking about the preacher's remarks about President Nixon. Someway the preacher had brought up the question of whether or not my alma mater, Duke University, would allow Nixon's Memorial Library to be put on the University Campus. In his sermon he had said several times, "May God forbid this to happen." I had just written a letter to the Duke trustees recommending acceptance. I thought whatever Nixon had done was a fact, right or wrong. Let those who see it determine right or wrong for their own lives. Well, whenever I could join a group I found they were talking about Noble and city hall.

Bert called me today to tell that he had a call from Don. He said Don told him to tell me and Jim the town would be willing to drop the suit for a token amount for the conventions we had attended. He had now given up on us paying for the land. I told him I didn't want to accept this, but I would see what Jim wanted. He was at the beach right now.

I told Dorothy about the proposal at noon. She is not happy about it or church either. There was a note in the paper stating that the Duke trustees had voted 9-2 to accept the library.

I have decided I am not going to let politics run me out of church. Certainly I will have a hard time on judgment day explaining my philosophy of religion, but for now at church it is mostly Democrats against Republicans, not religion, so I am going to continue to go to church.

Before judgment day I am expecting another judge to rule on our ABC mater. This is the third time it has progressed so far and been called off. The judge is due to decide Tuesday whether either side has a case to go to court. As far as Bert and I can find out Don and Sentelle are to meet before a judge named Farrell, the judge Wade said didn't like Don.

I have worried about the ABC thing for almost four years now. It has had a great effect on Dorothy and me. I feel sure it has done Dot and Jim the same way. For my part I have developed intermittent numbness in my left arm, my eyes water and burn, feeling like they are in a constant strain. My new glasses don't help. My ears ring like I have been exposed to a great explosion. I checked with the hearing people. They found I have lost 50 percent of my hearing. These are just some of the little things that have happened due to the continual anxiety.

Some of it might be aging. The intermittent numbness in my left arm is probably beginning angina. It runs in my family.

Hadley and his wife came in the office yesterday. They are the elderly couple that helped me run the theater. At one time he had lost the sight of one eye in a fight. Now he has glaucoma in the other eye and can hardly see. Mom, his wife, has developed diabetes and shortness of breath so bad it was necessary to send her to the hospital.

I sent another patient to the hospital Sunday with mild heart failure. Her daughter called me the first thing Monday morning to tell me that her mother had been suffering with heart trouble all along and I had not diagnosed it. She said I should have referred her to a specialist before now. When I got a chance, I told her I would have sent her to a specialist if she had been that sick. This didn't help any. Now her mother was confined to the hospital and would never come home because I sent her so late. She said her mother was not getting along well and almost died last night. She was going to report me to the authorities. She would come by the office this afternoon to pick up receipts so she could show the authorities how much I had overcharged her mother.

Now it was a little hard to start out Monday's work with such criticism. When I called the doctor who was treating the patient he said the daughter was calling him two or three times a day. He had found nothing else wrong than what I told him when I referred her to the hospital. He said he would be glad when he can discharge her.

Another event occurred a few days ago that has added to my tense-ness. I have gotten involved with the police about moving to the fire station. One of the policemen, the one with a big round face, came to see me with an earache. During the examination he talked about the meeting at the Rec Center. When I finished checking his ear I told him I couldn't see anything wrong with his ear. He was pretty insistent that I call Ted and Erby. They wanted to talk to me. After he left I called Bert and he called our attorney for advice.

Sentelle said I could talk to Ted, but not to Erby since he was named in the suit. Ted said he could help in the coming election and he could get the commissioners to drop the suit. I thanked him and let it go at that. Tuesday at noon, while having lunch, the front door bell rang. It was a policeman wanting to see me. Sarah went to the door and let him in to the dining room where Dorothy and I were eating. He had a clipboard and pencil and some yellow tickets in his hand. I thought he was going to file some more charges against me.

After a few remarks about how easily he could have broken into the house, he then asked about the security of the house. I started telling him about the front door and then I noticed he seemed to be leading me with various signs to the basement door. I followed his lead and when we were outside he suddenly needed to change pencils. He pulled from his left front shirt pocket a typewritten note on some light brown wrapping paper. The paper was about two inches wide and twelve inches long. There were four or five lines typed on it without any errors in the typing. He handed it to me and I asked him what he wanted me to do with it. He said read it and tell Bert what's on it.

I said I would give it to Bert, but he said no, the sender wanted the note back. This was a bit astonishing. Why would the sender want it back. The sender must have felt if the note got out of his control it could be traced. The note was an urgent request for me to tell Bert about the meeting tonight of the town board. Noble was going to pro-pose at the meeting that the policeman that had spoke up at the Rec Center be promoted to lieutenant. The note said this was Noble's way of paying off the policeman for speaking for the move to the firehouse. Bert was to contact his three supporters to block the promotion. Bert could break the tie vote. The note requested Bert to table the mater until after Noble had left town. In leaving he cautioned me not to call the police station, all calls were being monitored. I called Bert that afternoon about the note.

It was sometime late Wednesday morning when I got a report of the board meeting. They tabled Noble's proposal about the policeman. They had gone into executive session to discuss the ABC mater. Don had been instructed to propose a settlement of each party dropping their suit. Don held out for us to pay our convention expenses, but the board said no, just each party quit. They went into executive session so the reporters wouldn't know about it.

Tucker insisted on advertising for a new city manager. If Bert supports it he will have a hard time getting elected. The voters are opposed to a city manager now.

76

A bad way to begin a year

1-1-1982 ✓

I was called to one of the plants three nights ago at eleven o'clock. One of the men had got his arm caught in a machine.

When I arrived at the plant someone was standing under the light at the stairwell to guide me through the plant past the humming machines. We stopped at the end of one row. A large group of men had gathered around the end machine. Other men were standing about watching this group. One man was standing higher than the rest with his head twisted to the left just above the machine. His left arm was holding onto something above it and his right arm was fastened to something down in the machine. He was pale and sweating, but not complaining of pain.

There were some wooden crates on the floor. I climbed on these and then onto some part of the machine so that I could see that the worker's right hand had gone through some part of the mechanism that looked like a wringer on an old-time washing machine. The big difference was that these rollers had thousands of metal spikes about an inch and a half long spaced about a quarter of an inch apart.

Somehow he had got his hand caught and it had pulled his index finger between these rollers up to the first joint of his hand. Someone heard him screaming and ran over to stop the machine before it pulled his arm off. I was able to free his hand by breaking off the spikes. He is doing well.

I have waited until today to find out the name of the new police chief. The best I can find out is that the commissioners avoided the issue. It seems you wait a long time for tomorrow to bring the answers you want. On the other hand how far away is yesterday when you would like to correct some of the things you did that now appear wrong. Thinking of these things seems to point out how helpless we are to change the coming events. Perhaps our feelings are directly affected by the weather just like rheumatism.

Sometime during the night Dorothy awoke me to listen to the rain on the roof and running down the gutters outside the bedroom. I went back to sleep and resolved since it was a Sunday morning I would not get up until summoned by someone knocking on the door or the telephone ringing.

The telephone won out. It rang at exactly nine o'clock. It was a friend of ours calling to say that her husband had left her and would Dorothy please come to stay with her. We arose from our bed to a cold rainy day with a depressing task ahead.

Dorothy left to go see our friend. I went to the office where there were a few patients waiting. After seeing them I decided to go to church. I felt like the preacher would like to have as many people as he could on a cold rainy Sunday. Too, I didn't want to give the church up to my Democrat friends.

At the church Dot and Jim were greeters. They seemed right happy. Inside the sanctuary there were very few people and I was glad I had come. It was communion Sunday. I could tell from the white sheet the preacher had over the alter table.

When he started off the service he put me in a rather depressed mood right away. He first called for us to pray for sickness in his family. His young son was sick with a sore throat and possibly pneumonia with pain in his chest. This was depressing to me because I had seen his son on previous occasions and believed the preacher was satisfied with my services. Now he must be using another doctor. After the prayer and a hymn he read the text for the morning. He was about in the middle of it before I could get my mind off his sick son and back to his service. When I caught up to his reading he was emphasizing the part of his text where it says we should take no thought of tomorrow. You know the Scripture, the birds have nests, foxes have holes and flowers their colors, something like this.

How could I take no thought of tomorrow? I had trouble waiting for me today. My mind left him again until we were to stand in preparation to take communion. I thought of the coming events for the year.

The closest one being the possible settlement of the ABC suit. The town board is due to have a meeting Monday night and they might accept the settlement Jim and I offered them. The judge has set Wednesday for a pretrial hearing. If the town board accepts the settlement we will not need the trial.

Our children were home for Christmas and we have concern for them about finding jobs.

Certainly these seem like little problems now but they can be big ones tomorrow. Thinking of it now it someway reminds me of a time years ago when I was doing some duck hunting.

I was standing on a point on the lake watching for ducks. Three young men came up the lake in their boat. They had been members of the Boy Scout troop Jim and I worked with. When they saw me they came over to ask if I had had any luck. I told them no, and they replied they hadn't killed any either. They then invited me to join them in their boat and we would ride around the lake into the head of the necks and flush the ducks out over us. I was glad to see them again and accepted their invitation. As we entered the first neck the two boys in front stood up and fired at some mergansers that were pretty far away.

I remarked they shouldn't be shooting at these little ducks. They had a ready excuse. They thought they were big ducks far away. Soon my problems will be big ones not so far away, not even a tomorrow away.

I was called to the office several times. A lady that had strangled on cornbread a day or two before Christmas had trouble swallowing again. She frequently gets this way whenever she becomes depressed. This time she was thinking of her husband who committed suicide a few years ago on Christmas. She became frightened and called for help.

Another patient was a young girl who shot her finger with her new BB gun. I frequently have a case like this and occasionally one shot in the eye. Otherwise things went along about like this until New Year's Day.

Since it was New Year's Day I had given some thought to not going to the office and calling Sarah to stay home too. Dorothy said I had just as well go. Sarah was probably already there since it was nine o'clock now and I had not called her. Patients would be calling anyway. When I arrived at the office Sarah had opened up. There were no patients waiting so I decided to go to the hospital to check on Bert. I had not been in his room long until his telephone rang. He said it was Sarah calling to tell me Mrs. Hague was dead in my office and to come back right away. Mrs. Hague and her husband had come to see me and while sitting in the reception room she had suddenly felt faint and keeled over in the chair. Her husband had lain her out on the floor. Sarah had run to call me. I told her to call the ambulance and immediately left for the office about six miles away. On the way I hoped Sarah was wrong.

Perhaps it was just a faint and being prone on the floor she would revive. I even thought the ambulance crew might arrive in time to revive her. Then there was the thought of what was her husband thinking with his wife suddenly dying in my office. I had seen her about a week ago and given her medication for high blood pressure.

As I turned the corner approaching the office I saw the ambulance parked up against my office steps. There was again some hope that the crew had revived her and was taking her to the hospital. A little distance to the side of the ambulance was a police car and beside it a big red fire truck. There is a rule that when you call for the ambulance you also get police and fire protection. I parked beside the ambulance and hastily mounted the steps to the office door. It was locked and a fat ambulance attendant was sitting on the steps almost too close for me to get it open good anyway. Fumbling for my key I got it unlocked and open. In all the bumping around the door it must have jarred the latch loose so it locked.

Mr. Hague was standing over his wife looking down at her. An ambulance attendant was sitting in a chair near her feet. Mrs. Hague was stretched out on the floor with her head protruding from under a brown blanket from one of my examining rooms.

I bent down to check on her. There was no pulse. Her arm was cold and a little wet. Sarah handed me my stethoscope.

I couldn't hear any sounds in her chest. It was cold. Her face was blue and cold. The ambulance attendant said she was dead. I then stood up and asked Mr. Hague what happened. He said she felt a little faint this morning and wanted to see me. While she was sitting there she wanted some water, which Sarah gave her. After a sip or two she just slumped over and he eased her onto the floor. She didn't struggle or say anything else. He had tried massaging her chest to no avail. Sarah then called the ambulance. The crew came, checked on her and told Mr. Hague she was dead.

I expressed my concern to Mr. Hague and asked him what funeral home he would like for me to call. He named one in Lenoir. I started to make the call and the ambulance attendant said she had already made the call. I then asked her why couldn't she take the body back to Lenoir since they would be going there anyway. For reasons I didn't hear she said they were not allowed to move the body. Well, I wasn't going to leave Mrs. Hague stretched out on the floor in my reception room until the undertaker came.

I asked Mr. Hague to help me move her to one of the examining rooms. I took hold of the lighter end, the legs and the ambulance attendant and Mr. Hague the head and moved her to one of the examining rooms. Mr. Hague gave me some numbers to call for members of his family. While I was calling them I became aware of other patients in the reception room. It seemed strange to me that they could seem so jolly when unknown to them there is terrific grief in the next room.

When the undertaker arrived the crew was all dressed in white, neat and clean with rather frozen smiles. The chief undertaker gave me the death certificate to fill out while he talked to Mr. Hague about pertinent family history. I listed the cause of death a cerebrovascular accident (stroke). I gave it to the attendant and went to see about moving Mrs. Hague onto the cot.

Two undertaker attendants were on one side of the table pushing Mrs. Hague onto their cot. They exchanged my light brown blanket for a dark purple one. They tucked her toes in first and then pulled it over her head. Her eyes were still open. They strapped her arms down and carted her out through my reception room full of patients. I walked back of the cot out to the hearse.

There was now quite an assembly of people outside. The first one I recognized was the ex-mayor dressed in a light blue suit. He had come in a yellow cab to go someplace with Mr. Hague. Beyond the ambulance and fire truck was another police car. Mr. Hague had been a policeman several years ago. Now that he is a newly elected town commissioner he is expected to help put the present police chief out of office and put in one of his old police friends. Other people standing about were my patients waiting to see me.

The undertaker slid the cot into the back of the black hearse and hurriedly closed the door. It seemed as they sped away with Mrs. Hague a black curtain of depression descended on me.

I wanted to go someplace too, but I couldn't stop because of Mrs. Hague's death. The office was full of patients. I must continue to do the best I can. As the hearse sped out the ambulance crew left behind them. The police cars with Mr. Hague in the yellow cab were next and then the big red fire truck left rather slowly as if implying a funeral was next.

I went back into the office to see my patients. Sarah seemed undaunted by all the excitement. Her voice squeaks if she gets excited. After a few hours things went on as usual. I began to think of tomorrow. It will be the first business day of the new year. I will have to make some resolutions. One is to someway disengage myself from politics. It is a very vicious game that never ends. You can win one round and unless you are prepared to continually fight you may easily lose the next one. Just as with Mr. Hague in the yellow cab, it is politics as usual even in time of death.

Politics is so ingrained in some people that it is an obsession. Someone told me that the reason Mr. Hague didn't use the local funeral home was because Laney is a Republican. I don't know whether Laney is a Republican or not or whether Mr. Hague used the Lenoir funeral home because the owner is a Democrat.

Now, do you want a Democrat or a Republican funeral?

I think my only resolution is going to be to render service to all people the best I can. So far from the short time I have recognized this as my life's goal I have been gratified with the compliments of gratitude for my service. I find myself doubting the words to a song that goes something like this, "Ah sweet mystery of life, at last I have found thee. 'Tis love and love alone that rules the world." A different version might be, "It's service and service alone that gives the best life."

77

Life is unpredictable

3-7-82 ✓

Until today I had hopes the town board would agree to settle the ABC suit. After each board meeting they find some reason to delay settlement. In my spare time I have gone over again and again all my records preparing for the trial. Some reassuring things are a newspaper stating that it is the opinion of the attorney general that the ABC board could not be fired by the town unless we were found unfit to serve and there has been no law that I can find that says how much money an ABC store may hold. Since there has been no agreement the judge set a trial date for March 15th. In the paper tonight there was the picture of the judge, a Democrat and national delegate to the Democratic Convention. Perhaps we will get a Republican jury.

You can never tell just how thing will turn out. One summer our children were ages twelve down to two and had never had a train ride. At that time the train ran through Hickory around one o'clock in the afternoon and another met it in Old Fort. We planned to ride to Old Fort and then catch the next train to Hickory.

We thought we had time to get some ice cream in Old Fort. We had just sat down when we heard a train whistle and saw a passenger train pulling out from the station blowing clouds of smoke and steam along the track going east.

We hastened to the station and were informed that we had just missed the train. The next one would be sometime in the morning. Now it was three o'clock on a hot August afternoon. The children were hot and began to cry. Dorothy developed a severe throbbing migraine.

The bus station had a bus going to Hickory at eight o'clock. I couldn't wait. I went to the taxi stand. There was only one available and the driver appeared to be intoxicated. My only option for getting home was to call someone to come for us. Looking around for a telephone an ambulance suddenly came screaming down the street. Now another option had suddenly appeared. I crossed the street to a service station to look up the telephone number of the funeral home.

The undertaker answered. I told him I was a doctor in Granite Falls and had my children and wife with me. We had missed the train and needed to get home. Would he take me home? He asked where I was and where did I live. He said as soon as he could gas up he would be there in five minutes to take us home. Soon, as good as his word, a large black hearse slid to a stop at our street corner. An undertaker in a crisp white coat got out and introduced himself while opening the big black door on the back. We all climbed in, Dorothy lay on the cot, the five children found places around the cot and I rode up front beside the driver. With siren wailing we roared down the road to Hickory arriving almost as soon as the train.

I am telling you this to just show you how things change. Here I planned a nice train ride with the children on a Wednesday afternoon, eat a little ice cream in Old Fort, and have a nice ride back to town. I didn't foresee any difficulty with the trip. I found one needs to be resourceful in this life.

What would life be if it were all as a calm sea? I think it was St. Paul who said he wanted men helping him who had seen a lot of trouble. When this ABC thing is over I may be qualified.

But with all the tribulations life has there are some very pleasant moments. An hour ago I was called to see a lady about forty years old. I have been attending Zora for twenty years. She has had many operations and her abdomen is crisscrossed with many operative scars. At this time she had a strangulated hernia in one of the operative sites. I was able to reduce it and suggested a belt to prevent it from coming out again.

When I started to leave I remembered the last time I was there Zora gave me a quart of hazelnuts. She and her husband had picked them while rambling around the mountains near Iron creek. Her husband said there was another jar of them there on the shelf and for me to take them. I picked them up and had my hand on the door when he asked me about meat, what kind did I like, beef or pork. I said beef.

"Just sit there a minute," he said, pointing to a chair. He went to the freezer and handed me a three-pound roast.

"Now this is real good. I raised it myself. It is from a 400-pound bull, half Angus and half Whiteface. Its mother developed mastitis in the two back tits and he had to survive on the two front tits," he said.

I thanked Zora and her husband for the gifts and said I could repay them with some bluefish. You never know just when some pleasant thing will happen. Even in pain some people are very appreciative.

Now think of the contrast of the above visit and the visit the two policemen had with City Manager Noble when he fired them.

Barclay, the attorney for the policemen, had the last word.

"The decision to fire them was made by Noble," he said. "You all know that. Noble went above and beyond his capacity as town manager in wielding his power. He acted with malice, he knew what he was doing and he went after these fellows. We're talking about their constitutional rights. You got a man over there, Noble that doesn't want to defend freedom of speech. We all know the most disruptive thing in this department is brother Noble. He's the most disruptive thing I've ever seen or heard of. You know the misuse of power we had here. This could be the biggest moment in your life as American citizens. I think it's about time police officers had some rights. That's what this case is all about."

The verdict was for the former city manager to pay each of the policemen two thousand dollars out of his own pocket for punitive damages.

Again, things are not what they seem at first. Doris called for me to come quick yesterday to her rest home for women. She thought Pearl, a lady about seventy-two years old, was having a heart attack The rest home is an old house of wood construction with three chimneys. Years ago the family heated with wood, but when they converted it to a rest home they closed up the fireplaces and used central heating. When I arrived one of the ladies greeted me and showed me into the front room

On entering the room I couldn't tell whether they were doing their spring cleaning or had some kind of fire. Some chairs about the fireplace were loaded with drawers pulled out of the chest of drawers. The place where a stove flu went into the fireplace was pulled out and there was soot all over the floor.

Some of the ladies had soot on their hands and face so that they seemed to be going to a Halloween party. Doris showed me my patient. Pearl was sitting in a chair with her head resting on her bed opposite the fireplace complaining of chest pain and some numbness down the left arm. She had not slept any during the night because of the commotion they had with the soot.

All night long a bird had been chirping in the chimney. They had looked all over the house for it. I listened to Pearl's heart and took her blood pressure. I suspected she was having angina. I gave her a nitroglycerin tablet and a mild sedative. In a few minutes she began to feel better. While waiting for the medicine to take effect I asked Doris what had caused all the trouble; it looked like they had had a fire. She said no, they hadn't had a fire. A bird was lodged in the fireplace. They heard it chirping during the night and couldn't sleep for worrying about it. They had pulled out all the drawers, looked in the closets and even pulled out the coverings in the fireplaces trying to find it. They believed it was down in the fireplace where they couldn't find it. My patient Pearl had worried all night about it since her bed was near the fireplace.

While Doris was telling me of their trouble I heard the chirp too, only it wasn't a bird. I asked them to listen a minute to see if what I heard was what they were hearing. When it chirped again they all agreed that was the bird. I pointed to the smoke detector over the fire-place and told Doris that was their bird. Detectors often put out a high-pitched warning sound when their batteries are getting low.

They all laughed, saying they had been telling Doris she needed a man around the house.

Later in the morning Bert came by the office on his way to the post office. He said Don had made another proposition. If Jim and I would drop our suit, Don would drop the town's suit. We would have to pay our attorney fees. Noble would give us a notarized statement stating that Erby was the cause of the ABC trouble. We have declined and are preparing to go to court.

78

Land Ho!

3-10-1982 ✓

I am now in the position Jim Hawkins was when he was caught in the apple barrel in Robert Louis Stevenson's book, *Treasure Island*. It is at the end of the chapter on the Sea Cook.

"Just then a sort of brightness fell upon me in the barrel, and looking up, I found the moon had risen, and was silvering the mizzen top and shining white on the luff of the foresail; and almost at the same time the voice of the lookout shouted, 'Land Ho.'"

Last Tuesday night the town board met to make a decision about the ABC suit, whether or not to accept the proposal made by our attorney or go to court. Bert said it would be decided in executive session and since I was not a member of the board I would not be privileged to attend the meeting. All the old commissioners named in the suit and the new commissioners would be in attendance. Sometime around ten o'clock Bert called me. The board was still meeting. He had excused himself to tell me that the vote on the ABC suit had gone four to two in favor of accepting our proposal. Knowing this was like seeing land after a four-year voyage. Now it would be over soon, all the scheming, spying on each other, whispering about each other and searching for incriminating documents would be over.

I called Dot and Jim. They were thrilled, but had some regrets we were not going to court. I called Hamby, the man we had bought the land from to tell him we would not be going to court today. He was subpoenaed to appear in court to testify about the land purchase. He was upset that he was going to be bothered again after giving his deposition to the city attorney some months ago. He was now glad to know that the case was settled. He brought up the matter of Don having asked him about bringing his income tax report. I told him Jim and I had been audited for the year 1978–79. I was surprised when he said he had been audited for the same years. He suspected it was Don who had reported us.

He hopped someone would shoot him.

Wednesday morning around ten o'clock Bert called to say that the town had agreed to settle and had asked Don to call Sentelle last night.

All that was necessary now to finalize the settlement was for the two attorneys to get together Monday at the courthouse and sign papers in front of the judge. Until this was done there was the possibility the town board could call another meeting and reverse their decision. I knew this was true because I had seen them do it regarding a park for recreation. Now the anxiety of waiting began to return. I suspected there were other people waiting too. What about the reporters, will they make it look like the town is granting some concession to us by agreeing to settle. In the settlement we are asking for a public apology for our mistreatment.

All day I kept the matter on my mind. Just as I was closing the office and going to my car, Commissioner Clark drove up to talk to me. He is one of the new town commissioners. He said my troubles were over. Last night the town board agreed to settle the case. They are sure Don is the cause of all the trouble and they are going to get rid of him. Now all six commissioners are in agreement to fire him at the first opportunity. Erby had employed his own attorney and had been advised by him that the commissioners are individually liable. Clark accused Don of deliberately hiding this fact from them. With Noble having to pay each policeman two thousand dollars out of his pocket the commissioners didn't want to go to trial with the similar thing happening to them. Clark said Don told the board he had the ABC suit all worked up and could win, but Clay reminded him that he had said the same thing about the policemen and lost. Don denied it but Clay and Clark said he did say it and called him a liar.

Clark wanted to know now that the town had accepted the settlement would Jim and I sue the commissioners individually. I told him no; I was glad to get it settled.

Sometime after lunch Dot called wanting to know if I had heard anything more about the settlement. I told her I hadn't. She said she had not felt so well in years. She thinks all the anxiety has been causing her headaches. I agreed, saying I didn't think she would have them any more. Dorothy says that the settlement is due to my horoscope. She has been reading it in the paper for the last week. She says there isn't any bad luck in sight just now. I haven't any faith in it, but the last one almost makes me a believer.

"Pisces (Feb.19–March 20) You'll recoup recent loss. Legal matters claim share of scenario. Your position is stronger than originally anticipated. Law is written in a manner, which will favor you. Cancer, Taurus, Capricorn persons figure prominently."

Up to now I haven't given much mystics, the zodiac and stars. This though is such that I can't believe its accuracy. Marvin swears by the stars and signs. He watches them to plant his garden. I do well to identify the big dipper. For a time there was a constellation of stars that I called the square of Pegasus. About a month ago after the meeting of the Rotary Club a group of us were standing outside after the meeting. A new member, Tom who had recently joined the club was standing beside me and I pointed out the constellation to him. He said no it was called the Warrior, pointing out his belt and sword. Since then Tom and I have become good friends. He is into mystic things and knows the various levels of the mystic science. Today he brought me some flowers. He had found out that Don had accepted our settlement.

Now, like on a voyage, land is in sight and I will be ending this voyage soon. I believe if we had been in the apple barrel and heard fate talking of where it was taking us we would have jumped ship. I will try to summarize the voyage's effect on me and the town. With its conclusion there has come a profound change in my life in the way I look at my hometown and the people in it. The town seems to be an empty place now. I seem to have no goals now for the town. Once lots of things could be accomplished by working together. All of that feeling has been destroyed. There seems to be very few people that I can work with.

Tomorrow we will be honoring Chief Barlow who is retiring after thirty-one years of service as police chief. There was no mention in the announcement of any special services he had rendered to the town in thirty-years. I wonder if I were retiring now if they would say anything about me.

The official announcement of the settlement could not be made until the judge signed the papers Monday morning. Prior to this there was a bit of activity on the part of a few people. Clark came by the office Friday morning. He confirmed the settlement and wanted to know why he had been subpoenaed for the trial. It was because someone had asked him to serve on the new ABC board.

Another fellow came in to tell me if we had gone to court he was willing to testify that the had overheard in the barbecue stand that we were going to be fired on the Monday night at the town board meeting. I told him I was glad to know it but we were settling out of court. It seemed like hours until Jim finally arrived with the papers from city hall. We called our attorney to find out if we should sign. He assured us that it would be best for us to sign. We returned the papers to city hall and they sent them with a policeman to the courthouse in Lenoir. It was about four-thirty when Bert called to say it was finished. The judge had signed the papers, the town was to pay us one thousand dollars each and our attorney fees of $14,180.58. Bert was on his way to the town hall to make the announcement to the reporters. When we were fired it had headlined the news. I wondered if they would do the same now that we had won. The Hickory Record had a report of it headlined on the front of its second section; the Granite Press had a small write up on their front page in the lower left corner.

Conclusions

10-8-1999 ✓

It might be best to list things that may have been a mistake on my part in the affairs that took place from the beginning of 1978 until the voyage was ended in 1982. I think the biggest mistake was in believing the ABC Board was an autonomous body and not subject the town commissioner's rule except in some exceptional situations. I was led to believe this when I asked the attorney general if we were under the town authority or the state. From his answer I concluded the town commissioners had no further control over us after we were appointed by the town. This was a big mistake and probably led to us being fired. Had we have known this we would have kept the commissioners informed about all of our business since they were in effect the ruling body.

Another factor I failed to reckon with was the fact that one can't support someone for public office against another person without incurring the opponent's ill will. They will do their best to see that you do not do well in office and will try to get you out in the next election. There is also natural jealousy and prejudice against someone having a public office.

An office holder should have no secrets from anybody interested in the office. I failed to seek advice from the town commissioners so that they were not informed about activities of the ABC store. Since they turned out to be the ruling body they should have been kept informed.

All of these mistakes helped to make my life different. I learned that the majority had sway over the lesser number most of the time. The number of people against the ABC Board had gradually increased so that we lost our support. The town commissioners had support from the attorney general that we could not overcome.

I don't believe giving the town more money would have helped our situation; they wanted control of the ABC stern. It seems that money and time are the answers to most problems. If we had resigned and let them have the store it might have solved the problem. However when they accused us of buying the land illegally we could not resign and face a possible lawsuit.

From the lawsuit we had against the commissioners I have learned to be more patient. Things may not be as they first seem. One must know the whole story and then some to make a good conclusion. If it is possible, avoid conflicts. You can make an enemy in a second. You remember the chapter "Do what the Bible says?" Settle things as quickly and peaceably as you can. A lifetime may not erase bad feelings. One needs to be faithful, control his temper and don't argue with people. Find out the truth and let that settle the mater. Learn to know people, smart and dumb, big and little. People act according to their size and intelligence. There are many rules for living that are not written down. One may find them out by observation and acquaintance. Learn to watch body language. Listen carefully to people when they talk. What they are saying may have nothing to do with why they are talking. They may be just wanting attention, wanting to find what mood you are in or for lots of other reasons.

As you go through life it would be well to know where the leadership is and spend your time with this group. At the same time when one is trying to advance in life he must not forget about the natural jealousy, envy and greed of people. You learn a lot of these things by getting to be eighty-one years old. When you get that old you can recall the lines in the second verse of the hymn Amazing Grace. They go a little like this:

"I have come through many a danger, fear and snare."

I have held to a direction for my life, it being to always try to do better. I have always held to my faith regarding it as something like a compass, never changing, always holding me to a standard for my life. In addition to faith, one needs knowledge, wisdom and understanding.

There should be some point in the things one does. They should add to making you a better person.

These precepts might be considered one's religion, though I don't exclude the lessons in the Bible. One needs to study the Bible for the history of man, of man's behavior through the ages and for the rules for living a good life now.

One will always be confronted with the Scriptures, beginning with baptism, marriage and death. You will be better off knowing the Bible than just hearing the verses read on Sunday.

One should observe Sunday as a special day. You should reflect on what you have, remember your creator and parents, and be thankful that you are still living. Through observing Sunday you are showing others that you have a sense of belonging to something rather than just being a person without any dedication or principal. One should pray frequently for what they desire. Through prayer you keep your desires in mind and work to achieve them. With God's help you may often have your prayers answered.

I think the final conclusion of life is in serving your fellow man however you can. Let your religion be to fear God and keep His commandments.

About the Author

Born in 1918 in Granite Falls, North Carolina, Dr. Martin E. Jones is a graduate of Duke University Medical School. He interned at Gorgas Hospital in Panama C.Z. After a year there he joined the U.S. Army on active duty for two years, serving in the States in convalescent hospitals. He returned home to set up practice with a local doctor, and after a year accepted a residency at Rex Hospital in Raleigh where he met his future wife Dorothy. He worked about two years in the hospital and one year in Coats, N.C. before returning home again. He and Dorothy married in 1948 and set up practice in Granite Falls, N.C. where he served the community as a general practitioner for 42 years before retiring in 1985. Dr. Jones continues to be active in civic and community events and in 2000 was honored as "Rotarian of the Century" by the Granite Falls Rotary Club in recognition of his years of dedicated service. He and his wife have five children, four grandchildren and reside in Granite Falls.

0-595-26289-9

Printed in the United States
931900002B